Museums and Adults Learning:
perspectives from Europe

Museums and Adults Learning: perspectives from Europe

**Edited by Alan Chadwick
and Annette Stannett**

NIACE
THE NATIONAL ORGANISATION
FOR ADULT LEARNING

36,428

Published by the National Institute of Adult Continuing Education
(England and Wales)
21 De Montfort Street, Leicester, LE1 7GE
Company registration no. 2603322
Charity registration no. 1002775

First published 2000
© NIACE

CATALOGUING IN PUBLICATION DATA
A CIP record for this title is available from the British Library
ISBN 1 86201 021 8

Typeset by The Midlands Book Typesetting Company, Loughborough
Printed in Great Britain by Redwood Books

Acknowledgements

To convert an idea into a publication requires many contributors. Foremost among them are the ones who write chapters. We wish to thank our authors most particularly, both for their commitment to the undertaking and for their patience.

The Co-Editors

Contents

Preface   ix
1   Introduction   1
    Alan Chadwick and Annette Stannett
2   Conceptual framework   4
    David Anderson

Part I   Scandinavia
3   Norway   12
    Eva Maehre Lauritzen
4   Sweden   22
    Helena Friman

Part II   Baltic states
5   Latvia   28
    Aija Fleija

Part III   Eastern and Central European countries
6   Croatia   31
    Ivo Maroević and Tončika Cukrov
7   The Czech Republic   41
    Radka Schusterová and Pavel Hartl
8   Hungary   48
    László Harangi
9   Poland   59
    Daniel Artymowski
10 Romania   65
    Virgil Stefan Nitulescu
11 Russia   70
    Irina Mikhailovna Kossova
12 Slovenia   77
    Tatjana Dolzan-Eržen

Part IV   Mediterreanean countries
13 Cyprus   81
    Loukia Loizou Hadjigavriel
14 Italy   86
    Edi Fanti, Lida Branchesi and Paolo Orefice & Gianni Maria Filippi
15 Malta   103
    Carmel Borg and Peter Mayo

Part V Iberia
16 Portugal   115
   Ana Duarte

Part VI France and German-speaking countries
17 Austria   123
   Gabriele Rath
18 France   130
   Jean Galard
19 Germany   138
   Dorothee Dennert and Helena von Wersebe
20 Switzerland   147
   Flavia Krogh Loser

Part VII Benelux
21 Belgium   158
   Willem Elias
22 Luxembourg   172
   Bettina Heldenstein and Herbert Maly
22 The Netherlands   179
   Bastiaan van Gent

Part VIII The United Kingdom and Ireland
24 Ireland   188
   Ann Davoren and Ted Fleming
25 The United Kingdom   197
   John Reeve

Part IX Europe and beyond
26 European initiatives   210
   Alan Chadwick and Annette Stannett
27 Israel   213
   Nina Rodin

Part X Conclusions
28 Conclusions   221
   Nicole Gesché

Abbreviations   227

Notes on contributors   228

Index   232

Preface

Elizabeth Esteve-Coll

Over the last 200 years in Europe, museums have been constructed around a range of ideas which have quite closely reflected the prevailing social, political and economic climate of their time. The notion of collecting natural and man-made objects together in specific categories, whether for public display or private pleasure has proved to be the underlying *raison d'être* which has translated into a concept now described as a museum. There are so many different kinds of museum, displaying diverse collections ranging from archaeology to zoology, contemporary art to science and technology – some narrowly aimed at specialist visitors, others seeking to appeal to as broad a visiting public as possible – that generalisation is impossible: a point abundantly demonstrated by the contributions to this volume.

These chapters focus on the contemporary European experience of museums and, reading them, one is instantly struck by the shared aspiration to involve the visiting public in partnership. At the end of the second millennium, we are witnessing a deliberate movement in museum philosophy which aims to create a learning environment; an environment which, being outside the formal educational structure, allows adults to participate at their own speed and in their own way. Unlike school or college, there is no sense of competition. Successes or failures are not measured, so there is nothing threatening in a museum learning experience. Indeed, one could argue that museums provide a near perfect setting for the adult learner. Unfortunately, for far too many adults museums are exclusion zones, either because of an early childhood introduction badly handled, or because, mistakenly, they are viewed as elitist temples of knowledge inaccessible to ordinary men and women. In order to break down these barriers, museum staff and museum educators have demonstrated a wide range of creative approaches in devising innovative ways of encouraging museum use. New museum buildings often include activity areas, old ones are refurbished to become more welcoming, and staff are trained to deal with all aspects of public inquiry. It is this common drive across Europe to engage with the visiting public which makes the contributions to this volume so heartening. There is a wealth of experience to draw upon, and a range of good practice to follow up. Different countries are at different stages of development, but all are moving towards a shared goal of quality provision for lifelong learning, of which adult learning is a substantial part.

There has been a common acknowledgement that many adults want to learn and, equally, an awareness that each individual has a unique learning style. Learning style may be characterised by visual memory or by aural impression. Some people learn best when they are physically involved, and active participation reinforces the written or spoken word. On a recent visit to Russian museums, I was particularly interested at one museum by the way staff used activities designed for children to draw the parents into active engagement and participation. From being onlookers at egg-painting sessions, parents and relations of all ages joined with the children in a shared experience where oral community history fitted seamlessly into Russian folklore, creating a rich family experience.

The issues raised by the Maltese contributors concerning the training of museum educators highlight the responsibility which museum professionals bear to the visiting public. All museum educators, both paid and voluntary, need to be aware of their role as mediators in questions of cultural politics. To date, in Europe, the new approach to education in both local and national museums has been to emphasise the role of the museum educator as animateur, as mediator rather than as an agent of 'ideological pressure'. Such informed 'neutrality' demands appropriate specialist training of considerable sophistication. It is clear that in some countries progress towards such training is well advanced, whereas in others work on defining curricula and gaining acceptance for suitable courses within traditional academic frameworks is just beginning. Likewise, across Europe there is varied recognition from funding agencies, both local and national, that such work is important.

Reports on problems associated with an ageing population, on community disintegration, on the place of information technology in the next century frequently touch on the desirability both of improving the quality of life for adults in a society where the working week becomes ever shorter (35 hours proposed in France, compared with 43 hours in the United Kingdom – the longest working week in Europe) and of improving use of leisure time. One of the dangers of official reports is often the emphasis placed on achieving a technologically literate population. Although this is a vital factor in the work-place, it can lead to a mistaken focus on technology in the learning process. Clearly, Europe needs a computer-literate workforce, skilled in a diversity of applications for business and industry, in order to compete with the trading blocs of America and Asia; but, equally, governments must value the satisfaction and enrichment of their people.

The route offered through museums to personal learning and enhanced enjoyment of life is still too often ignored by governments and community leaders. If the lives of our citizens are to be enriched, we in the museum world must take care not to be seduced by funding grants which are wholly associated with technological advance. We must not lose sight of the powerful appeal of real objects and their attraction for ordinary people in the learning process. The image of museums in society has radically changed in the last 10 to 15 years. There is a recognition that whatever the type of museum – local, regional or national – all have a role to play in adult education. At the local level the museum may be the repository of community memory; it may be the only explicit link to a past forgotten and undervalued. At a national level it can be a key both to understanding our heritage as human beings and to a more tolerant (because informed) view of how Europe came to be shaped as we find it today.

Throughout these chapters there is the common thread of collaboration and partnership. As a profession, museum educators need to work together, learning and adapting experience from one country to another. In attempting to enrich the lives of our citizens through an open, multi-stranded approach to adult learning, the lesson must be absorbed that we have to work in partnership with adult educators and, most particularly, our public. The assumption that adult learning in museums is a one-way process needs to be challenged: museum staff have a great deal of knowledge to share, but they must also be receptive to learning from the public. Adult learners are often able to impart information and experience-based knowledge to curators, and from mutual receptivity a new understanding can develop. There is much to learn from this approach and the results need to be monitored and evaluated, but already it is clear that an equality of purpose must guide adult learning in museums. If we are to enfranchise the disenfranchised and do it with integrity, we must be open about our purpose and honest in seeking collaboration with the learner. Our European society will be the richer for our efforts in the coming millennium.

The terms 'educator', keyworker, 'mediator' or 'cultural mediator' and 'mentor', and similar terms used in this book describe facilitators who work as intermediaries between museums and the public.

1 Introduction

Alan Chadwick and Annette Stannett

In July 1997 the Fifth International Conference on Adult Education was held in Hamburg, Germany, under the auspices of UNESCO.

The 10 themes that reflected 'the broad and complex spectrum of adult learning' contained statements of commitment, of which several have particular meaning in the context of this volume, such as:

> Adult learning provides an essential opportunity for adult learners to participate in all cultural institutions, mass media and new technologies in order to establish effective interactive communications and to build understanding and co-operation between peoples and cultures...

and

> International co-operation and solidarity must strengthen a new vision of adult learning which is both holistic, to embrace all aspects of life, and cross-sectoral, to include all areas of cultural, social and economic activity.
> (UNESCO 1997: 35, 37)

The key importance of culture in the learning process was stated, with the accompanying recognition that adults had an inalienable right to it, and that museums and similar agencies had an important role in this process.

The purpose of this volume is to offer a prospect from European experience and expertise which cross-refers to some of the important principles identified above. It has its origin in a presentation made to the General Assembly of the European Association for the Education of Adults in 1995 where the idea of a project leading to a publication was mooted (Chadwick 1995). It was argued that a growing awareness of the need for collaborating with and utilising museums for adult education was emerging, and that greater opportunities for collaboration between educational and cultural agents should be created. These proposals led in due course to the mounting of, first, the *Adult Education and Museums* project under the guidance of IIZ/DVV, and, second, to the *Museums, Keyworkers and Lifelong Learning* project, both financially assisted by the European Commission under its SOCRATES funding scheme.

The individual chapters in this book illustrate differing areas of experience and expertise, both external to and within European countries. Yet there are also many similarities which echo sentiments expressed above. A specific example is the notion of constructing opportunities for various forms of co-operation, between cultures and between agencies with adult learners. A more general recognition which, implicitly or explicitly, permeates the contributions is the developing realisation that museums, as well as adult education providers, act as important learning resource centres – in the former case, throughout life; in the latter, for its most substantial part.

In the process of compiling the book we issued identical invitations to museum education and adult education providers in 35 European countries. Not every country responded, and of those that did, not every one finally submitted a contribution. As will be seen, there was a greater response from museologists than from adult educators; interestingly, this mirrors our experience in a prior volume, which restricted its coverage to the United Kingdom (Chadwick and Stannett 1995).

Conversely, our appeal for contributions in *ICOM Newsletter* attracted a response from one non-European country, Israel, which we decided to include, as it echoes many of the concerns and aspirations of other contributors, particularly those in Eastern and Central Europe, many of which also submitted case studies rather than historical overviews and were, predictably, heavily influenced by political changes entailing shifts in populations, resulting in emphasis on national pride and on museums as heritage centres.

Generally speaking, colleagues in the West provided more historical overviews, possibly reflecting a more uninterrupted continuity of development. It was refreshing to receive such variety of themes, formats and styles – and, exceptionally, candour, as witnessed through descriptions of aspirations unmet. On balance, the relationship between museums and adult education providers is, to quote two contributors, 'sporadic'. In some countries there appear to be no clearly defined links; indeed, in one case museums remain 'rather passive' regarding the adult public. In others the potential is 'considerably under-developed'. Alternatively, one contributor states that adult education provision in museums 'is one of the most exciting trends' within that country's museums. The picture is uneven but, as will be seen, much important work is being done or considered, not least for socially excluded groups.

The increasingly important element of collaborative activities between educational and other cultural organisations and, particularly, of those concerning museums and their communities, is stressed in a number of contributions. Others discussed the perennial issue of training and development of staff, although there was very little evidence of evaluation, of principles which govern policy, of policies that determine programme provision, or of pro-activity in terms of community aspirations.

We hope that this text of shared current experiences in the related fields of museum and adult education by theorists and practitioners alike may go some way towards aiding awareness and understanding throughout Europe, and, most particularly, will provide to, and receive benefit from, adult learners.

References

Chadwick, A, 'Museums and the education of adults: a European perspective', in European Association for the Education of Adults (ed), *Innovation and adult education*, February 1995, EAEA with the support of the European Commission, Directorate General XXIII, pp. 52–3

Chadwick, A and Stannett, A (eds) *Museums and the education of adults*, Leicester: NIACE, 1995

UNESCO, *Final Report, Fifth International Conference on Adult Education*, 14–18 July 1997

2   A conceptual framework

David Anderson

In *The Island of the Colour-blind*, the neurologist and writer Oliver Sacks describes the atoll of Pingelap, where there is a community of islanders born totally colour-blind (Sacks 1996). The condition is not, of course, limited to that island; there have been other isolated communities in which it has been concentrated (Sacks cites Fuur in Norway as another example) and a significant proportion of the general population throughout the world is also to some degree affected. But disorders such as this can affect small, in-bred populations much more extensively than larger, more open ones.

I use this as a metaphor for museums and their awareness of adult learning. That the metaphor relates to a deficiency in visual perception (a sensibility that lies at the centre of the function of museums) is a deliberate irony. It is not that museums and galleries do not perceive that adults learn, or that they do not respond to or actively provide for the learning they perceive: the problem is rather that the perception and response are so narrow – in a sense, monochrome.

To be explicit, museums and galleries continue to perceive learning as mainly the communication of information, the transfer of a given body of knowledge from one person (generally 'the expert') to another (generally a member of the public).

In the United Kingdom the principal evidence for this assertion comes from the questionnaire surveys conducted for *A Common Wealth: Museums and learning in the United Kingdom*, the 1997 report on museum and gallery education for the UK Department of National Heritage (now the Department of Culture, Media and Sport), together with more recent data from the Museums and Galleries Commission's DOMUS [Directory of Museum Statistics] surveys.

The detailed results of the first (and main) questionnaire survey in 1994 for *A Common Wealth* showed that 64 per cent of visitors to museums are adults. However, given that the remaining one-third of visitors are children, mainly in family groups, many adult visitors must also have a child focus to their visit. Nearly half of museums responding to the questionnaire provided lectures or courses for adults, and 43 per cent provided print publications and other published resources. For those adults who are students in further or higher education, the level of provision was significantly lower. Direct teaching/lecture programmes for these users were provided by 20 per cent of museums, and publications by 18 per cent. Provision for adults with special educational needs or from minority communities was not identified separately, but was conspicuously low for all age groups together.

When asked to rank different audiences for provision of education services, museums said that their order of priority was as follows:

1. schools;
2. local and regional adult visitors;
3. children aged 5 to 12 years;
4. families with children;
5. teenagers aged 13 to 18;
6. further and higher education students;
7. adult tourists;
8. retired people;
9. academics and other specialists;
10. people with special needs;
11. children aged 0 to 5 years;
12. unemployed people; and
13. people from minority communities.

(Of course, these categories are not entirely mutually exclusive.) There are wide variations in the priority given to different adult audiences between types of museums; students in further and higher education are a particularly important audience for university museums (but, surprisingly, still a lower priority than schools).

The survey also looked at the level of employment of adult volunteers in museums, and found that overall they accounted for over one in three (35 per cent) of all staff. Their numbers were significantly greater than those of paid professional staff and only slightly lower than those for paid, non-professional staff. Many museums are, then, dependent to a significant extent upon the skills of unpaid staff from their local communities. Not surprisingly, therefore, museums are also heavily dependent upon paid and unpaid staff who are not specialist educators to deliver education services to adults. In museums, 41 per cent of lectures or courses for adults, and the same percentage of gallery lectures and tours, are either organised or delivered (or both) by non-specialist educators (Anderson 1997).

Once again in the United Kingdom, the Museums and Galleries Commission (MGC)'s 1997 public services survey, conducted as part of its DOMUS general survey of registered museums, included some questions which were almost identical to those in the 1994 questionnaire for *A Common Wealth*. It found that provision of lectures and courses for adults was unchanged since 1994, but provision of publications in print and other media had fallen from 43 per cent of museums in 1994 to 19 per cent in 1997. The nature and reason for this fall is hard to define, especially as nothing similar has occurred across the rest of the spectrum of museum education (indeed, the level of services for schools seems to have increased). It should, however, be remembered that the MGC's 1997 survey covered only registered museums, whereas the 1994 survey was sent to all UK museums, registered or not.

The data listed above are consistent with a hypothesis that, in the main, museums and galleries see the dissemination of curatorial knowledge, through lectures and publications, as their main responsibility in support of adult learning. But these statistics have little to say about methodologies and theories of adult learning which underlie such provision in Europe. No sustained research has yet been conducted which might explore this in detail, and the evidence available remains largely anecdotal. Such evidence is, however, also widespread, as can be observed and experienced by any adult user of museums, and by any museum professional engaged in debates with other museum colleagues about the kind of services museums should provide for visitors.

At the time of writing, the processes of democracy in Europe are subject to renewed examination. There is a strong movement towards regionalisation and a questioning of national identities. Within the United Kingdom, for example, Scotland has a new parliament and Wales a new assembly, each with responsibilities for educational and cultural development in their nations and for achieving a new synthesis of these two dimensions of public life.

In all Western European countries, the institutions of parliament, the civil service and an independent judiciary are widely recognised as foundations of the democratic process. It could be argued that in the long term, the operation of our cultural and educational institutions (print and broadcasting media, digital media, performing arts institutions, archives and libraries as well as museums and galleries) is almost as important for the health of our democracy as are its more immediate judicial, parliamentary and executive bodies. This is because it is through the educational and cultural sectors that adults as well as children learn the practical meaning of democracy. A democratic society is not just one where people have the right to vote every few years; it is one where as many people as possible contribute actively and creatively to the cultural and other development of their communities and to society as a whole.

A model of learning and engagement in cultural activities which is based on dissemination of the knowledge of experts – the model which still drives much adult education in museums – is antithetical to the fostering of participation in cultural activities and, therefore, contrary also to the fostering of a democratic civic culture. The contemporary Scottish philosopher George Davie (1991) has warned against the emergence of a 'cultural apartheid' which would result from encouraging the intellectual backwardness of the masses. Instead, Davie argues the case for a 'common sense', in which the expertise of individuals is illuminated by and accountable to the understanding of the public.

'Common sense', as public property, is a necessity for a democratic amd critical culture in which educated lay people no less than specialists have a contribution to make. For Davie, 'common sense' is a fundamental requirement for a democratic society. 'Common' may be read as synonymous with 'democratic' and refers to the social distribution of knowledge and understanding, and the processes of their generation. As such the meaning of 'common sense' is not the same as the colloquial usage of the term as 'widely shared gut feeling'. This more developed definition has deep roots in Scottish, Scandinavian and some other European cultural traditions (but perhaps less resonance in England where the class system and inherited privilege remain powerful social forces). The role of museums is, then, to foster skills and creativity in learning through their resources, and to provide a space for exchange and debate for and with a wider public.

Museums and galleries, which have a reputation in public perception as dusty and dysfunctional environments, can be (and often are, when operating properly) centres for creativity. Since the election of a new government in the United Kingdom in 1997, there has been a fresh emphasis on the value of the cultural sector in the economy, but as yet only a limited understanding on the part of policy makers of the significance of products of past creativity as a source of inspiration for contemporary creators, whether for economic development or for wider educational and social purposes. Like all education, museum education is people-intensive work and requires a long-term investment of resources if it is to achieve transformation in people's lives. Because, in addition (as seen above), most museums provide adult education services for their existing adult audiences rather than as a means to engage excluded groups in their activities, there are few models of good practice for work of this kind, and little research on the effectiveness of such programmes.

We also still have much to learn about the precise processes that define the change for adults from non-participant to participant. A few years ago the Arts Council in a consultation paper, *The Creative Abilities of Young People* (Arts Council 1996), identified three stages in encouragement of young people's participation in the arts. The first of these was the *inspirational* stage, for those who might have had little previous (positive) involvement in arts or a cultural activity, and would offer increased opportunities for quality creative interaction and participation which are meaningful and relevant to young people's own experience. The second, the *aspirational* stage, was intended for young people already involved in some form of creative cultural activity and who wished to broaden their experience and understanding or to develop their skills and abilities further. Third came the *entrepreneurial* stage, for young people who are already highly confident and motivated, and who have achieved independence and expertise in their chosen field; this last stage would support young people in realising their potential and putting their talents to use in a cultural initiative or artistic enterprise. The Arts Council were, however, quick to emphasise that the levels they identified were not exclusive, and that there might be overlap or progression between them.

The validity of this three-stage model, interesting though it is, has yet to be properly tested. Research in these areas will be essential if museums are to be successful in moving towards achievement of education, access, social inclusion and community regeneration. It is, however, evident that individual institutions can only have limited success in opening opportunities for adult learners in this way if their efforts are part of a concerted development of new provision for adult learners within a local, regional and national framework.

The breaking down of the traditional distinctions between 'experts' and 'the public' is, therefore, an educational as well as a social and political necessity. Museum users and museum professionals are engaged in the same – not different – activities, and museums need working methods that support this process.

There is limited quantitative evidence of the nature of provision for adult learning across some countries in Europe, as shown in this volume, and a significant issue for European museums about their role through adult learning in the rooting of democratic educational processes in their communities. What other developments of philosophy, theory or practice can be identified that are of significance to European museums?

It should be said at once that it is almost impossible to make generalised statements about the nature of policy and provision in museums across Europe. It is part of the richness of museums that they are often deeply embedded in their cultural contexts, which in Europe are extremely varied and which, in turn, depend upon the policies of the political groups in power at any one time in local, regional and national governments.

Nevertheless, some trends can be discerned. One is an increasing willingness of policy makers to look to the cultural sector as an engine of social and economic regeneration in their communities.[1] Another, related development is the search for evidence of the impact or outcomes from the arts experience upon individuals. Such evidence will remain limited, however, until substantial longitudinal studies are undertaken.

In European museums there is also an increased interest in the spiritual and religious dimension of museum collections and museum provision. Rather than being a product of millennial anxieties, this is an inevitable result of the increasing sensitivity of museums to the cultural diversity of both their collections and their audiences. There is, too, growing (if still unwilling) acknowledgement by museums in Europe of their unavoidable engagement with oral history, traditional beliefs and other manifestations of non-material culture in local communities in Europe, without which material cultures (including museums collections) have no meaning.

This is, in turn, part of a wider recognition of the significance of differences among adults in European museums. In the Irish Museum of Modern Art, for example, the distinctive needs of older adults have been explored and articulated through a series of innovative projects that recognise that, unlike young people, they have no further stage of active life to move on to. Likewise, the Municipal Museum in Sobralinho, Portugal, recognises that, although relatively small in number, members of the African community who are first- and second-generation migrants from former colonies in Africa have very distinctive cultural backgrounds. Taken together, these trends indicate a growing awareness and sophistication on the part of at least some European museums of their audiences and their complex role in society.

These are all potentially significant developments. There is, however, another which is likely to have the most rapid and extensive impact on the nature of adult learning in museums. This is the emergence of digital media technologies. Use of the Internet in homes, offices and educational institutions is increasing exponentially, and it will only be a few years until half of all homes in Western Europe have personal computers. Already a majority of home computers in the United Kingdom are used for educational purposes (Department of Trade and Industry 1997).

At present, the greatest number of museum staff and funding streams established by the European Union make the assumption that the most important application of these technologies will be to enable museums to put their collections on-line. The old fallacy – that learning is about absorption of information, that it is curators' expertise which will provide most useful information, and that this information will flow one way, out from the museum and into the minds of the public – is thus resurrected anew in the digital age.

A fallacy is always a fallacy, and in this case it is likely to be a visible one. Users of museum web-sites are already showing their preference for information on creative resources over that concerning collections. A recent report to the UK Government by the Conference of National Museums Directors urged that at least as much investment of staff time, resources and spaces should be put into the development of museums as participatory public digital spaces as into curatorially driven on-line services. It indicated that digital media would bring into museums a tide of ideas, resources and expertise generated by society, greater than those which individual museums themselves could possibly contribute to the sea of learning around them.

As a centre for digital learning, the future museum will contain participatory digital exhibits incorporating responses and meanings contributed by the public, as well as digital cameras, 'smart cards' and other portable personal media for use during a visit. Both on-site and on-line, content created by users will be an important part of museum provision to the wider community. The public will expect to search the museum's collections and other resources according to their own criteria of interest for self-directed learning, not according to categories created by museum staff, which are irrelevant to them. The public will, therefore, need staff who are trained to help them develop their skills and creativity through the new media (National Museums Directors' Conference 1999).

An example of the way in which the public can make creative use of museums is *Going Graphic*, a project of the Victoria and Albert Museum in London. Over a two-week period in 1998 the museum invited visitors to borrow digital cameras, use these to capture images in the galleries, then use graphics software on computers provided by the museum in a public space to design posters about the V&A. Altogether about 3,000 people took part in the project. Every night, the posters designed digitally by the public that day were posted on the V&A's web-site, so that participants and anyone else interested in the project could access, download, change or re-send the posters they liked best. The freshness, originality and quality of the results, and the evidence they provided of the natural creativity of humankind if given an opportunity, were clearly visible to anyone who saw the results. During the first year after the project, these obscurely located pages on the V&A's web-site were visited by well over half a million people.

The creative potential of the new media is, then, exceptional. As with any other new technology, it was inevitable that in the first instance early applications would replicate traditional models (just as the first fired pots in pre-history copied the forms of leather bags). Control of technologies is now passing from technologists and collections managers to creative artists and educators, as well as the public. One of the clearest manifestations of this is the annual Arts Electronica Festival in Linz, Austria (Arts Electronica Centre 1997). Once again, there is potential for learning through museums to be developed through the informed 'common sense' of the public.

Over the last two decades, European adult education policy and provision have focused mainly on colleges, higher education institutions and other traditional adult learning networks. Where their role has been recognised at all, museums and galleries have been perceived to be marginal and inconsequential. In a sense, the European Commission and many other adult education agencies have been as colour-blind to the potential of museums and galleries as centres of learning, as museums and galleries have been colour-blind to the richness of the adult learning that is taking place, or could be developed, through their institutions. But European Community policy is now changing. The significance of the cultural dimension of many of the EC's education programmes is increasingly recognised and encouraged, and the cultural programmes include an increasingly developed education dimension.

The UK's Secretary of State at the Department of Culture, Media and Sport, Chris Smith, said in a speech in 1998 that 'without education there can be no culture'. In saying this, he reflects a growing awareness in Europe that learning and culture are two sides of the same coin.

Note

1 See, for example, F. Bianchini and H. Parkinson *Cultural policy and urban regeneration: the west European experience*, Manchester: Manchester University Press, 1993

References

Anderson, D, *A common wealth: museums and learning in the United Kingdom*, London: Department of National Heritage, 1997, p.12 (2nd edn, 1999, published as *A common wealth: museums in the learning age*, London: The Stationery Office on behalf of the Department of Culture, Media and Sport)

Arts Council of England, *Lottery new programmes: creative abilities of young people*, London: ACE, 1996

Arts Electronica Centre, *Fleshfactor: Informationsmaschine mensch*, Vienna/New York: Springer, 1997

Davie, G, 'The social significance of the Scottish philosophy of common sense', in *The Scottish Enlightenment and other essays*, Edinburgh: Polygon, 1991, pp.51–85 (see also Davie, G, *The crisis of the democratic intellectual*, Edinburgh: Polygon, 1986)

Department of Trade and Industry, *Is IT for all?* London: DTI, 1997

National Museums Directors' Conference, *A netful of jewels: new museums in the learning age*, London: NMDC, 1999

Sacks, O, *The island of the colour-blind and cycad island*, London: Picador, 1996

3 Norway

Eva Maehre Lauritzen

With a population of 4 million and more than 800 museums, Norway has a greater museum density than many other countries. The number of permanent employees in Norwegian museums is approximately 2,000 people. In addition, approximately 1,000 people work on a temporary basis. The museums show a great variation in themes and sizes, and most communities have their own local museum. Among Norwegian museums 77 per cent have a staff of three people or fewer in permanent positions; some are small and unmanned, often taken care of by local history societies, and open to the public only in the summer. These museums document the history of the population in the area, and in a way they are looked upon as the people's property. This creates a very tight bond between community and museum in many areas. Since the early 1970s children and young people have been given the highest priority as museum visitors. Most large museums have employed museum educators to develop programmes and undertake educational work especially for these groups. Some museums have few regular programmes for adults, others none at all. In most museums, however, the museum educators are responsible for programmes for all types of visitors.

Museum authorities publish annual museum statistics. The total number of visitors in 1996 was close to 9 million. This is approximately two museum visits per inhabitant per year, and exceeds the number of visitors to football matches. The number of participants in educational activities and special arrangements was 710,000, of whom 472,000 were young people and children (Museumsstatikken 1996).

University museums

Norway has four universities, in Oslo, Bergen, Trondheim and Tromsö, founded between 1811 and 1968. All universities have museums for archaeology and natural history, as well as botanical gardens; some also have a museum for ethnography. Some of the university museums are older than the universities themselves.

In Oslo, the museum's oldest collections (mineralogy) were used for teaching purposes at an Academy for Mining, established in 1757, connected to the silver mines at Kongsberg. When the University of Oslo was established in 1811, the Academy became part of it. The university museums, as well as many other museums, still play an active role in university studies. Students use museum exhibitions, objects, data and libraries, and many members of the professional museum staff work as tutors and give regular university lectures.

Thus the university museums have for a long time played a very special role in adult education.

The university museums are important. They are among the biggest museums in the country and of the total number of objects in Norwegian museums, the university museums' collections include 12 per cent of the country's art objects, 43 per cent of the cultural history objects, 99 per cent of the natural history objects and close to 100 per cent of the archaeological objects.

Further education and in-service training

Over the last 20 years the universities have gradually become more engaged in further education and in-service training. The university museums' role in this has mainly been that of providing in-service courses for teachers. These courses do, to some extent, use museum artefacts, although many of them are oriented towards fieldwork. Several courses have been arranged with financial support from the Ministry of Education's section for continuing training (Statens Laererkurs).

The Norwegian Association of Museum Educators

Most major Norwegian museums have museum educators. The Norwegian Association of Museum Educators (Norsk museumspedagogisk forening) was established in 1976 and has played a significant role in the professional stimulation of museum education and museum educators. The Association has been an important source of inspiration and knowledge. By means of several seminars and courses it has also focused on adult groups and initiated co-operation with adult education organisations as well as with organisations for the disabled. Some museums have established permanent collaborative projects with these groups. Today the Association is a group within the Norwegian Museums Association (Norges Museumsforbund).

Lectures and open days

Many museums have regular lectures for their public. Staff members and other specialists give open lectures in their specialist subject. This is probably the most common form of adult education offered by museums. Often these lectures are part of a series focusing on a special theme, and most will have an audience that is different for each lecture. Some series require registration and are only for a limited group. Art museums in particular have presented series of lectures for adult audiences covering a part or period within the history of art as seen in their museum. For example, in spring 1998 the Museum of Applied Art in Oslo

(Kunstindustrimuseet i Oslo) offered lectures in history of design styles for which participants registered and paid a fee.

Most museums regularly arrange demonstrations, activities, lectures and games for the public, aimed at families and adults. At the cultural history museums these arrangements frequently focus on old traditions and techniques in housekeeping, handicrafts and farming. Visitors are often given 'hands-on' facilities, and sometimes courses are offered for those who want to learn more. This has been especially important for old trades and crafts like smiths, coopers, plaster casters and others. Some of the crafts are facing a renaissance, and demonstrations like these are an important means of directing attention to them and recruiting new apprentices. In similar arrangements in natural history museums the public is offered help in identifying the specimens and objects they bring along. Lectures and demonstrations are also available, with opportunities for interaction. When the Botanical Garden in Oslo advertises demonstrations on, for example, how to prune trees, the garden is crowded with amateur gardeners eager to increase their knowledge of this particular skill. Many museums in different fields have a general service for identifying objects and explaining their name, age, use and suchlike.

Special courses and work for the unemployed

Some museums offer courses in old building techniques, or techniques used in farming, handicrafts and housekeeping. Several of these courses have been part of programmes for unemployed people, with the idea that they may lead to better qualifications for future employment outside the museum. Courses like these have been arranged specifically during periods of high unemployment and were developed mainly in open-air museums where it is possible to obtain practical experience of restoring or rebuilding houses. Furthermore, a large group of unemployed persons has been offered temporary work within museums in a special programme, again with the aim of later transferring their experience to permanent work elsewhere. In 1996 they numbered more than 400. They perform a variety of work dependent on their skills and demands of the museums; many of them, however, are carrying out data documentation of collections or maintenance work.

Elderly visitors

Regular links with elderly people have been forged by many museums. For those which focus on cultural history, elderly people represent an important source of information. They are also important as instructors in old techniques for special events in museums. In addition, organisations for the elderly are eager museum users, and frequently lay on group visits.

Among younger pensioners there are many active participants in lectures offered by a variety of organisations. The University for the Elderly (Eldreuniversitetet) is decentralised and gives lectures and courses, many of which are in co-operation with museums and/or museum employees.

Some museums have direct contact with homes for the elderly and invite them to programmes especially planned for this group. In the winter of 1997/98 the Kon-Tiki Museum in Oslo ran a successful special programme for which invitations were sent to organisations for the elderly as well as to residential homes and care institutions.

However, not all such initiatives are successful: some years ago museum educators in Oslo decided to focus on elderly people. Realising that many of them living in homes were not able to come to their museums, the educators planned to take parts of the museum collections out to them. This plan involved a short lecture and presentation of slides and objects from most major museums in Oslo, and was to be cost-free for the pensioners or the home. Each of the museums found someone willing to visit the homes and suggested some actual themes connected with their museum. The response from the administrators of the homes was disappointing: they refused the offer, indicating that they were not interested in the scheme. Thus the plan had to be abandoned.

Immigrants

The population of Norway was relatively homogenous until guest workers, mainly from Pakistan, Turkey and Morocco, began to migrate about 30 years ago. Later, groups of political refugees arrived, chiefly from Vietnam, Chile, and countries in Africa and Eastern Europe. These groups are now living all over Norway, the vast majority in the Oslo area. All immigrants participate in language classes to learn the Norwegian language. These classes are frequent users of museums as environments for concept formation, for learning about Norway, and for discussions and experience.

The Norwegian Council for Cultural Affairs (Norsk kulturråd) has initiated programmes to develop co-operation between the different ethnic groups and the Norwegian population and society. In recent years a very active foundation, the International Cultural Centre and Museum (Internasjonalt kultursenter og museum, IKM), situated in Oslo, has worked as a link between many ethnic groups and other cultural organisations, including museums. The main goal of IKM is to promote respect and understanding between people with different cultural backgrounds (IKM 1996).

Examples of co-operation between IKM and museums

Since IKM was established in 1990, it has proved to be a very creative institution. Despite its name, it is not a museum in the strict sense of the word, but has arranged several cultural festivals and exhibitions. Since 1993, it has received financial support from cultural authorities, schools and museum authorities and the city of Oslo, as well as ministries and state councils. The collaborative projects with museums have been successful and have resulted in several travelling exhibitions dealing with cultural diversity. IKM is situated in Oslo and has worked mainly with museums in Oslo, the Ethnographic Museum of the University of Oslo (Etnografisk museum), Oslo City Museum (Oslo bymuseum) and the Norwegian Folk Museum (Norsk folkemuseum).

The exhibitions have often focused on cultural similarities and differences in life and rituals, through childhood, youth and adolescence. The exhibition 'Similarity in the differences: rituals marking the transition from childhood to adolescence' was presented in 1994 after a seminar with the same title. In 1995/96 IKM presented 'Wedding: an exhibition about wedding customs in different cultures'. These exhibitions have been important sources of information about the various cultures.

Outside Oslo, Tröndelag Folk Museum in Trondheim (Tröndelag folkemuseum) presents programmes aimed at immigrants and refugees, children and adults. The museum co-operates with local theatres in this project. The programmes for adults combine language lectures with practical work like weaving, sewing and wood-turning.

Disabled visitors

In 1980, the Norwegian Association of Museum Educators initiated a co-operative programme with the organisations for blind and visually impaired people. This resulted in a seminar in 1981, 'Museums and the handicapped'. The aim of this seminar was to increase the knowledge among museum educators about the special needs of visually impaired museum visitors, and to provide advice for adapting museums and improving educational services for this group. The disabled participants described their experiences, which were very valuable. During group work with different themes, the blind and visually impaired were participants as well as experts in planning how to improve museum exhibitions, buildings and education services. In addition to the usual seminar report, a booklet giving a systematic presentation of improvements was edited in Norwegian and in English (Norwegian Association of Museum Educators 1985).

Some museums have a programme for disabled visitors. The Botanical Garden at the University of Oslo has a fragrance garden with elevated flower-beds, easy access for wheelchairs, and labels in Braille.

Museums and amateur organisations

There is a tradition that natural history museums have close contact with amateur scientific societies in fields such as geology, botany and zoology. The address of these societies is usually linked with that of a natural history museum; there are museum staff members on their board; and they make use of the museum facilities when arranging meetings. They also regularly have staff members as speakers and excursion leaders. This is an important and effective way of conveying knowledge and the results of new research to people with an interest in a particular field.

There are amateur organisations in subjects such as geology/palaeontology, botany, mycology, zoology, entomology and ornithology, and most of these are connected to museums. Some have local groups scattered around the country and are in this way linked to most natural history museums. Museums of local history, varying from large city museums to small rural museums, are closely connected to local history societies. Especially in the small museums with very limited staff resources, local history societies often participate in museum work, particularly in interpreting history in the museum.

Factories, ships and railways which have been converted into museums often benefit from making close connections with groups of amateur enthusiasts. Frequently these groups have been the initiators of the conservation, and they continue doing restoration work and giving demonstrations for the public. Those involved often possess and develop valuable technical knowledge from their profession and practical life experiences.

Internet

In recent years most major museums have presented their own information on the Internet. This is an important knowledge source that should not be underestimated. In addition to the presentation of exhibitions, a diary of events and useful information for the potential visitor, many museums also offer a good deal of information about their specialism. Some museums prepare special exhibitions or information programmes for the Internet. For instance, the Mineralogical Museum of the University of Oslo presents a geological encyclopaedia developed by one of their curators. This gives more extensive and easily available information about geological facts and terms than any book on the topic in Norwegian. The Palaeontological Museum gives the public access to their collections on the Internet, and it is possible to study fossil finds of a given species, locality or period. In many museums computers are available for public use.

In 1997 Norway established a new National Curriculum for grades 1–10, which focuses on new methods for learning, especially through projects and topics. Museums are important learning environments for many students working on projects. Some museums now present frequently requested information on the Internet. Several have also provided the opportunity to ask questions of staff through a direct answering service. Information made available in this way is of interest to everybody, regardless of age.

Many museums are now registering their collections on databases, and the process was initiated and decided on programmes by museum authorities and organisations. Two programmes are running, one for registration of cultural history objects and the other for natural history museum objects. In the future, parts of the databases will be available to the public and the museums will function as knowledge banks for the whole community.

Norwegian Association for Adult Education (Voksenopplaeringsforbundet)

Museums often have limited possibilities for offering courses as most of them have only a small administrative staff, and may experience difficulties in finding suitable rooms. Frequently museum staff members are engaged by institutions and organisations to give lectures at courses they offer. Museum staff members teach on practical and theoretical courses as parts of formal and informal education. Topics include dyeing, identifying edible mushrooms, furniture styles, antiques and gemstones. Usually museum visits form a part of the course.

Education outside the formal school system is undertaken by a variety of organisations united in 22 study federations. They include hobby activities such as music, dance, folk culture, handicrafts, philately, photography and political organisations. Some schools also offer formal education. The study federations were formerly gathered in one unit, the Joint Committee for Study Work (Samnemnda for studiearbeid), now incorporated in the Norwegian Association for Adult Education. The members of this Association offer courses on a wide range of themes for many different groups in society. Their courses may be preparations for an examination and a part of formal education, sometimes at university level. Mainly, however, they arrange courses independent of curricula which people take to broaden their minds generally or because a particular topic is a hobby. The total number of participants in 1997 was close to 700,000.

Collaboration between the Joint Committee for Study Work and museums was formally established in the 1980s. In the following years some seminars were arranged with the aim of increasing co-operation. The result was very promising and in some areas good relationships were established. One example is the area Sogn og Fjordane, a county in the fjord area on the west coast, with mainly small local museums. In a collaboration between museums and sports clubs, handicraft organisations, music and folk dance organisations, arts clubs and political organisations, several interesting projects were developed which were beneficial to all parties. These programmes included work with local folk costumes, folk music and folk dance, exhibitions, and a variety of courses and concerts. In some areas this work has continued, so that museums function as local cultural centres, an important focus for many kinds of activities in the local community. However, due to organisational changes, such promising collaboration between museums and educational organisations quietly faded away after a few years.

Lifelong learning

The Norwegian Official Report on lifelong learning (NOU 1986: 23) does not discuss the role of museums within the informal learning system. Similarly, the trade unions now working on programmes of continuing and paid training for all groups of employees, which they want to make a legal right, have not to date discussed the role of museums in this connection.

Training and staff development in museums

There is no clearly defined educational path for museum work. The opportunities for training and staff development are limited and have been important issues for a long time. So far there is no organisation taking full responsibility for staff development – neither for the general education of staff for museums, nor for the continuing education of existing staff.

Members of the professional staff in museums have university degrees, which provide limited background for many of the varied tasks a museum position requires. For students wanting to prepare for future careers in museums there are some possibilities: in the last few years it has been possible to take a course in Museum Studies at the University of Oslo as part of a university lower degree, lasting one term. This course is mainly intended for students in ethnology, ethnography, archaeology, history and history of art. There are a few related courses at other universities and colleges, and the University of Oslo announced the start of a conservation course in 1998.

Since 1947, the natural history museums have had a programme for museum training offered to four candidates every year (one in each of the subjects geology, palaeontology, zoology and botany), after completing a master's degree. This arrangement was initiated and for many years administered by the Norwegian Association of Natural History Museums (Norske naturhistoriske museers landsforbund 1993), but was later left to the universities. The candidates are employed for one year at one of the university museums for natural history and follow an in-service education programme focusing on the different aspects of working in a museum. Due to a change in the doctoral system, this programme has now been changed to four years' employment, with the aim of completing a doctorate degree in a biological or geological science. This will probably strengthen the research part, but may lead to an impairment in general museum work.

The University of Oslo runs courses in Science Education. For those with a master's degree in Science, it is possible to continue studies by undertaking a doctoral thesis in Science Education. A few candidates are at present working on their doctoral degrees by doing research on museum education and museum exhibitions in museums of natural history and technology.

Museum organisations offer courses for the continuing professional development of museum staff, and some large museums run courses for their own staff. Quantitatively, the museum organisations are the most important training organisers. The Norwegian Museums Association, of which most museums and many museum employees are members, arrange courses, conferences and seminars in many different subjects for many groups of museum staff. Some recent themes include security, public relations work, cultural laws and museums as part of community development.

In 1989 the Norwegian State Council for Museums (Statens museumsråd) initiated a report on the situation for training and staff development within museums in the Nordic countries. It recommended establishing a Nordic academy for museology, but this has not been realised. The Norwegian Official Report on Museums (NOU 1996: 2) suggests the establishment of a one-year course in Museum Studies at one of the universities, and that, after this is developed, a full academic programme should be considered. This course should focus on different types of museums. The Report also suggests programmes for continuing professional development for museum staff.

Potential for progress

The potential for progress is mainly dependent upon initiatives and economics. The 1996 Official Report (see above) recommends developing a programme to preserve for the future knowledge from old trades and crafts relating to buildings, ships and landscape, by establishing temporary positions at museums. The craftsmen engaged would also be responsible for apprentices preserving and developing trades for the future. This is a means to secure knowledge and skills that many museums need for the care, maintenance and presentation of their collections. If this comes to pass, it means that museums, probably in co-operation with the school system, will educate people in old trades and give them formal qualifications. To date it has been tried with good results by a traditional shipbuilder working at Tromsö Museum, constructing and working on a wooden fishing boat in the exhibition area.

Today most of the adult education provision offered by museums is sporadic and not part of a planned programme; it is mostly informal and offers no formal qualifications, although it gives a great deal of pleasure to visitors. There is a need for a thorough discussion of the role of museums in this field. Many Norwegian counties are at present working on plans for the development of museums, and this ought to provide an opportunity to include plans for museums and adult education.

One problem is that the Norwegian museum landscape is very complex, and that museums belong to different museum organisations and many different ministries. It has been suggested that an annual meeting be instigated, where these ministries are represented on parliamentary secretary level to exchange information, to avoid duplicating work and to discuss co-operative projects/ activities. If this takes place, adult education in museums is a theme that ought to be a subject for discussion in this forum. It should also be discussed within the museum organisations. It is hoped that such initiatives will lead to an increased focus on the theme and on plans for future development.

Bibliography

International Cultural Centre and Museum (IKM) *Museumsformidling i et flerkulturelt samfunn*, 1996

Museumsstatikken, *Norsk museumsutvikling*, 1996

Norske naturhistoriske museers landsforbund og Norske kunst- og kulturhistoriske museer, *Museums in Norway/Museer i Norge*, 1993

Norwegian Association of Museum Educators, *Adapting the museum for the blind and the weak-sighted*, 1985

Norwegian Official Report on Museums, (NOU) *Livslang laering*, 1986

—— *Museum Mangfald, minne, motestad*, 1996

Statens museumsråd, *Kunnskap à jour*, 1989

—— *Musea og opplysningsorganisasjonene*, 1989

4 Sweden

Helena Friman

'Stockholm Education': a personal account of a public education project

Stockholm is a capital on the outskirts of Europe. It has the salt sea, the Baltic, to the east and sweet water, Lake Målaren, to the west. It is a city where the historical layers are unusually evident and easy to 'read', and one where the authorities are at great pains to develop a public space where people can meet and experience the world around them together.

Europe is sometimes called the 'Old World'. In an article in *Nordisk Museologi*, the well-known museum critic and museum lover Kenneth Hudson writes about Europe as the Great Museum:

> From a museum point of view, I see every town, village, landscape, country and even continent as a Great Museum in which everyone can discover their own roots and see how they fit into the chain of human activities which stretches back over the centuries.
>
> (Hudson 1993: 55)

This metaphor has been a strong inspiration for me.

I worked in Stockholm City Museum for over 20 years and taught many things. Above all, I taught that the museum's main task and arena is the city itself; that a local museum must take part in the never-ending discussion about changes to the built environment and the social life of the city, not just by collecting and reflecting objects and actions, but also through the exchange of ideas, communication and confrontation. The museum is there to make the citizens interested in and curious about the world outside.

In the 1980s I organised courses on the cultural history of Stockholm for the city's traffic wardens and for policemen. These groups are not usually the most frequent visitors to museums, and I thought it might perhaps be better to reach them by means other than exhibitions and lectures. They are the only uniformed occupational groups who move around the city on foot. They are asked all kinds of questions and, among many other duties, their work has an educational and social side which involves great strain. It is tiring to be a representative of the authorities, as any uniformed person will automatically become. If, at the same time, their work situation is full of stress and conflict, it is easy for them to regard the general public and visiting tourists as a troublesome element, rather than as the most important part of their work. I found that they responded very positively, with a newly aroused interest in the city and issues connected with it.

It was while working on this programme that the idea of a special Stockholm education for specific occupational groups began to take shape in my head. Another strong inducement for me was meeting Havana's town antiquarian, Eusebio Leal, who gives lectures at street corners about the ongoing large-scale renovation of the old city. Moreover, the educational methods used by my friend and colleague in the Musée de la Ville de Paris, Catherine de Bourgoing, have also influenced the project.

Swedish cultural policy

Before I begin to describe the project, it may interest the reader to have a short outline of current Swedish cultural policy and the ideas that enable a special museum project like Stockholm Education to be implemented.

During the 1960s and 1970s the perception of culture as one instrument among others for achieving social change was widely accepted in Sweden. Equal access to culture was seen as a 'right', no less important than social and economic equality. Accordingly, national cultural policy was supposed to:

- help to protect freedom of expression and create genuine opportunities for the use of that freedom;
- give people the chance to engage in creative activities of their own and to promote personal contacts;
- counteract the negative effects of commercialism in the cultural sector;
- promote the decentralisation of activities and decisionmaking in the cultural sector;
- make more allowance for the experiences and needs of disadvantaged groups; and
- promote the interchange of experience within cultural sectors across linguistic and national boundaries.

These goals have been important for formulating the direction of cultural policy, establishing common values and raising national ambitions, but they have probably influenced opinion rather more than action. They have certainly been important at the local level in areas that did not previously have any debate about the arts.

Circumstances change, and today reference is still made to this kind of objective in budget statements and in regional and national debates. But the references have become more selective, perhaps reflecting a declining political consensus about the goals for cultural policy: for example, the negative effects of commercialism are very rarely mentioned today.

For many professionals like myself, working in the cultural sector the goals are still in place as commandments with a lasting influence on the evolving debate.

Museums in Sweden

The official statistics list 204 museums. There are national, regional and municipal museums, and the rest are classified as 'other museums'. Independent museums are rare in Sweden. In 1997, the official museums attracted around 16 million visitors.

Sweden has more museums than this, although they are neither covered by official statistics nor seen as part of the museum system. Different sources estimate the total number as more than 750, if various local collections and exhibitions, science centres and similar enterprises are included. These museums are often found in rural areas and in smaller towns; they are often organised around industrial sites or have ecological objectives.

The official museums are visited mostly by the more prosperous and well-educated part of the population. Of all cultural activities, visiting museums is the one which is most defined by social class. Only a few local museums go against this picture. It is also significant that museums are visited mostly by people living in the capital, in the larger cities and in the regional centres.

In 1994 a commission of inquiry presented a National Report on Museums. Its analyses and recommendations for future museums were widely discussed. As the Report argues:

> Systems in evolution need a memory, and societies are evolving systems. The museums are part of the collective memory of human beings: they are not *the* collective memory, but they may well be the leading elements in societies' collective memory..
>
> The definition of memory holds the key to the museum's objectives. Memory is not a building, it is not a structure. It is first and foremost a process whereby information is gathered, processed, communicated, and used. Note that memory includes communication and use, by definition memories are remembered, i.e. communicated, and the only means of verification is to observe usage...
>
> There are those who claim that museums are mostly for fun, or that the preservation of artefacts from the past is an end in itself.
>
> We [the Commission] argue that museums are in the service of society and consequently must offer both learning and entertainment, but the single most important objective of memory is to help us learn, as individuals and in society. Learning is about changes in knowledge structures, and the museum's main objective is to provoke and facilitate such changes. Learning is most effective when it occurs under conducive circumstances, and we do not underestimate the importance of an aesthetic dimension in museums. In addition, knowledge is an end in itself, irrespective of how it is used. However, the strategic implication is that the museums should first and foremost cooperate with schools, universities, and adult education organisations for the purpose of learning.
>
> (SOU 1994: 216)

Stockholm Education

In 1993 the Ministers of Culture of the European Union decided that Stockholm should be Cultural Capital of Europe 1998. When the decision was announced, I saw my chance to implement a special educational programme for people working in the streets of the city of Stockholm: policemen, traffic wardens, workers in public transport such as bus- and subway-drivers, ticket collectors and controllers, public library staff, taxi drivers, firemen and similar groups. I called it Stockholm Education.

In spring 1996 the Cultural Capital Office asked me to investigate whether the companies and institutions who employ these people would be interested in training of this kind and to submit a proposal as to how to initiate the project. In my proposal I wrote:

> It may be assumed that Stockholm Education will arouse attention both in Sweden and abroad. Nothing similar has ever been done before on a large scale. It could be said – somewhat facetiously – that there is something typically Swedish about an adult education project aiming to educate a whole capital city.
>
> The entire ongoing discussion about the concept of *lifelong learning*, that is, continuous training and further education, going beyond the narrow confines of subjects and occupations, can be distilled in the project, the content of which represents humanist values. Stockholm Education provides a chance for the participating companies to present their services in a positive light to the people of Stockholm and simultaneously to tourists during the year when Stockholm is Cultural Capital of Europe.

Implementation and purpose

Stockholm Education became a large adult education project. Its successful establishment depended on companies and public sector institutions in Stockholm realising the value of this special kind of training for their employees. The education is offered to them free of charge. The cost to them (which can be quite high) lies in letting their staff take part in the programme during working hours.

When I began working on Stockholm Education in October 1996, I had already met several directors and education managers of the prospective companies. In August I informed them all that the decision to implement the courses had been taken, that the project would come to fruition, and that they could contact me if they wished to begin during the autumn.

I had several preconceived opinions. One was that I would have trouble in enlisting co-operation from the police. Their education manager had had reservations about the plan, and I had the idea that police officers are mainly interested in sport and motor vehicles, not in history or culture, and that it would be difficult to catch them in the educational net. This proved to be a total misconception: the mounted police and local police of Stockholm, my target groups, were among the most interested of all.

I also thought that I would be able to arrange the courses in roughly the same way for all the different occupational groups. This turned out to be impossible: no two courses were the same.

It was interesting to see how the different companies reacted. The greater the independence of the management, the greater the possibilities of their grasping the opportunity. However, hierarchies can make themselves felt. People are cautious and often refer a matter upwards to someone else who can take the decision or express an opinion. Sometimes it was difficult to obtain the go-ahead for a simple matter such as convening a meeting, even though everyone agreed that it would be the best thing.

The work required me to attract more and more institutions and companies as time went by, getting them interested and willing to take part in the courses. The project has grown slowly, taking up much time. It requires roughly the same effort to reach groups that are unaccustomed to culture as it does to persuade them to come to a theatre or a museum. I have always worked in this way: there are no short cuts.

Through Stockholm Education people learn about the city and learn to see the city. The training is tailored to each participating group. It can vary from a short course lasting one day to a number of sessions of a few hours a week over a longer period.

Together we study the cultural history of Stockholm, with particular emphasis on people, social conditions, architecture, the names of streets, places and famous buildings, and the ongoing debate about the development of the city.

I plan, organise and lead the training myself, in close collaboration with the commissioning companies and institutions.

Key resources for the project are the museums and cultural institutions of Stockholm, many of which work in close partnership with me. Naturally enough, in view of the content of the training, the Stockholm City Museum is particularly significant. All groups meet there for their first (and only) study session, when they examine maps of Stockholm dating from the Middle Ages to the twentieth century.

The museums serve as a starting point for the discovery and exploration of Stockholm. Eighty per cent of the teaching takes place on walking tours of the city. The city itself is the real museum.

It is not my intention to train my 'students' to become guides. That is not the point. I want to arouse their curiosity. My idea is that, if they have a basic knowledge about the history and development of the city, if they are at home in their own parts of the town, then they will feel more assured and confident to meet the general public and tourists in a more responsive way. Their working days might be more interesting. Stockholm Education is an exercise for the mind, as important for the health and well-being of employees as physical exercise is for the body.

There is also a deeper meaning behind Stockholm Education: it is the idea of an open society, where one feels secure, is met with knowledge and respect, and where the intellect is activated.

I regularly contribute a column to several staff newsletters, where I write about the names of streets and places and about events and people in the history of Stockholm. I have also recorded a number of short television programmes for the Swedish Educational Broadcasting Company, covering various significant places in the city. The programmes were broadcast during 1998 and are directly associated with Stockholm Education.

As I write this, in mid-1999, some 1,550 individuals working in the infrastructure of Stockholm have participated in courses and received the special Stockholm Pin which serves as certificate of attendance. Many more people have attended lectures and taken part in walking tours and other activities arranged as part of the project. New, unexpected participant groups have requested the education after hearing about it, such as the street vendors of food who wanted a course in order to raise the status and educational level of a very specific occupational group whose members meet many people.

The project created a large 'Open University' in Stockholm. Many of those who had participated stated that Stockholm Education was the best in-service training that they had ever had; that it changed their working lives. They have begun to read about Stockholm, and 'when there is something historical on TV' they watch – something they had not previously done.

Thanks to an educational project within the SOCRATES programme – *Museums, keyworkers and lifelong learning* I am able to continue the project for at least another year. Stockholm Education will certainly survive – in one way or another.

References

Hudson, K, 'The great European museum', *Nordisk Museologi* 1993(2): 51–60

Swedish Government Official Report (SOU) 1994: 51, *Minne och bildning: Museernas uppdrag och organisation* (Memory and learning: the museums' commission and organisation), Stockholm: SOU

See also Myerscough, J, *National cultural policy in Sweden: report of a European group of experts,* Stockholm: Allmanna forlaget, 1990

5 Latvia

Aija Fleija

The development and functioning of a museum is directly dependent on the level of education, culture and economic wealth in society. The museum, as a part of society, increases the level of education in that society and its development. In the museum the individual obtains knowledge of 'collective memory', which is never gained from personal experience. Museums form the cultural environment. The higher the level of a society's culture, the wider and more differentiated is its museum system.

The present state of development of Latvian society can be characterised with the word 'leap'. We are in transition from one society model – closed, regulated – to a free and democratic one. However, these processes are not evolutionary: they are revolutionary, like a leap. Processes that would normally take decades now occur much more rapidly.

The traditional utilisation of museums by society is through visits to the museum to see collections open to the public. The following comparison of two museums in Latvia – the War Museum and the Museum of Revolution – may illustrate such a 'leap'.

The main theme of the War Museum is Latvia's fight for independence during the period 1916–41. As a result of Soviet occupation, however, the museum was shut down, and, instead, the Museum of Revolution was founded by Soviet officials in 1940. The main task of this museum was to demonstrate the superiority of Soviet society. As such, it functioned in the building of the former museum until 1990, when the War Museum was re-established.

There are two aims of a museum visit: education and entertainment. The former is usually realised by pupils, students and other organised groups of society. Visits to the Museum of Revolution had a hidden agenda in that they were, in essence, directed and supervised from the top ranks of the political party. The public and the museums had to follow instructions imposed from above on 'the improvement of ideological education in museums'. During the year 1985, there were 1,324 excursions to the Museum of Revolution, while 10 years later, there were 280 to the re-opened War Museum. This drop in numbers may be partly connected with the freedom of choice given to the people, even if the poor economic situation overall has to be the main reason.

It might be expected that visitors to museums of military history should be mainly those connected with the military. This is not so: in 1995, only 0.75 per cent of the total number of visitors were from the military, while during the first period of the existence of the War Museum the total was 10 per cent in 1933, and 12 per cent in 1936. There is no logic that indicates that museums of art are visited mostly by artists, natural history museums by biologists, history museums by historians – that is not a criterion. In my view it would be very disappointing if only specialists visited their own specialist museums.

How can our museum stimulate the public? One way of raising interest is the information about exhibitions which is sent out to schools and military units. Soldiers are extremely interested in the weaponry on display. However, as it is one thing to look at a weapon, quite another to handle it, the museum has prepared specific programmes for soldiers about the history of weapons which contain a survey of the museum's collection and a detailed examination of its shooting weapons.

Our museum as an institution for education and entertainment is used mostly by the citizens of Latvia. There is to date no successful co-operation with tourist companies, but the museum is now directed towards integrating more possibilities for relaxation which will make it more attractive to tourists. The exhibits provided in our museum are as extensive as in other social history museums (exhibition space covers 2,500 sq. m.). We are aware that such an abundance of displayed objects does not correspond with recent recommendations by museologists, but our Friends of the Museum and others who actively participate in the collection of artefacts want as much material as possible to be exhibited. We thus sacrifice the principles of exhibit design to an expansion of the museum's collection. However, in the future this policy may pay dividends.

Collaboration with the public is organised by the museum's Division of Information and Science Education. Its responsibility is organising visits and educational programmes, informing the public of historical events, co-operating with public organisations and arranging theme-based activities. Of these, the last two are the most important. The museum plays host to the five largest organisations relating to participants of World War II. They not only hold their meetings there but also visit the displays arranged by the museum and take part in different activities. The museum has a special hall holding 150 people.

One of the recent activities organised by the Museum in midsummer was devoted to the organisation Helsinki 1986, the first organisation to raise the national flag at the Monument of Freedom, and the hall was crowded. This may seem strange, but I would like to stress that this support was the free choice of the participants in response to advertisements on radio and in the press. During the existence of the Museum of Revolution the hall was also full – but that was 'voluntary obligation'!

What does such an activity contain? It is led by a member of the Division who gives an overview – the evolution of the event, or the actions of some individual; it is continued by contemporaries, participants in the event under discussion, and relatives. Sometimes these activities are connected with the design of the exhibition, the sequence of events; bands participate by playing old military music. Emotions aroused by such activities are sometimes so high that you can see tears in the old soldiers' eyes; and usually someone among the participants donates a gift from the period or topic under discussion.

Of course such activities are topical, and currently they are directed towards targeted groups. They offer an opportunity to meet and revive memories of participants' younger days.

One specific type of activity is with those Latvian emigrants who have become professional soldiers in foreign armies. They come to the museum and tell young Latvian soldiers about military service in different countries. At the recent exhibition 'Latvians in the Western military forces', we also displayed two uniforms of officers in the British Royal Air Force. The visiting soldiers gave advice and provided material aid.

In order to ascertain the views of visitors to our museum we have devised special questionnaires. I hope that comments will prove to the politicians that the museum is vital for our society.

6　Croatia

Ivo Maroević and Tončika Cukrov

The educational role of museums is becoming ever more important, both in theoretical and practical terms. In many countries it is, to an ever-increasing extent, gaining equal importance with other museum activities, regardless of the traditional differences that can be discerned between museums. However, in some countries it has a dominant role. In Croatia we have various experiences, but they are always in harmony with the Central European and Mediterranean milieu to which Croatia belongs, both geographically and culturally.

The suffering of the people in Croatia during the recent Patriotic War, the great migrations of the population, the loss of homes, the attempts at making a new home in some other place, as well as a number of processes that appeared during efforts made to normalise the situation – all these created a number of challenges for the museum community in Croatia. The answers that had to be provided to problems that had been only recognised recently were neither easy nor simple, and museum education covers only a part of them. We could say that this is the part that fulfils some of the aspirations of people who had left their homes and are now trying to adapt to new surroundings, as well as those who returned and are trying to find a lost reality in the reality of museums, regardless of the level of abstraction with respect to reality evident in museums. The span between the aspirations of museum visitors and that which museums offer is the unknown quantity which needs to be solved as successfully as possible, although the solution to this problem is neither static nor linked with a particular moment but is, rather, dynamic and stretches through time in which both the museum educator and the visitor are subject to change.

Adult education in museums is firmly linked with two elementary assumptions: on the one hand we have the museum holdings and the range of the representation of knowledge with all its specific features and secondary effects, while on the other we have the visitor as an individual and a part of a particular social group, with their cultural identity, personal characteristics and leanings, which are frequently insufficiently recognisable, and their needs and aspirations. After times of crisis – and war is certainly one of them – museums have an irreplaceable role in promoting the return of trust between people, reconciliation in the broad sense of the word, as well as in the creation of a new identity.

Museum education

According to the information gathered for this paper,[1] museum education in Croatia is experiencing new levels of popularity; it is changing the former closed nature of museums and is taking an active position with respect to visitors. If we consider this from the historical point of view, until recently the model that was developed was based on the co-operation of museums and educational institutions, and, to a much lesser degree, the museums were also co-operating with tourism workers. This orientation was the result of the educational policy of society, and it was, for the most part, limited to the younger generation. Adult education was sporadic and was aimed mainly at the education of teaching staff, for which lectures were organised to inform them so that they themselves could lead schoolchildren through museums or prepare them for museum visits. With respect to other age groups or social groups, museum education was limited to guided tours through the museum's permanent or temporary exhibitions.

. A few museums have a long record of devoted educational work and significant results in this field. Among them, the one with the longest tradition is the Archaeological Museum of Istria in Pula which has, since 1969, had an active museum education department (Girardi-Jurkić 1975), the first of its kind in Croatian museum practice. All large museums have had an organised education department; for example, the Ethnographic Museum, the Museum of Arts and Crafts and the Technical Museum in Zagreb, the Modern Gallery in Rijeka, the Municipal Museum in Varaždin, the Museum of Slavonia in Osijek and others.

During the Patriotic War (1991–95) most museums did not present exhibitions and, unfortunately, some museums suffered damage, both to the buildings and, to a great extent, museum holdings. Out of a total of 204 museums, galleries and museum collections in Croatia, 66 museum buildings were damaged or destroyed, while 45 museums and collections recorded damage to museum holdings (Museum Documentation Centre 1998). After the end of the war, the first task in the process of establishing peacetime conditions was the restoration of permanent exhibitions. In the early 1990s, all the achievements of museum education had become a thing of the past because of the war, so that the younger generations had lost the opportunity of coming into contact with museums as institutions, with their content and the other educational aspects they offer.

Educational activities in the mid-1990s

A survey carried out by the Museum Documentation Centre (MDC) during 1995 in museums in Zagreb had shown that the state of educational activities was indeed very bad. The survey questionnaire was made up of two parts: the first contained 23 questions concerning the number of staff professionally involved with educational activities in the museum, the way in which these were organised, their financing and co-operation with curators; the second part dealt with general information about professional staff and their qualifications, for example. The questionnaire structured in this way was aimed at realistically identifying the state of these activities in the most representative sample in Croatia.

According to the survey, 61 per cent of respondents stated that they had no professional staff devoted to education.[2] On the other hand, we have the prominent example of the Technical Museum which has for many years organised its educational activities in such a way that educational tasks are carried out not only by the teaching organiser and two museum educators, but also by 12 professional staff members during one-third of their working hours. The survey sought responses concerning experiences with respect to plans and programmes. They were gathered only from museums that had a professional museum educator, while such planning in the case of museums without one is 'unknown'.

We find the data concerning the share of the educational activities of museums with respect to age groups of visitors to be interesting. In the younger age groups, most of the visitors come from secondary schools, and in the adult group, most of the visitors are students. Few museums record a prevalence of pre-school age groups. Little attention is devoted to family education, specialists and collectors. In this context, the results of the survey show that museum education is for the most part restricted to the education of schoolchildren and students, and that the earlier model has again been implemented. In this respect we also have data concerning teaching activities in museums that show that they are regularly carried out in 44 per cent of cases, and in a further 25 per cent on an occasional basis. On the other hand, museum educators teach more frequently in schools (in 67 per cent of cases) than in their regular work (13 per cent). Teaching is carried out with the combined use of traditional and modern media, such as photographs, slide-shows or videos. Additionally, visitors use computers at the Museum of Arts and Crafts, the Archaeological Museum in Zagreb and others.

The data collected from the survey show that neither professional museum staff nor most of the museums have a clearly elaborated view of educational activities, so that in this respect the strategy of museums is not defined. It is for this reason that the MDC has initiated a number of educational projects, organised seminars and professional trips for museum staff with the aim of developing an awareness of the need for greater emphasis on the educational activities of museums.

Modern tendencies

In recent years, Croatian museums have carried out interesting educational projects. A major contributing force in this has been the MDC, which, through efforts led by Želimir Laszlo and Tončika Cukrov, has initiated two educational games intended to promote individual visits by children and young people to museums. In 1996, 15 of Zagreb's museums gathered around the project *What thrilled Professor Baltazar in the Museum?*, led by the MDC, while as many as 19 museums from Zagreb participated in the *Flower* project in 1997, led by the Archaeological Museum in Zagreb. The funding for the projects was provided by the Ministry of Culture and the City Department for Culture and Education, while the *Flower* project received financial support from the City Department of Culture and various sponsors. Prizes for both projects were also provided by sponsors.

Museum educators also carried out other educational projects intended for children and young people, such as the *Remembering history and culture* project of the Teaching College in Pula and the Archaeological Museum of Istria (1992–98), aimed at children from day-care centres. This project served as part of the practical training of students at the college. Similarly, the educational project organised on the occasion of the exhibition 'Cartographers' geognostic projections for the 21st century' by the Museum of Contemporary Art in Zagreb included 10 well-thought-out workshops where children and young people 'played' at raising the consciousness of modern artistic expression. These workshops ended with a quiz and prizes for the lucky ones.

Some international institutions also took part in the promotion of museum educational projects in Croatia. For example, in 1998, by participating in ICOM-CECA's international project *All roads lead to Rome*, Zagreb's museum educators led by Vesna Leiner from the Museum of the City of Zagreb organised a project titled *On our way*, intended for children from secondary schools. Every museum organised workshops: for example, a mosaic workshop, a workshop for the making of Roman hairstyles, weaving. Lectures and archaeological research were also arranged. The organiser planned a final event in Rome with a gathering of young people from participating countries, at which they all presented their projects in order to draw attention to the bonds that are the result of a joint heritage.

The Natural History Museum in Rijeka was, together with the Naval School in Bakar and the 1st Croatian Grammar School in Rijeka, involved in the SEMEP ecological project for the south-eastern Mediterranean. This interdisciplinary project looked into the ecological aspects of the sea through lectures about the sea and field trips.

Another international project worth mentioning is UNESCO's project *The participation of youth in the preservation and promotion of the world's heritage*, organised in co-operation with the Ministry of Culture and the state Administration for the Protection of the Cultural Heritage, as well as educational institutions of Split and Zagreb and the Cultural Centre of the Stari Grad Municipality. Within the framework of the projects, workshops were organised for students of the humanities where they would study the history of the oldest Greek town in Croatia – 'Pharos' (now Stari Grad on the island of Hvar). Along with research in the archaeological workshop, the newly discovered objects were conserved with professional assistance, catalogued and presented within the framework of the archaeological section of the museum exhibition at the Cultural Centre of the Stari Grad Municipality. The mosaic workshop made copies of original artefacts that were placed at their original locations, while the originals were moved to the museum exhibition. There were also history workshops that were organised for the study of Latin texts that deal with this region. These educational events have regularly taken place for the past three years (1996–98) during the summer holiday recess.

Museums in the promotion of adult education

In the post-war period, museums in Croatia have had, for the most part, no clearly defined programmes for adults, although all of the regular activities are primarily intended for them. As in the period before the Patriotic War, museums in most cases feel that it is sufficient to cover current events and presenting their public with exhibitions that it wants. Guided tours are provided for the public, but are rarely accompanied by other events.

Exhibitions organised in the early 1990s were for the most part aimed at the subject of the war, as borne out by their titles: the exhibition of photographs 'SOS for the Croatian Cultural Heritage' (1991) or the exhibition of photographs 'Vukovar-VukoWAR' (1991), presented at the MGC Klovićevi dvori in Zagreb.

Displaced persons: refugees and museums

The war caused numerous problems and, unfortunately, there was a growth of a population that had been a tiny minority up to this time. These are, for example, displaced persons and refugees; namely, people who have in some way been socially endangered or have suffered as the result of the war, such as invalids and the blind, widows and mothers of those who died in the war. The organisation of reception centres and refugee camps was very important for these people. Apart from providing basic protection and assistance, there were also events that helped this part of the population to participate in the life of the local community. A great part in this was played by our own Suncokret (Sunflower) organisation – a non-governmental organisation founded in 1992 with the aim of providing psychological and social assistance to such displaced persons, refugees and returnees and to the local populations in order to alleviate the effects of the war and re-integrate the community. The work was organised for all age groups and included educational, creative and entertainment aspects, as well as the aspect of socialisation.

Creative workshops were organised in the camps, mostly for women skilled in handiwork (weaving, embroidery, sewing, knitting), with the aim of reproducing old decorations and motifs from the folk costumes of their home communities. This work was also aimed at preserving the identity of the displaced persons and refugee population. Exhibitions, such as that of handiwork 'This too is Love', organised by the Society of Croatian Widows of the Patriotic War from the County of Dubrovnik and Neretva, overseen by the MGC Klovićevi dvori in Zagreb (1994), were not only the outward presentations of a way of life, but were also experienced as integral cultural events.

Of particular importance, especially for the population displaced from eastern Slavonia, were the newly organised old museums: the Vukovar Municipal Museum in Exile and the Ilok Museum in Exile that continued their cultural task in Zagreb even without their museum holdings. They became the agents of the preservation of the cultural identity of the people of Vukovar and Ilok at the most basic level, and they did this by gathering objects like folk costumes, books, works of art, photographs, old postcards and historical documents. The local community assisted in various ways, and the most frequent events were travelling exhibitions for donations. They were regularly organised in museums throughout Croatia, and in this way strengthened support and the hope for eventual return to their homes and way of life.

Invalids and museums

Most museums in Croatia have not yet developed programmes for the invalid population. Although their number rose, unfortunately, during and after the Patriotic War, they receive only guided tours depending on the interest they show and the level of activity of their local Association of War Invalids.

A more meaningful contribution for the blind is provided by a specialised museum, the Typhlological Museum in Zagreb. In the Tactile Gallery it has, for example, organised the exhibition 'We look with our hearts', accompanied by an auction, and the receipts from the sale of works donated to the blind were used for the purchase of equipment. The same museum organises various exhibitions intended for this population, mainly of sculptures, artistic and educational exhibitions. It has also, in co-operation with the Archaeological Museum in Zagreb, organised an exhibition of copies of archaeological objects titled 'Touching into the past' (1996).

Regular educational activities of museums

Apart from organising exhibitions and guided tours, museums frequently arrange lectures or scholarly discussions or scholarly symposia on given themes. The Technical Museum in Zagreb is an example of a museum that organises some 40 lectures ranging from astronomy to space science (in the Planetarium), as well as popular science discussions on technology every year.

Museums have also organised other events. They arrange book promotions as well as literary, musical and other cultural presentations. Most notable among these museums are the Museum of Arts and Crafts and the MGC Mimara Museum in Zagreb, the Museum of Croatian Archaeological Monuments in Split, and the Dubrovnik Museum in Dubrovnik.

Museums as advisers and organisers

Local museums are also small cultural centres in their towns. They are places where advice is sought concerning various cultural subjects. At the same time, the museum professionals are advisers of mentors for those writing their bachelor's, master's or PhD papers. Their capacity as advisers is evident in the organisation of cultural events, including those that bring together amateur artists in creative workshops or colonies. These are a part of the regular annual activities of several museums in Croatia, the most notable of which is the one organised by the Vinkovci Municipal Museum, aimed at academically trained artists and founded as the 'Nuštar Art Colony'. It began in 1993 and is held every year for a week in mid-June. At the end of the 'colony' there is an exhibition of works produced during that 'season'.

Local museums also play an important part in the promotion of educational activities through the organisation of various ethnological events, such as those held during the carnival season, or accompanying the Days of Bread. 'Autumns in Vinkovci' are an example of an event that is at the same time ethnological, cultural and economic. The Vinkovci Municipal Museum is only one of the organisers of the event, but in the educational sense it is the most important, especially in the expert section linked to a display of folk costumes (from Croatia).

Other museums perform a similar educational function, depending on the events with which they are involved, particularly events linked with International Museum Day. On that day museums provide free admission for all visitors, and organise free expert valuations and other expert services. This day is thematically defined each year, so that the public is informed through the mass media and can take part in discussions concerning particular museum themes. The theme is recommended by ICOM, whose instructions are further coordinated by the MDC, the central museum institution in Croatia.

Workshops and the demonstration of skills

The Ethnographic Museum in Zagreb is one of the few museums to have an adult education department. Although its activities are for the most part linked with educational work with the young, work with adults is based primarily on the organisation of creative workshops. Especially popular are public workshops that make traditional Christmas decorations or Easter eggs. During the exhibition 'Furniture in Croatia', for example, there were workshops for educators and art teachers, 'Making furniture from cardboard'. The museum co-operates with other museums with ethnological holdings, most notably with the museums of the Croatian Zagorje and its member the 'Old Village' Museum in Kumrovec. Through their joint efforts they have organised workshops for educators such as 'The straw-weaving skills of the women of Bunjevci'.

The demonstration of skills is another way of providing assistance through which museums aim at attracting the interest of the public at large. The above-mentioned 'Old Village' Museum in Kumrovec is one of the few open-air museums in Croatia that, during the summers of 1990 to 1996, regularly organised weekend demonstrations of various traditional crafts. The characteristic feature of this museum is that each of the 30 buildings that belong to the museum demonstrates a different traditional economic activity or living function. They also present various crafts, thus making visits especially interesting.

The Prints Cabinet of the Croatian Academy of Science and Art has, for example, organised a calligraphy workshop that is educational in that it demonstrates the making of prints. However, it is also a new form of work for this institution since it rents out rooms to print-artists for their needs.

New elements in the museums' approach to the public

In the 1990s it became popular among museum professionals in Croatia to organise societies of the Friends of a museum, societies that primarily attract adults who find an incentive for a broader education in museums. Exceptional results were achieved by the Gallery of Modern Art in Rijeka, which, since the founding of the 'Club of the Gallery of Modern Art' in 1992, has organised for its members free information about events, free admission to the museum, free copies of exhibition catalogues, special lectures and excursions. The Mimara Museum in Zagreb has also reaped good results with its 'Mimara Club'. Museums also co-operate with professional and expert societies, the one with the longest tradition being the 'Coin Collectors' Society' under the auspices of the Plaster Cast Collection of the Croatian Academy of Science and Art.

Croatian museums have recently gained public interest through well-prepared exhibitions. The exceptionally successful ones that were well marketed include the 'Biedermeier in Croatia' exhibition (April–August 1997), organised by the Museum of Arts and Crafts in Zagreb. The exhibition provided an integral view of events in the political, social, economic and cultural life of Croatia in the first half of the nineteenth century. Marketing activities linked with the exhibition involved several levels: co-operation with the professional staff of the museum, co-operation with sponsors, promotion of the project, a programme of souvenirs and accompanying events (Jurić-Bulatović 1966). A great media campaign, a rich programme of souvenirs, promotional events, a competition for the best Biedermeier photograph, as well as a competition for visitors (admission tickets were drawn to select the lucky winner of a car donated by a sponsor) resulted in 35,000 visitors. It has been a long time since a museum drew such numbers of visitors in Croatia.

Who were these visitors? This, among many other questions, was the subject of a survey organised in the closing days of the exhibition.[3] Most of the visitors (29 per cent) were between the ages of 18 and 30. The second largest group was that of people between the ages of 30 and 45. Persons between 45 and 55 made up 18 per cent of all visitors. Seventy-nine per cent stated that their reason for coming to the museum was their interest in the subject, while only 2 per cent responded that they came by chance. The same survey attempted to elicit visitors' views about the exhibition.

Conclusion

It is with great pride that we can say that, in spite of the hard times and the destruction inflicted on the cultural heritage during the Patriotic War, Croatian museums have been able to provide a number of quality programmes aimed at a select public. However, they still need to work on raising their quality to that of the great European museums. An indication of this is an evaluation in the survey mentioned above, where only 9 per cent of the visitors responded that Croatian museums today are neither worse nor better than the majority of European museums.

Croatian museums are still searching for the best path to take in regard to education and for better organisational solutions. The results that have been achieved so far indicate the potential of both the professional staff and museum holdings. However, adult education remains an insufficiently recognised field of activity, although there are many valid reasons why there should be an orientation towards it. The promotion of collecting, the discovery of meaning in the material world of objects, the development of emotional relationships within and between various cultural traditions can help adults not only in gaining new knowledge, but also in providing them with a meaningful way of spending their free time. Furthermore, and especially in Croatia, it can help in overcoming the trauma of war and, in the process of creating a new national identity, may, through museum education, add a cultural element.

Notes

1 The data used in this text have been taken from the database of the Museum Documentation Centre, Zagreb.

2 At the time of writing, the number of museum educators differs from that indicated in the survey data.

3 The survey was carried out by Vesna Jurić-Bulatović, Head of Marketing at the Museum of Arts and Crafts in Zagreb.

References

Girardi, V Jurkic (1975) *The development and the results of the museum education department at the Archaeological Museum of Istria in Pula*, Pula.

Jurić-Bulatović, V, 'Marketing projekta Bidermajer u Hrvatskoj' (Marketing the Biedermeier in Croatia project), *Informatica Museologica* 1996, 27(3–4): 7.

Museum Documentation Centre, *War damage to museums and galleries in Croatia*, 1998

Organisations

The Modern Gallery, Dolac 2, Rijeka

Museum Documentation Centre, Mesnička 5, Zagreb Ethnographic Museum, Mazžuranićev trg 14, Zagreb

Museum and Gallery Centre at the Mimara Museum, Roosveltov trg 5, Zagreb

The Museum of Arts and Crafts, Trg maršala Tita 10, Zagreb

The Technical Museum, Savska cesta 18, Zagreb

7 The Czech Republic

Radka Schusterová and Pavel Hartl

Chimney and mushroom museums

A visitor from Bohemia interested in museums and visiting England for the first time might be surprised on finding many unusual exhibitions, such as a private museum of chimneys. Similarly, an English visitor coming to the Czech Republic might be surprised on finding not one, but a number of museums of mushrooms. We Czechs, despite the fact that about 50 of us get mildly poisoned by mushrooms and two or three die as a result of our passion, still love to seek, pick, eat but also watch all kinds of mushrooms.

Educational efforts are always connected to culture and traditions, and the extent of the educational process is difficult to measure. Nevertheless, it would be difficult to find anyone in our country saying that our contemporary museums, galleries and monuments do not participate in education of both professionals and the public. They do, and their activities are quite substantial.

According to a documentary survey published by the Association of Bohemian, Moravian and Silesian Museums and Galleries (1998), there are currently 566 active museums, galleries and monuments in the Czech Republic. They give evidence of history and the present time, they work with collections of exhibits, prepare both permanent displays and temporary exhibitions, organise lectures and concerts, and publish a number of periodicals and other publications. They address a wide spectrum of visitors in all age categories. Their offer is truly broad: from permanent displays and short-term exhibitions documenting a specific historical event or personality of the given region to the whole range of different programmes discussed later in this chapter. All of this contributes to a certain educational milieu. What does it look like today in the Czech Republic?

Belief in the value of education

Strong belief in the value and power of education has been traditional for the population. This fact was supported by the results of the international Delphi study of 1995. Education as a value appeared very high compared with the other countries surveyed – namely, the EU members, Estonia and Slovenia. Such a view of Czech citizens may not come as a surprise to an Internet and CD-ROM surfer. In the Encarta *World Atlas* 1996 one can read the following characteristics:

> Czechs generally value education, intelligence, social standing, modesty, and humour. The Czech sense of humour is often dry and ironic, and

reflects an attitude of realism rather than pessimism. Jokes and parables are commonly used in conversation. Professionals (doctors, engineers, etc.) are admired, but so are skilled manual workers.

(Similarly flattering assessments could undoubtedly be found as characteristics of other European countries. Were we take to them literally, the world would be in harmony, and all nations would want to be neighbours of all other nations.)

A comparative study of Czech Republic citizens, also dated 1996, ordered by the Ministry of Education, offers the following characteristics: traditional belief in the power and value of education, a very good level of general education of citizens, a high level of workforce qualifications, strong motivation to enhance one's qualification, and flexibility and promptness in the supply of educational opportunities for adults.

The labour market

Such surprisingly good prerequisites can be explained by contemporary trends on the labour market. Fewer and fewer people are employed by the government, a diminishing number of people work in industrial production, there is a decreasing number of large enterprises in favour of smaller ones, demand for a flexible workforce is increasing, wages tend increasingly to reflect economic prosperity, gaps in incomes between different professions and industries widen, most working people realise that they cannot keep one job for their entire life, that they will have to retrain and continue to learn.

Unfortunately, there are also less positive data and trends. The rate of unemployment is growing. In the worst affected areas, the unemployment rate of the least well-educated people can reach 30 per cent, while the global percentage is between 5 per cent and 6 per cent. Changes in labour organisation and time management evokes stress in many people. One of the results is decreasing trust in politics, loss of purpose of living and problems with identity. In accordance with tradition, adult education can best help in enabling people to gain qualifications and re-training, to cope with new technologies, and gain access to information. It is less successful, yet still helpful, in solving health problems, problems of personal identity, purpose of living and so on. Yet issues such as unemployment and poverty remain outside the influence of adult education, as they are of a political-economic nature.

Historical background: establishment of the Republic

Historical data can give us evidence on the synergistic power of good adult education legislation. In 1919, only one year after the establishment of the Czechoslovak Republic, two special laws on courses in civic education and on libraries were passed. In the country's individual districts, towns and villages, adult education commissions were formed. Indirectly, they also affected the establishment of regional and municipal museums. In 1925, Masaryk's Institute for People's Education was established. The Government widened and reorganised the structure of people's high schools, and they became the institutional basis for people's systematic education on the level of municipal or secondary schools. They were of excellent standard; the poor had free access to them. Education became national property. Only professional training courses were charged for. General and other education and administrative costs of these institutions were covered by government subsidies. Schools for the unemployed were organised; they were compulsory for everybody on the dole.

The nation, enjoying its freedom and independence regained after 300 years, valued work for the Republic, and was eager to learn. This situation reached its peak in the 1930s and the period immediately following World War II.

The second half of the twentieth century

From 1948 and the total dependence on the Soviet Union, the country became isolated from information, the expansion of adult education stagnated and the gap between the country and the fast-developing Euro-American society widened. Most people were working for the Government, directly or indirectly. Over 40 per cent of labour was in large, state-owned industrial companies. Wages were fixed centrally. There was no geographic mobility but there was full employment and this was, naturally, accompanied by low productivity of work and low competitiveness of Czech products on Western markets.

The collapse of the Soviet empire starting from the 1980s has brought an immense influx of knowledge of all kinds, information technology, and harsh free-market competition into the liberated countries of Central Europe. On the one hand, this strengthened the importance of education for qualifications, and as a result, hundreds of private adult educational agencies were established. On the other hand, such private or public activities which focused on less vocational-oriented areas of adult education were scarce. The Government reacted only reluctantly to legislative needs in the area of national heritage preservation, including the activities of museums, in spite of the fact that it is one of the most traditional educational and research areas in the territory of the Czech Republic.

The Czech National Museum

The National Museum in Prague is the oldest museum in Bohemia and the biggest and most important museum in the Czech Republic. It was established at a ceremonial meeting on 15 April 1818, following efforts by the *illuminati*, members of the aristocracy and Czech patriotic scientists, led by Earl František Libštejnský of Kolovraty. The first exhibits were based on collections of Earl Kašpar of Sternberg and a number of other noble benefactors; many patriotic donors also contributed financially. Originally, there were collections focused on mineralogy, palaeontology and numismatics, as well as a library and an archive. *The National Museum Journal* was established, the first issue being published in 1827, edited by the renowned Czech historian and representative of the Czech National Revival, František Palacký. The journal has been published ever since, and is the oldest professional journal in the Czech Lands.

Collections of the National Museum were originally placed in various palaces in Prague. With the increasing consciousness of the nation and the growing number of collections, a grandiose project originated to build a dignified representative seat for the institution and its exhibits: a grand palace on Wenceslas Square in Prague – that is in the very heart of Prague, both from a historical and a cultural point of view. The building was constructed between 1885 and 1891 and became one of Prague's dominant features. It also bears symbolic value for the nation, as it was built as a glorification of Czech science, history and culture. In the past, most important cultural, political and historic events took place there.

Current activities of the National Museum

The current fund of the National Museum (NM) consists of 14 million exhibits, covering the areas of natural sciences, history, fine arts, music and librarianship. It is a cultural heritage of immense value as well as an endless source of information for local and international scientists, and an educational resource for schools and the public. Twelve specialised institutes and offices are also administrative parts of the NM, each offering specific information and knowledge. These are: the Náprstek Museum of Asian, African and American Cultures, the Ethnographic Museum in Prague, Lobkowitz Palace in Prague, Tyrš Museum of Physical Education and Sports in Prague, Museum of Bedřich Smetana in Prague, Museum of Antonin Dvořák in Prague, Lapidarium in Prague, Exposition of Asian Culture in Liběchov, Antonin Dvořák Monument in Nelahozeves, Josef Suk Monument in Křečovice, Smetana Lodge in Jabkenice, Exposition in Vrchotovny Janovice Castle.

In 1997, 78 exhibitions were organised in the individual premises of the NM, and 519,463 adults and children visited its collections and exhibitions. Compared with 1996, this represents an increase of 12,081 visitors. For example, 'The Homeland of the Pharaohs' held in Náprstek Museum was one of the most successful exhibitions.

Publication activities the of NM mainly focus on its 12 periodicals, most of which enjoy a long tradition and popularity among readers, the most popular being *The Numismatics Papers* (Numismatické listy). It was first published in 1945, produces six issues per year, and has a circulation of 3,600. In all, there are 1,650 subscribers to NM periodicals,

The NM is very active in organising lectures, concerts and other cultural events. The range of lecture topics is wide, and the most frequently represented areas are: preservation of the national heritage, anthropology, librarianship and fine arts. The concerts organised in the historic building of the NM are also very popular, both for the atmosphere of the new renaissance style of the building, and the repertoire on offer. In 1997, there were 106 concerts, attended by 48,000 listeners.

In 1996, the College of Information Services in Prague, specialising in informatics management, widened its study offer with a new specialisation, Services of Museums and Galleries. This is a unique study programme in the whole network of secondary and higher education. Under a special contract, specialists from the NM provide part of the tuition. There are some 50 students in a class who study for seven semesters, including one of compulsory practical training. The technical background of the school is of good European standard, seeking international certification and the status of university study level.

For the future work of the NM, it is very important to win the Japanese Government Cultural Grant, which would open up new possibilities in the use of audio-visual and presentation technologies.

Regional museums

As an example of activities in the regions, we have selected the Polabské Museum in Poděbrady (PMP) with its eight branches. At the moment, they have no systematically scheduled educational programme, providing the traditional, well-tested activities: printed materials, lectures, collections, exhibitions and accompanying programmes. The PMP started with printed materials and gave lectures in 1969 and the activities have continued ever since, with few changes in character or audience. The most popular are lecture topics concerning the history of the region, travelogues, natural sciences and history of art, illustrated by slides and videos.

Statistics for 1997 are as follows:

- 24 lectures in its own premises;
- 37 lectures by PMP specialists in other institutions;
- 1 programme dedicated to celebrating the millennium of St Vojtěch;
- 3 concerts;
- 1 bicycle trip tracing local monuments;
- 3 bus trips tracing local monuments; and
- 1 excursion for biology teachers.

Unfortunately, a number of hobby clubs were disestablished, such as history, fungology and numismatics. This means there is only one club attached to the

PMP at the moment. This is called Field–Club Polabí (established in 1991), whose aims are the preservation of nature and other environmental issues. As an illustration, let us look at the table below, which compares attendance of visitors to the PMP and its branches in 1996 and 1997:

Museum, branch	1996	1997
Poděbrady	8,613	9,779
Monument of King George	12,375	12,004
Přerov nad Labem	46,247	45,802
Sadská	534	904
Lysa nad Labem	1,135	1,234
Nymburk	6,206	1,585
Rožďalovice	1,856	1,200
Městec Králové	(closed)	(n.a.)
TOTAL	76,966	72,508

There were 115 visits by researchers, and 8 diploma studies.

Children visiting collections and exhibitions with their classes often draw pictures reflecting their impressions, which enhances the educational impact of the event. The results are then usually also exhibited. Recent examples are set out below:

- 1993 'Come and Play in the Museum – or Toys Yesterday, Today and Tomorrow'
- 1995 'Guilds, Crafts and Entrepreneurs': the latter part was prepared by students of the private School of Economics in Poděbrady. It was very interesting for the visitors to see and find connections between traditional and current crafts and businesses.
- 1996/97 an auction of works by fine artists to a children's home in Nymburk. The donated works of art provided an opportunity to exhibit a range of various art techniques (enamel, encaustics, painting on silk, etc.).

It is a common practice to organise an opening seminar before each exhibition for teachers of all grades from the regional schools. The idea of creative workshops for each exhibition (typical, for example, of French museums) has not yet succeeded in practice.

Seniorgymnasium

Since 1992, the Museum of Beskydy in Frýdek Místek has been implementing a project entitled *Seniorgymnasium*, a kind of non-traditional educational programme for the Third Age, in the specific museum environment. At the moment, there are two classes, each of some 70 senior citizens. They meet every fortnight to attend lectures, guided walks (history, nature), guided exhibitions, film shows and so on. At the beginning, the topics were more professionally oriented; the current focus is on popular education, with issues such as travelling, gardening, health, and discussions with popular personalities, with local politicians. There are also regular trips to natural and historic monuments. The study programme finishes with a special examination. Subsequently, the graduates may become members of the SeniorClub where they meet once a month.

Reference

Asociace českých a moravských muzeí a galerií, *Adresář muzeí a galerií v České republice pro rok*, 1998

8 Hungary

László Harangi

The Hungarian National Museum, which recalls so many historic memories, houses Hungary's very first public collection and dates back to 1802 (45 years later than the British Museum), when Count Ferenc Széchenyi presented his library and collection of medals to the nation. Hearing the word 'museum', the hearts of the Hungarian people leapt more than those of many other nations because the National Museum became, somehow, one of the country's patriotic symbols.

The glorious revolution and war of liberty of 1848–49 commenced on 15 March 1848 when a mass demonstration in front of the National Museum was held and 'The Twelve Points' of the group of radical young intellectuals were proclaimed, stipulating the freedom of the press and independent government. From the ceremonial stairway of the museum, Sándör Petofi (1823–49), eminent Hungarian poet, recited his famous 'National Song'. During 1848–49 the upper house of Parliament met in the ceremonial hall of the museum, and sessions were again held there after the compromise of the Habsburg monarchy in 1867, until the Houses of Parliament were dissolved in 1902.

The other factor which raises patriotic feelings about the museum and generates visitors from all walks of life is that it houses and displays the 1,008-year-old Hungarian 'Holy Crown' which was returned to Hungary on 8 January 1978 in person by Cyrus Vance, then Secretary of State of the United States of America, where it had been kept since the end of World War II. In that sense the museum is a place of national pilgrimage.

Apart from the Hungarian National Museum, the nineteenth century was the period during which the large representative museums, such as the Museum of Fine Arts and the Museum of Applied Arts, were established. It also witnessed the foundation of county and city museums across the whole of Hungary, located, in most cases, in neo-classical buildings with professional staff. Until the 1950s museums had principally been scientific research institutes tasked partly to explore, collect, classify, store and preserve different kinds of artefacts for succeeding generations, and partly to exhibit these collections to the public. With very rare exceptions the museums could be characterised as having some kind of aristocratic aloofness from our recent, holistic view of the education of adults. The exhibitions were very stable, almost permanent.

My father and I had seen the same bones of ancient bears and suits of armour in the same places, accompanied by the same texts with all their benefits and drawbacks. Although the Third Universal Conference of Public Education (1928) declared that museums should also cater for visitors other than schools, this met with little success (A III. Egyetemes 1997).

The role of museums in school education and the education of adults changed radically during the last decade of socialism when the state generously supported cultural issues and organisations; in this regard, museums and the 'museum culture' began to flourish as never before. The facilities of museums have been modernised, the collections have expanded, as have techniques and methodology, and the graduate training of museologists has been extended. A large number of new institutes have been founded, most of them 'off-beat museums' like the Paprika Museum in Kalocsa, the Museum of Hungarian Naïve Artists in Kecskemét, the Blue-Dyeing Museum in Pápa. The old representative county and city museums, as well as the specialised and local museums, have covered the country with an accessible network and their number has exceeded 700 in total.

In the framework of this 'museum boom', museum education and museum adult education were introduced in the early 1970s. The direct aim was the expressive and experiential display of the materials of museums (collections, research, exhibitions) in order to increase adult learning through a systematically designed connection of primary 'museum communication' with the services of university extramural or community-centred adult education providers. Since then, departments and sections for adult education or community education were set up in the major museums − or rather 'adult education officers' were installed in the Department of Youth Education. The main focus of these activities were:

- museum lessons as integrated units of the curriculum of second-chance education for adults;
- museum visits by study circles;
- series of lectures based on and illustrated by special collections of museums;
- test-sheets for targeted studies and observations leading to relevant quizzes (Lovas, 1997).

Such activities were often conducted through systematic cooperation between museums and community centres, as well as evening schools coached by specially trained museum staff members.

A unique form of collaboration between adult education and museums had been the relationship between the museums and the so-called 'socialist brigade' movement. The slogan of the 'movement' was to work, live and learn in a socialistic way. In the course of such learning activity of the brigades, many workers' groups had visited museums. These were registered in their 'brigade diary' and were highly regarded in the eyes of the communities. Museum visits were formally discussed, but frequently ended rather more informally in pubs or cafés over the weekend! Nevertheless, it is true that never before or since have such a great number of workers and lay people visited museums in Hungary as they did in the 1970s and 1980s.

The present state of museum andragogy

In the long history of museums and adult education the above relationship between museums and adult education lasted only for a short time, due to external difficulties. In short, social, political, economic and cultural changes have not, for the present, been favourable to liberal adult education and museums. Both public and private funding agencies have identified vocational and professional education and training as priorities. The first victims of this overall austerity are the general education and cultural education sectors. In addition, the motives and drives for learning have also changed, with courses which give qualifications and/or of practical use dominating. With the public funding of the community centres, the major partner of museums in adult education activities, having been cut all over the country, the former wide range of general and liberal education provisions have been restricted; moreover, the centres have also entered labour market training.

Among the losers in this uneven competition are the museums. They have to bear the greatest burden of the austerity measures indicated above. This obviously poses problems for curators: they are responsible for valuable artefacts, and yet they are tasked with using their severely reduced budgets to keep and maintain these treasures, often belonging to the national heritage, so as to ensure survival for better times, at the cost of museum education, including adult education. All museum departments of education have experienced a major reduction of professional staff. The programmes for children and young people are prepared and carried out by museum staff in parallel with research, cataloguing and administrative duties (Bereczky 1997).

Last but not least, there is one more important point that diminishes the social and cultural functions of museums: since 1989–90 free admission to museums has ceased. For that reason museums are not as well attended as before; compared with the year 1985 the number of visitors in the 755 museums decreased by 50 per cent (Müvelödési évkönyv 1993). This is a great loss and has reduced the former democratic character of museums.

In such a socio-economic environment we cannot give a coherent, comprehensive survey of museums and adult education in Hungary. However, there have been sporadic initiatives where premises and conditions were favourable and some fairly strong traditional activities and movements were able to be maintained.

Below are some examples of such initiatives in a number of different museums.

Museum Friendship Society of the Jósa András Museum in Nyiregyháza

The Society was founded on 21 May 1976 with 72 members. Its main aim was the popularisation of the museum generally and to raise interest in the exhibitions of the museum, principally through publicity by the members. The constitution of the Society stipulated the range of activities. Thus, with the exception of the summer months, on 'every second Monday of each month lectures were held, given by museologists, lecturers at the local Teachers' College, as well as by members of the Society'.

During the past 20 years, well over 400 lectures have been organised by the Society. These have concerned topics connected with the local history of the town of Nyiregyháza and the region of Nyirség, which is rich in cultural, historic and ethnographic heritage. The aim of these talks was to make the museum's artefacts on display more interesting. The presentations were attended by 9,100 interested members of the Society and also by non-members. Every year they had at least one or two museum-focused county and country trips combining social with educational elements. These ventures have only been partially financed by the museum, the larger expenditure being borne by the Society. Two visits have been to Ópusztaszer, the site of the first National Assembly of the seven tribes who were the first settlers of Hungary. Here they could admire the famous circorama gallery of 'Feszty Körkép', which portrays the conquest by means of very imposing three-dimensional paintings, accompanied by musical, sound and text effects. The Society regularly arranges graded museum and local history quizzes which are open to the public. At the end of such events valuable awards are presented to the competitors. One of the most popular activities occurs when members have an opportunity to take part in and study excavations, thus sharing the joys of discovering relics and artefacts. Over the past 20 years Society members have had a number of excavation trips which, with the co-operation and support of the 'mother museum', have concluded with an evaluation of their experiences, both educational and social.

The biggest problem faced by the Society is that of an ageing membership. Of the 65–70 members, 80 per cent are retired and/or elderly people. The Society has found that recruitment from the middle-aged and younger genera-tions of adults is difficult. The active section of citizens in the town are very busy in their occupations and with their family and household obligations. Similarly, young people are either engaged in studies or are not interested in the kind of leisure activities offered by the Society.

Apart from this Society, several other museum friendship societies exist in the country. On 6 May 1996 the National Association of the Friendship Societies of Museums was established. The main aim of this umbrella association is to safeguard the communities of visitors for museums, reasoning that, 'in the course of changing the system, conditions for visiting museums became worse'. At the outset, the Association comprised 15 Friendship Societies of Museums (Papp 1996).

The Press Coffee House of museums

This is a voluntary organisation of journalists specialising in museum issues, and was founded in October 1990. Its permanent venue is the lecture hall of the Hungarian National Gallery, and meetings are held on the first Monday of every month. The Association is a joint venture of the museums in Budapest and those journalists who are eager to promote information relating to the activities of museums throughout the media. The existence of the organisation is assured by the large national museums which provide regular support for it, and it is hoped that minor museums and galleries will also give proportionate donations.

The museums, represented by those staff members who are most competent in public relations and the establishment of innovative exhibitions, give monthly presentations of their new programmes to newspaper and media people. This forum has also debated more recent problems of cultural life with special reference to museums. On many occasions, producers and specialists concerned with the latest exhibitions, publications and excavations have also attended, thus ensuring that all participants receive thorough and up-to-date information. Among well-tried methods at these events have been CD-projects or computer or short-film presentations concerning current topics. There is also the custom that the press group visit the exhibitions of the museums and galleries, guided by professional staff or experts from the museums in question.

In fact, the Press Coffee House has acted as a social link between museums, the press and the media. On the one hand, the main museums and galleries are able to gain more publicity in the press; on the other, the link also leads to friendships between museum people and the press: it is a network which benefits both museums and the media.

The term 'Coffee House' is not just a name but expresses the atmosphere and mood of the meetings. These are very informal and intimate, reminding one of the cultural ambience and also the workshop character of the literary coffee house popular in the nineteenth century and at the beginning of this one. Here everybody may pass comments and has the right to vote if that becomes necessary. Many a time have various TV stations linked up with the Coffee House for reports and interviews. Regrettably, the recent rise in travel costs to the capital has inhibited activities.

A recent meeting of the Association focused on the theme of the misappropriation of treasures by the Soviet Army during World War II. The topic was introduced by László Mravik's presentation 'What happened to the Hungarian art treasures in the Sadovaia 302/B House in Moscow?' The Coffee House hopes that themes such as this will serve the interests of museums during these 'Seven lean years' more successfully – to be followed, one hopes, by seven good years (Demeter 1997).

Programmes for adults in the Museum of Military History

In the 1,000-year history of Hungary, its wars, battles, revolutions and counter-revolutions had great impacts which live on in people's folk memories. The intense interest shown in military history is met, to a large extent, by the Museum of Military History. This is housed in the Buda Castle District. In front of the building cannon and historic cast-iron guns are on display, while inside the exhibits range from pikes, swords and crossbows to a self-propelled missile launcher and a Mig-27 aeroplane parked in the courtyard. Selected documents and relics illustrate some of Hungary's efforts at self-defence over the centuries (Bernstein 1990).

The great interest in the museum shown by children, young people and adults has helped to maintain the range of educational services for children and adults. The youth programmes have been differentiated according to age groups and interests. For example, nursery school children are able to build castles of the Middle Ages from models; primary school children are given drawing assignments; secondary school students engage in solving test-sheets, and undertake special archives and map studies. There are also film shows and demonstrations of how to cast model soldiers in lead.

While such programmes for young people are relatively varied, offers for adults are much more modest. The Institute of Military History runs a study circle entitled 'What does the museum do?' The aim is to show the museum's main activities: namely, how to collect, conserve, classify, exhibit and educate. During the meetings the members of the group can visit a special collection, stores and conservation workshops where they can familiarise themselves with the phases of the process required for producing an exhibition. The meetings are held once a month, during the early afternoon and evening. Membership is free of charge, and sessions are run by staff members of the museum as part of their official duties.

The other service for adults is the so-called 'Film Club in the Castle'. The title of the film series follows the slogan 'On the battle-line of peace'. The club is a joint arrangement between the museum and the Friendship Society of Army and Society, a voluntary organisation pledged to strengthen the relationship between the Society and the Army, and consisting mostly of veteran soldiers. The aim of the film club is to inform people by means of films of the different kinds of 'brute force' organisations developed during the years of dictatorship. Prior to the main feature, club members can view military news films drawn from the period of the 1950s and borrowed from the film archive of the Museum of Military History. The films are accompanied by commentaries by researchers, lectures by film connoisseurs of the Institute of Film, and talks by historians from the Institute of Military History. The club is very popular and attracts the older generation (Hadtörténeti 1995).

Drama and concerts in museums

In February 1998 the Museum of Hungarian Literature, situated in Budapest, established a drama studio and arranged performances entitled *Poets and Muses* based on the documentation of manuscripts held in the museum. The aim is to give an insight into the conflicts and internal lives of prominent Hungarian writers and poets, and thus lead to a thorough understanding and appreciation of their output. Basically, the performances aimed at exploring the complicated psychological and social background of the artists and the power of motivation inherent in the creative process which resulted in the production of literary work.

This presentation of documents differs from the passive display of objects in the exhibition halls, and by comparison is much more alive and attractive. The chief editor of the series is the project leader in co-operation with university lecturers in the Department of Literature, grammar school teachers, drama directors and actors. The plays have been performed by only two or three people; in most cases, these have been the director or editor of the play, plus another actor or actress. The sources of information have been correspondence, diaries, notes, papers, official applications, all selected and conscientiously edited and then presented in the form of dialogues and monologues.

The first play was entitled *The love correspondence*, and refers to Gyula Krúdy (1878–1933), the famous novelist, chosen because his unconventional lifestyle almost immediately gave rise to a legend about him. The performance portrayed the writer's inner conflicts in his love for a mature woman, and for her daughter who later became the writer's second wife. This presentation of that – until then unknown – correspondence between the three partners forming the triangle, enhanced the authenticity of the writer's deep romanticism and impressionism. A further example concerned the love between Sándor Petöfi and his wife Julia Szendrey, using the letters written to each other, their diaries, and their friends' recollections. Some of the most beautiful love poems in Hungarian literature were Petöfi's poems written to his wife (Petrányi 1998).

The theatre has also planned documentary plays about Imre Madách (1823–64), the author of *The Tragedy of Man*, Attila József (1905–37) and Ferenc Molnár (1878–1952).

Since the 1980s there have been annual concerts in the historic Kiscelli Museum and Municipal Gallery. The beautiful internal spaces and its court with excellent acoustics are very suitable premises in which to hold concerts, the Board of Trustees having agreed that the architecture and atmosphere of the museum could enrich the concert life of Budapest. Programmes have included works by Beethoven, music from the Renaissance and Baroque periods, and also compositions by Joplin and his contemporaries. Thanks to these very popular evening concerts, those attending also develop an interest in the museum and its exhibitions.

The concerts are managed by the museum. Because of their long tradition and reputation they have attracted sponsors and are supported by, among others, by the local Borough Council, the Municipality of Budapest, the Budapest Bank and Samsung Electronics. They are hopeful that this tradition is so strong that despite current economic difficulties they will be able to maintain the musical offerings. The public, too, has voiced its appreciation of the museum and the concerts (Koncz 1997).

Art Gallery of the Grassalkovich Community Centre in Hatvan

Hatvan is a small agricultural and food industry town in the centre of Hungary, with a population of 25,000. The cultural, social and educational centre of the town is the Grassalkovich Community Centre, well-known because of its innovations and ways of seeking innovative approaches in adult and community education. Apart from its traditional services, it has established a handicraft school for young adults, a youth camp and an art gallery. The main facility of the institute is a well-renovated castle which was formerly privately owned.

The gallery was established in 1971 and initially operated in the main building. There followed one year's construction work, generously sponsored by firms in the town acting as a kind of Maecenas, and in 1980 the gallery was re-housed in a beautifully restored two-storey former burgher's house. Over the past 27 years the gallery has made a name for itself in Hungary and even in international circles. This was due to a man of genius, now deceased – its director Győző Moldvay (1925–96), otherwise known as poet and *literatus*, and his worthy successor, the recent woman director of the centre, Éva Horváth Matiszlovics, who was also curator of the gallery.

The main characteristic of the gallery, unusual compared with similar institutes, is that it is deeply embedded in the local society of the town. By a long and systematic process the work of the community centre became that of a 'community art gallery' in the best sense. This means that the inhabitants of the town feel it to be their own; they like and appreciate it; they feel responsibility for it and endeavour to understand and internalise the splendours, pleasures and conceptions that the exhibitions are intending to communicate.

Over time, the community centre has publicised and arranged Free University of Arts programmes in order to develop the basic knowledge and appreciation of less well-educated people. The courses have been closely related to the exhibitions and paintings of the gallery. These classes have offered a general introduction to a basic knowledge of art and have dealt with world-famous masters, followed by presentations of the most representative domestic workshops of the arts. Discussions have also been held by noted art historians from the Museum of Fine Arts and by lecturers from the University of Budapest.

In January 1980 the first 'Gallery bus' of the community centre was made available: regular visitors to the gallery have used the bus to visit towns with many historic monuments; they have undertaken regular trips to Budapest to visit the National Gallery, the Museum of Fine Arts and the Museum of Applied Arts, where well-informed guides have received them. Where possible, they have had opportunities to meet artists personally in the galleries. Since the mid-1980s the range of services has been extended, with art study trips abroad by special bus being offered. The main stages of such itinerant learning have included the neighbouring countries of Austria and Greece, and also Spain. This mode of learning resulted in a European round-trip which was unique and so impressive that the group was accompanied by a Hungarian TV crew, and a documentary film on the group's travels was made. Meanwhile, their horizons were extended and they developed a sense of community and partnership relating to the gallery and the love of art. On returning to their home town the travellers felt more at ease in the gallery.

Most recently, the many changing exhibitions of the gallery have given the public more and more surprises: every year, some 16 to 18 nationally famous artists and scholars, including holders of the Kossuth Prize, the highest national award in art, visit the gallery. They introduce themselves and lecture on the current exhibitions in the halls of the gallery. These memorable events have aroused and maintained the interest of both and less well-educated members of the public alike.

Since the foundation of the gallery, the ceremonial opening of exhibitions have been important events in the life of the town, and the honour and accruing prestige is shared by the community. This high day or 'cultural mass' is celebrated by the Lord Mayor of the town, and the opening speeches are always given by well-known art historians or scholars praising the artists' merits and initiating the public into the 'mystery' and meaning of the paintings, graphic arts or small sculptures on display. A good atmosphere is created by the programme of local amateur ensembles (recitations, choir, solo or chamber music) associated with the exhibition. Such cultural programmes have been held both at the opening ceremony and also on other occasions.

The municipality of Hatvan and local firms, such as the canning factory and sugar refinery, are supporting the gallery financially as best they can. The city council has established an award which is given to outstanding artists on the themes of 'Hungarian Landscapes' and 'Faces and Fates'. The biennial exhibitions which include this competition have been endorsed by the National Art Association. This initiative strengthens the gallery's bonds with the locality. Furthermore, the local cultural quarterly journal *The Southern Island* regularly presents and commends recent exhibitions at the gallery (Horváth Matiszlovics 1996).

Programmes for adults at other museums

Brief mention should be made of some of the special programmes for adults and families offered by a number of Budapest museums. The Transport Museum holds regular club meetings for retired people. At the Museum of Applied Arts, established in 1872, there are Sunday morning choir performances in the 'Family weekend' programme. The Hungarian Agricultural Museum, Europe's largest agricultural museum, offers folklore programmes for visitors every Sunday and arranges specific programmes on request. And the Education Department of the Hungarian National Gallery runs advice sessions by telephone on museum education and the preparation of museum lessons.

References

'A III. Egyetemes Tanügyi Kongresszus Határozatai, 1928, június 8-án' (The final resolutions of the 3rd Universal Congress of Education, 8 June 1928), *MNT (Müvelödés, Népföiskola, Társadalom) (Hungarian Folk High School Society)* 3, (1997): 6

Bereczky, L, 'Elöadás az országos múzeumpedagógiai konferencián' (Lecture at National Conference on Museum Pedagogy, 6–7 October 1997), *MH (Múzeumi Hirlevél) Newsletter on Museums*, November 1997, pp. 277–8

Bernstein, K, *Hungary*, Lausanne: Berlitz, p. 256, 1990

Demeter, J, 'Múzeumi sajtókávéhaz minden hónap elsö hétföjén' (The Press Coffee House of the museum every second Monday of each month), *MH,* March, pp 70–1, 1997

Hadtörténéti Múzeum Budapest' (Museum of Military History, Budapest) *MH*, p. 282, October 1995

Horváth Matiszlovics, É, 'Negyedszázados a hatvani galéria' (The Gallery of Hatvan is a quarter of a century old), *Délsziget* 35, pp 104–21, 1996

Koncz, E, 'Kiscelli zenei esték. Egy sikeres rendezvénysorozat margójára' (Music nights in Kiscelli: on the edge of a successful series of performances), *MH*, p. 249, October 1997

Lovas, M, 'Múzeumpedagógia' (Museum Pedagogy), *Encyclopaedia of Education*, Budapest: Keraban Publishing House, pp. 518–19, 1997

Müvelödési évkonyv (Yearbook of Education), Budapest: Department of Culture and Public Education, 1993

Papp, A, '20 éves a nyiregyházi Jósa András Múzeum Baráti Köre' (20 years of the museum friendship society of the Josa Andras museum in Nyiregyhaza), *MH*, July/August, 1996

Petrányi, I, 'Szinház a múzeumban' (Theatre in museum), *MH*, p. 178, July/August

Organisations

Directory of Cultural Heritage
1053 Budapest, Magyar u.40

publishes *Calendar of Museums,* updated in English on Internet: http://www.ace.hu/MNM/MN

Hungarian Folk High School Society
1011 Budapest, Corvin tér.8

Hungarian Institute for Culture
1011 Budapest, Corvin tér.8
national centre for methodology, research and training in adult education

Hungarian Pedagogical Society, Section for Adult Education
1067 Budapest, Csengery u.68

professional–scientific NGO for lifelong learning

Pulszky Society: Hungarian Museums Association
1087 Budapest, Könyves K. krt. 40

National Association of Friendship Societies of Museums
1053 Budapest, Magyar u.40

Society for the Dissemination of Scientific Knowledge
1088 Budapest, Bródy Sándor u.16

9 Poland

Daniel Artymowski

Although in this chapter I cannot attempt to describe the educational work with adults in all 500 Polish museums, I aim to bring out the pattern as exemplified by the information we gathered from 25 museums across the country.

Traditionally in Poland the word 'education' is associated with children and teenagers rather than with adults. Hence the former two groups are taken to museums as part of their school life, and students of certain courses, such as history of art or archaeology, visit museums as part of their professional training, whereas adults, unless they are participants in a teachers' course or a guided tour, are left more or less to themselves.

The museums which we contacted, both large and small, have very little to offer an adult who is not a member of an organised group and would like to learn more about the objects on display. It seems to be easier for our museums to organise film shows, concerts, lectures, even fairs, than to develop a policy of systematically showing their collections to interested individuals. There are, however, some noteworthy exceptions.

The National Museum in Poznan (a large art museum in a major city in west Poland) offers a monthly cycle of lectures with a concert, called 'Meeting a picture'. The aim of this enterprise is to present single objects of special interest in a setting of the music of their historical period or artistic milieu. Furthermore, the public can meet the curator of a given exhibition at a set time every week for a guided tour. The Museum of Warmia and Mazury (a castle and art museum in a medium-sized town in north-eastern Poland) organises weekly afternoon guided tours by exhibition curators for interested adults.

The Royal Castle in Warsaw (a major royal residence in the capital of Poland) offers workshops to both adults and teenagers. There is a monthly cycle of workshops focused on art objects on display, as well as an art course workshop and a cycle of encounters with oriental culture in the impressive Oriental Rugs and Carpets exhibition. This form of activity is accessible to all interested adults. The aim of these workshops is different from both lectures and guided tours, where stress is laid on imparting knowledge: the participants are encouraged to look at different works of art with the fresh eye of, for example, someone walking through a forest and admiring it more for its charm than for the botanical names of the trees. A typical workshop generally begins with a series of observation exercises, often connected with simple sketching, followed by a session where the participants are expected to produce some form of artistic expression, such as drawing, collage, movement, sound or speech, depending on the character of the given workshop.

The Asia and Pacific Museum in Warsaw (a small semi-private museum specialising in Far Eastern art) offers to those interested cyclical meetings concentrating on Far Eastern religions and spiritual traditions (Buddhism, Taoism, Yoga, I-Ching). This programme is largely independent of the exhibitions in the museum, though subjects sometimes overlap.

It would seem that members of organised groups have a much greater opportunity to participate in some form of museum education than individuals. Generally, Polish museums appear to be prepared to provide educational programmes to such groups upon request. Thus several of our museums conduct activities with the University of the Third Age, a type of university for retired people eager to continue their education. The National Museum in Poznań has weekly lectures for the University of the Third Age in two parallel groups, 'Ancient and medieval art' and 'European art at the turn of the nineteenth and the twentieth century''. The Museum of the Earth (a medium-sized geological museum in Warsaw) and the Castle Museum in Lublin (a large museum in a big city in east Poland) also organise cycles of lectures and museum visits for this institution.

Target groups

The only target group which often appears in adult education programmes in Poland are teachers. Many museums organise courses for local teachers which are intended to help them guide their classes through the exhibitions. Various groups of the disabled, adult or otherwise, are served, but no special facilities are offered to them other than allowing the blind to touch certain objects, and the simpler language used when guiding the deaf. The University of the Third Age is a notable exception, but it is more of an example of an organised group asking for at least semi-professional tuition. Groups such as ethnic minorities, unemployed adults, immigrants or refugees, or adults seeking literacy and numeracy skills do not appear to be regarded as special target groups in any of our museums – with two noteworthy exceptions: the Masovian Village Museum in Sierpc (an open-air ethnographic village museum in a small town in central Poland) organises special programmes for groups of Polish emigrants visiting their home country. These mostly old people are deeply moved by the possibility of rediscovering traditional Polish culture, and are considered to be a very good and interested public. The Archaeological Museum in Biskupin, a branch of the State Archaeological Museum in Warsaw, organises courses for the local unemployed. They are trained to be potters and mediators during the annual Archaeological Festival which takes place in Biskupin. Thus, besides participating in pottery workshops they are taught the history of pottery and basic skills in communication and public relations.

Occasional events for families do take place in Polish museums. These are generally Sunday events intended to attract a mixed public. The museum in

Olsztyn organises such events regularly. They are usually a mixture of entertainment – such as people in medieval costume shooting with bow and crossbow, and re-enacting duels and tournaments; arts events, including concerts of classical music and poetry recitals; art workshops at which the public is encouraged to draw and paint certain subjects; and traditional museum education – guided tours. Some other museums offer such events to children rather than to families. The Centre of Contemporary Art (a large modern art gallery in Warsaw, mainly avant-garde) endeavoured to launch a special educational programme for families on Friday afternoons. Workshops were planned for children while the adults were to visit the various exhibitions with curators. The enterprise was, however, only a partial success: the parents left their children to take part in the workshops while they went shopping.

Also of note are seasonal events at the Ethnographic Museum in Warsaw (one of the largest of its kind in Poland). It organises monthly 'Museum matinees' with workshops on traditional folk crafts and customs which, though primarily intended for children, actually attract whole families. The largest offer of all, however, is the Archaeological Festival organised once a year by the State Archaeological Museum of Warsaw in Biskupin (an important prehistoric settlement and probably the most famous archaeological site in Poland). The festival takes place in September every year and lasts nine days, of which the two weekends have programmes intended for families. Each day is organised around a specific theme, such as everyday life or traditional handicrafts, and consists of a wide range of workshops including clay pottery, basketry and cooking; competitions such as archery and javelin throwing; demonstrations of ancient hunting and fishing techniques; concerts, games – of which bathing with an Amazon in a stave tub is the most striking example; ram and pig roasting; beer brewing and drinking; and others.

One may well ask whether many of these events belong more to the world of entertainment than education. Yet one may equally argue that experiencing new situations is a form of education, especially when this happens in surroundings which constantly remind one of the ancient past, and when even uncouth games have archaeological associations. In 1997, the Archaeological Festival in Biskupin attracted 80,000 visitors. A similar festival on a smaller scale is organised by the District Museum of the Kalisz region.

Museums for local communities

Museums in large cities in Poland rarely, if at all, have special educational programmes for the local community. In most cases they are intended for the public in general, local or otherwise. Respondents to my inquiries were slightly puzzled at the idea that an educational programme could be devised especially for the neighbourhood. Smaller museums in smaller towns or villages are more closely connected with the local community which supplies most of its visitors.

These, however, consist mainly of schoolchildren, not adults.

The Masovian Village Museum in Sierpc is a noteworthy example of the role a museum could play in a local community. It runs a cycle of meetings especially for the inhabitants of Sierpc. The nature of these meetings varies – sometimes lectures on the past or the folklore of the region, at other times reminiscences of the older inhabitants of the town, or meetings with folk artists and their art. These, and other activities among the inhabitants of the region, have the consequence that people who until now have felt rather ashamed of being 'peasants' and were eager to rid themselves of anything old-fashioned, are beginning to value and cultivate traditional crafts, and are discovering that their local tradition is something worth cultivating, something that will add to their self-esteem.

The District Museum in Bydgoszcz (a medium-sized museum in a large city in central Poland) has, for the last few years, run a special programme for the socially disadvantaged teenagers and children of its rather run-down neighbourhood. During the summer and winter vacations art workshops are made available to them, free of charge. Out of about 100 random participants a group of about twenty young adults forms lasting ties with the museum and its staff.

Training and staff development

While many museums in Poland have education departments, being an education officer is not, as yet, a fully recognised profession. The general practice is to employ graduates of all kinds of humanistic studies (although historians and art historians predominate), who are expected to mediate between the exhibitions and the public. Over the past few years, however, an effort has been made to help those educators who wish to improve the quality of their work.

The Laboratory of Creative Education, an experimental museum workshop studio at the Centre of Contemporary Art in Warsaw, and the Workshop of Museum Activities of the Royal Castle in Warsaw have independently offered cycles of workshops for museum educators. In the course of these cycles (which have no formal, rigid programme) an effort was made to show participants the different possibilities offered by such active forms of education as workshops and mapping, and to discuss with them the problems which might arise from adapting such methods to the needs of different target groups.

The Laboratory of Creative Education has been running a programme called 'A different museum' for the past five years. The final workshop of this programme, 'Hidden – discovered', which concentrated on preparing instructional aids facilitating a lively and interesting museum visit, was levelled at education officers from museums and art galleries.

The Workshop of Museum Activities has been offering a parallel programme for museum educators over the same period of time. After working for three years with a group on a monthly basis, it now organises art workshops conducted by professional artists (a musician and a painter), intended to give some form of art training to education officers, and to promote new methods in museum education. Museum staff were also able to participate in workshops organised principally for art teachers.

Potential for progress

Polish museums today are in a difficult position as they work their way towards a more effective model of serving their visitors. Over the past 50 years they have traditionally relied on state funding only, and had to satisfy, firstly, authorities and, secondly, the academic milieu. This was a highly demoralising situation as the public had to assume a role similar to that of schoolchildren in a traditional school. Theoretically, the school was for their benefit, but it was not they who decided what and how they were going to be taught. Similarly, the public was expected to enjoy the Polish museums and their educational programmes as they were, and little effort was made to understand their needs and to adapt to them. Thus what we can observe today is a general lack of a planned museum education programme aimed at the public at large and adults in particular.

Museums are increasingly aware that they should assist schools in the process of education, and many Polish museums have produced lists of lessons and special guided tours. However, they seem to be afraid of tackling the non-organised adult public, and very few museums in Poland offer any kind of educational programmes, especially those connected with the displays. What is offered are mostly lectures (often without reference to the displays) and concerts – as if our education officers, afraid of the public, were anxious to keep them at arm's length!

Fortunately this situation is slowly changing: many museums recognise the necessity of attracting visitors, which is especially important at a time when, on the one hand, public institutions are expected to prove their efficiency, and, on the other, potential visitors are busier and find many other attractions to fill their time, often much more enticing than an old-fashioned museum which offers little, if anything, to the individual adult, the family or the local community. The 'good examples' quoted in this chapter, as well as many others, show that a growing number of museums in Poland realise this and are moving in the right direction.

One other example of attempting to modernise the museums can be offered: the Royal Castle in Cracow (the largest and most famous residence museum, a very popular national monument) has installed a computer in a small room with a large monitor which demonstrates a 'virtual' visit to the now non-existent residence of the eleventh century.

However, the financial situation of the public sector, a certain conservatism on the part of curators, and the rather passive attitude of both organised groups and individual visitors, not used to formulate and express their views and expectations, are all reasons for the length of time that will have to pass before the state of museum education generally, and adult education specifically, can be considered satisfactory.

10 Romania

Virgil Stefan Nitulescu

During the years of communism much emphasis was officially placed on adult education. However, not only was the quality of such education poor, especially during the last decades of the regime, but also the number of students decreased year by year: the Communist Party realised that they no longer needed adult education since the leaders themselves were able to obtain diplomas at university level, despite the fact that their knowledge was only basic. Adult education, in the form of high school and university evening courses, and 'popular university' evening programmes, was a myth of the communist regime, abandoned during the reign of Ceausescu. For museums, adult education concentrated on ideological aspects, especially – but not exclusively – in history museums, and on a vulgarisation of the understanding of the arts. For curators, 'working with the public' was regarded almost as a punishment; it was an activity which, as was generally known, frequently contained half-truths, if not lies. The public's enthusiasm for visiting museums reached its peak during the so-called 'liberalisation' period (1964–71), but was followed by a period of increasing apathy and disappointment (1971–83), which intensified and ended in a complete lack of interest in museums (1983–89).

The anti-communist revolution, begun in 1989, found museums unprepared for change. After 45 years of imposed adult 'education', the public, free for the first time, refused to visit museums: activities in the streets, such as anti-government marches, strikes and meetings, were far more interesting. Everything had to be re-invented, and museums, like all other artistic and cultural institutions, followed almost the same line of development. During the first three years (1990–92), public attendance fell dramatically, at least officially: it was known that since 1984 the number of visitors had been used as an indicator for calculating salaries and, consequently, falsified so as to adjust to the required level. This custom was maintained even in 1990, despite the fact that by then salaries were no longer dependent on visitor numbers. Annual visitor numbers show a sharp decline between 1989 (18,217,000) and 1992 (8,941,000); however, from 1993 onwards people became increasingly disenchanted by current politics, and more interested in their own free time. Gradually the public returned to theatres, cinemas, exhibition halls and museums.

The first three years coincided with the years of 're-settlement' in the museum world. Some curators left for better jobs, some retired – and almost noone replaced them. Political debate was intense among curators and took up much of their time; similarly, debate concerning a new law on protecting the cultural heritage and a law for museums and collections was passionate and time-consuming. These were years of confusion: the old style of exhibitions and museum events no longer attracted the public. Those curators who were genuinely interested in their work tried to revitalise their views, travelling abroad, reading and establishing contacts with foreign partners in a search for new meaning in their activities. A new type of management, more dynamic and efficient, began to replace the old one, which needed approval from the 'tutors' for almost everything. A small group of curators who agreed to be not only museum directors but also managers, in a 'commercial' sense, started to look for methods to attract the public back into museums.

In fact, this new generation rediscovered two well-known truths: *there is no museum if there is no public,* and *museums mean education* (as stated very clearly by ICOM in 1988). Correspondingly, the educational methods used in Romanian museums today are also not new. However, one thing is new: there is no ideological pressure of any kind, and the public comes to museums if and when they wish.

The main methods are as follows:

1. *The lesson in the museum*: usually used in primary and secondary schools, especially in history, biology and literature classes. Some university courses in archaeology and art history are also held in museums. Lessons include visiting one or two exhibition halls.
2. *The organised visit*: guided by a curator, this includes at least one department, if not the entire museum.
3. *The thematic visit*: also guided by a curator, the visit focuses on a certain theme or idea throughout the entire museum.
4. *Museum trips*: organised by teachers and curators together in specific regions, including visits to several museums and/or historical sites.
5. *Competitions*: subsequent to museum visits, enhancing and assessing what has been learnt during the visits.
6. *Museum Friends' circles*: members have usually completed at least elementary school. They receive further explanations on the exhibits and help curators with some work and activities inside the museum.
7. *Archaeological research*: young people help museum archaeologists in fieldwork, learning at the same time.
8. *Formal courses*: usually organised for mature audiences, mostly by arts museums. Courses are arranged in sessions of at least two to three hours.
9. *Museum soirées*: Targeted at the mature audience, but not exclusively. They include short conferences and performances, followed by meetings with the protagonists.

The list above describes the main methods used; imagination may play an important role in creating new ones, combining them in a number of ways. While curators are engaged in one form of education (aesthetics, technological and professional, and physical), they are, in fact, creating (often unconsciously) another form which combines them all: museological education.

Concerning the target groups of museum education, as seen in the above list, these are mainly children and teenagers. For adult education, there is usually no further delineation. Some 'universal' categories do not need further education because they do not exist in Romania or are extremely weak. For instance, there are almost no adults needing encouragement in basic skills such as numeracy and/or literacy, because more than 99 per cent of the mentally healthy adults in the population have these competences. The number of immigrants and refugees in Romania is extremely low (fewer than 2,000 in the entire country, mostly Somali and Albanians), so that there are no special programmes provided for them. The ethnic minorities in Romania are, histori-cally, constituted in certain regions: the only minority group spread throughout the country is that of the Roma (Rroma or Gypsies), although this group is not the most numerous – that is the Hungarian minority. However, Romanian museums show no interest in programmes for specific ethnic minorities *per se*. In a town like Miercurea Ciuc, for instance, inhabited predominantly (more than 95 per cent) by Hungarians, all the programmes in the local museum are, in fact, for Hungarians. In a city like Targu Mures, inhabited half by Romanians and half by Hungarians, the educational programmes are targeted at one or the other ethnicity only if the group is organised on an ethnic basis and requests a certain language preference. Otherwise, programmes are not directly addressed to minority groups. Thus we may say that programmes may be offered in a specific language if the public asks for it, but are not designed to deal with the problems of ethnic minorities. In the ethnographic museums, however, we may recognise the existence of some features of adult education connected *with* the ethnic minorities, but not *for* them. Many open-air museums have fairs where craftspeople from minority groups are invited to perform. During such fairs they have the opportunity to 'teach' the public about their craft, with curators assisting them. However, they are doing this not especially for their co-nationals, but for the entire public.

A group only recently catered for in our museums is that of handicapped people, although museums are not ready yet to make educational efforts for them. At present, only the most important museums in Romania have introduced access facilities. A few museums, especially of natural sciences, are asked to prepare special guided visits for handicapped children – if they are institutionalised. There are no reported programmes for adult people with disabilities. As with other categories of the adult public, museums are rather passive. Curators are willing to prepare special educational programmes for certain categories of adults, but only if they are asked to do so by other public institutions or non-governmental organisations.

For unemployed people, we may say that despite the fact that since 1990 unemployment has been spreading, now reaching about 9 per cent of the entire adult population, museums have no special educational programmes; nor are they trying to attract the unemployed as a deliberate policy.

There is also no special focus on young adults or elderly people, the only differentiating criteria on age from a museum viewpoint being those for teenagers and adults.

We may conclude that the only target group reached by Romanian museums in the adult education process is the most convenient one. This includes family groups – if these families are composed of employed adults, with no special needs. For them, museums organise conferences and lectures, performances and special forms of guidance. The art museums and the open air museums are the most industrious in this area.

The Ministry of Culture has an institution under its authority, known as the Centre for Training and Education for the Personnel from Cultural Institutions, which organises courses for curators in basic museology and in some specialities. The first-ever course in museum education is scheduled for 2000 and is due to last 40 hours. Adult education in museums will be one of the subjects tackled during the lectures. The Centre is interested in organising such programmes, since university courses in museology are still very rare in Romania, and there is no other special form of training for curators in museum education.

Since 1990, the Ministry of Culture, in conjunction with local museums, has been organising a yearly colloquium on 'museum pedagogy'. From 1998, the ICOM Romanian National Committee has also been involved. From the very beginning, this colloquium has been concerned with many more issues than intended. As all the national regular sessions for curators in Romania are devoted to certain specialities (archaeology, ethnology, natural sciences, conservation/restoration, classification), important branches such as marketing, management, museum legislation, new media and even museology itself have found themselves located inside the colloquium on museum pedagogy. We may say that half of the papers presented each year are not connected entirely with museum pedagogy, let alone adult education.

During the past year, the Ministry of Culture has begun to draft a law on museums and collections. The draft bill (as it is today) mentions the educational dimension of museums, listing museum specialists such as curator, conservator and so on, but omitting the educator. However, there is still time to introduce this role into the draft, and museum educators will certainly press the Ministry of Culture to do so; officially, there are no 'museum educators' as such in Romanian museums. All the educators are 'curators'.

Very recently, the Ministry of Culture has created, inside the Centre for Training and Education for the Personnel from Cultural Institutions, a special department called the Danish-Romanian Institute on Adult Education. The Institute was planned for more than three years before being established. However, to date it has shown no interest in collaborating with museums. The only cultural institutions targeted are the cultural clubs (especially those in the rural parts of the country). Still, there is a possibility that the Institute will co-operate with other institutions, including museums.

Despite the extremely low interest in adult education, I think that Romanian museums have a good opportunity to develop this part of their activity. There are two reasons to think so: firstly, public subsidies are decreasing year by year. For the museums, there is no chance of surviving without considering the needs of the public; sooner or later, all of them will be forced to do so. The second reason relates to the democratisation and (post)modernisation of Romanian society. A new generation of curators is emerging in the museums. They are more concerned with the needs of society and what they consider to be the real duties of their profession. Significantly, they are not referring to the inhibitions and taboos inherited from the older generation, marked by the 45 years of communist dictatorship. This new generation is sensitive to the problems of permanent education and has an interest in being involved in it. It is only the beginning of real adult education provision in Romanian museums – as we understand it in the western part of Europe.

Bibliography

Antonesei, L, *Paideia. Fundamente culturale ale educapiei*, Polirom: Iaoi, 1996

Cojocariu, V *et al*, *Pedagogie muzeala*, Bucharest: Centrul de Pregatire oi Formare a Personalului din Institubiile de Cultura, 1998

Comunicarile prezentate la Colocviul nabional de pedagogie muzeala, Sibiu: Muzeul Civilizabiei Populare Tradibionale 'Astra', 1997

Cuco, C, *Pedagogie*, Polirom: Iaoi, 1996

Florescu, R, *Bazele muzeologiei*, Bucharest: Centrul de Pregatire oi Formare a Personalului din Institubiile de Cultura, 1999

Nicolescu, C, *Muzeologie generala*, Bucharest: Editura Didactica oi Pedagogica, 1979

Lucrarile Colocviului nabional de pedagogie muzeala, Baia Mare: Ministerul Culturii, 1994

—— Deva: Muzeul Civilizabiei Dacice oi Romane, 1996

Revista muzeelor oi monumentelor (Romanian Journal of Museums), 1974– (ISSN 0035–0206)

11 Russia

Irina Mikhailovna Kossova

Adult education in museums was one of the most exciting trends in the cultural and educational work of Russian museums at the end of the twentieth century. It arose from a growing interest in questions of education, culture and leisure, and is based on the considerable scientific and educational potential of national and small, provincial museums.

This chapter is based on publications from Russian sources and also materials provided by the Director of the Museum Education workshop in the Institute for Retraining Workers in Art, Culture and Tourism in the Russian Federation (Kossova 1997, 1999).

Adults visiting museums come from different backgrounds, educational and professional, different age groups and with differing interests. By studying their requests and needs, special cultural and educational programmes are devised, taking into consideration specific museum collections and the expertise of museum staff in the form of process skills, such as lectures and excursions, both occasional and long-term.

Work with adult audiences demands regular changes of theme. We have stopped any form of 'ideological pressure', which had existed for decades, and this has helped us to re-examine the potential of museums in helping to find answers to the many questions about specific historic events, and the life and work of famous Russian writers and statesmen which arise, in varying degree, from the displays in many museums.

For example, weekend lectures in the Museum of Moscow Kremlin have had a long tradition. This is not only a museum *per se*, but also the seat of government where many important issues were dealt with. The lectures have recently taken a new direction towards 'The individual and history: historic portraits of statesmen in Russian history'. The authors of this programme decided to follow the theme of 'Psychology of power' from Countess Olga (tenth century) to Nicholas II (twentieth century). The programme runs for several years and consists of a cycle of lectures prepared by the museum staff, the Russian Academy of Sciences, Moscow University and so on.

Questionnaire surveys showed that the majority of visitors are middle-aged (44 per cent) and older adults (38 per cent). Thirty per cent of the total have been coming to lectures for at least 10 years, and 10–15 per cent consider them to be a family entertainment/leisure activity and bring with them children and grandchildren. Seventy per cent of the respondents are scientists, engineers and economists. The majority of them aim to widen their knowledge of the humanities (Faizova 1996: 33–4).

Regionally, the local inhabitants are attracted by folklore or ethnographic events in museums which are usually held at the time of national, traditional or religious celebrations or around some important dates in museum calendars. Practically every museum in the country has such a programme which is aimed at active and creative adult participation. These events take place in museums themselves or outside them, and include expositions, new exhibitions, concerts of folklore or ethnographic groups, olympiads and traditional entertainments.

In a number of museums there are clubs with members from different backgrounds united in their interest in the study of the history, culture, art or nature of their territory. These clubs have their own charters and programmes of 2–3 years' duration, consisting of plenary lectures and seminar courses, meetings, evening events and excursions to other museums, and also preparation of case studies for specific topics.

The Moscow State Biological Museum has acquired much experience in dealing with club networks. At present three clubs are functioning: Moscow Club of Stone Lovers, Moscow Club of Cacti, and 'Biofitum' which has been in existence for a decade. One of the sections of this club has courses on drying and arranging flowers in the European style. There are also distance learning programmes for educators and club leaders. The section has close links with a similar club in Falmouth (UK). In the winter a special exhibition "New Year Bouquet', takes place. In 1996 a special seminar based on the exhibition took place as well as competitions for flower arrangements.

Another form of club activity relates to private exhibitions of collections/ parts of collections of club members. Some of these collections are for sale, and visitors are attracted by the possibility of obtaining information from an expert, acquiring literature or buying some of the exhibits.

Museums of literature organise competitions of literary readings, usually dedicated to the lives of famous writers and poets, or to historical events at national and regional levels. Anyone can take part, provided they fill in an application form at a specified time, and many do: factory workers, office workers, teachers, students from different towns and regions all participate. Information about such competitions is usually announced on radio and television and in the local press. The jury usually consists of members of the acting profession and museum staff. The winners take part in a gala concert at the end of the competition.

We view museums as additional educational establishments and, therefore, use them as another means by which adults may study. Museums are keepers of unique national traditions. There are museum schools and studios of national art forms such as clay toys, objects made of straw, tree bark and wood painting.

Russia is rich in forests, and wood has traditionally been one of the most popular materials for artistic expression, always combined with high practical applicability of the objects produced. The northern parts of Russia are particularly well endowed in collections of peasant life and their creations.

Vologda Museum has had a wood painting studio for the last 15 years, where a course given by professionals with their own developed methodology takes two years to complete. Old methods of work are introduced, based on museum research. Students enter the world of folk images and bright colours. They participate in exhibitions, fairs and town celebrations. On graduation they obtain a diploma and many of them join workshops or work on their own. Their creations are usually painted bread boards, salt cellars or boxes made of birch bark. Our contemporaries are amazed by the talent of these artists.

Every programme is inspired by one or more individuals. The initiator of this particular one is the head of the Art Department of the Museum. The programme is based on a detailed study of painting on wood techniques, involving a study of archives and other museum materials.

In areas where traditional handicrafts are widespread, the role of museums in the initiation of the adult population into the history and knowledge of these crafts is very important. The Kargopol', Kursk and Penza museums of local folklore, history and economy are among the best popularisers of these crafts.

Apart from studios, programmes of excursions and lectures on the subject, folklore and ethnography events are organised, in which specialists in pottery, wickerwork, and so on take part. Products of such events are usually sold in museum souvenir shops.

In a number of regions museums are used as bases for master classes. For example, in the Kaluga region, renowned for its pottery, a private museum run by an adult couple with children (a so-called family museum) was created. This is a new form of museum work, as indicated below. This particular course concentrates on the study of Kaluga's cultural heritage. Among its activities are the training of pottery specialists and the organising of special programmes for mentally and physically handicapped children.

Kaluga traditions in clay toys are known to go back to the seventeenth century, but recent excavations have revealed that as early as the twelfth century toys were made there. The clay toy workshops take place in the museum's building, next to the historical display of these toys. An understanding of the ethics underlying these crafts, of local traditions and ceremonies may help both children and adults to develop more balanced personalities. The revival of traditional crafts is a complex process which has a beneficial impact upon the development of a nation's spirituality. The participation of museums in this process is a very responsible mission and should lead to a strengthening of family ties and a better understanding between generations.

Family problems occupy a key position among issues which museums deal with in their role of adult educationalists. In a number of museums, programmes for families have been developed. For example, in the Polytechnical Museum in Moscow one such programme, entitled 'A family at the museum', as well as a programme of the History Museum in Tol'yatti called 'Museum visiting for the family', aim at bringing children and their parents closer together at exhibitions and on special museum occasions.

There are new museum guidebooks for families. These are aimed at helping parents to guide their children around museums. In addition, they include tasks/games for children to do at home, so that parents can also participate (and learn).

Some guidebooks are written in the style of an individual participating in an event, such as a soldier at the time of the Napoleonic Wars (guidebook; *Battle at Borodino in 1812*). This book includes questionnaires, theme topics, crosswords and so on which aim at helping both adults and children to learn more about Russian history.

A special programme, 'Family labyrinth', which takes place at weekends, was developed in the State Biological Museum. Botanical and zoological questions set by the museum may be researched by all members of a family. The events are conducted as competitions and winners receive prizes, but the main benefit in the process is finding out new things about different species of flora and fauna and their habitats. In the process of learning, adults and children may also get on better together.

Approximately one-third of all museum visitors in Russia are students (Kossova 1989: 56). They come for different purposes (educational or leisure). Students of the humanities show the greatest interest in the educational aspects of museums, as their art and history displays and exhibitions serve as main sources for their coursework and final projects. In a number of Russian museums there are student placements; for example, at Abakan Pedagogic University, Kazan State University, Moscow State University, Saratov University, and Yaroslavl' University.

At Kazan University students reading history start participating in the museum's activities from their first year. Placements can involve any of the museum's activities: resource management, exhibitions, educational work. Students learn to organise museum events, to lead guided tours, to design and organise exhibitions, to conserve exhibits. At the State Museum of Tatarstan, university students also participate in archaeological and ethnographic expeditions (Nurutdinova 1995: 87–9). Half of the research staff of Russia's museums are recruited from university graduates (Kossova 1989: 58).

The Department of History at Moscow University has long experience of providing graduates for such work. The Russian history course traditionally consists of lectures and seminars but also includes work with museum exhibitions and memorials. This encourages individual interpretation of history as well as of national and folk traditions. A number of Moscow museums own magnificent medieval Russian collections, among them being the State Museum of History, the Museum of Moscow Kremlin, and country estates 'Kolomenskoe', 'Ostankino' and 'Kuskovo'. Many museums in Moscow and in the Moscow region are dedicated to the lives of famous public figures and writers, scientists and artists. Visitors to these museums enter the worlds of those people and learn to understand their characters and talents. Their lives are much better portrayed in context than in any books.

Students, after conducting an in-depth literature search on a chosen topic and consultations with museum research staff, are expected to develop their own tours for other students in their groups. These tours are then actively discussed and analysed, thus making them a practical class, which stimulates the students' creative work.

In the Novozybkovsk Regional Museum a special course has been introduced for primary education specialists at the local teacher training college. The aim is to teach them how to optimise the potential of the museum for their pupils. For the students of the humanities, museum education is a valuable part of their professional training although it falls outside their curriculum.

There is a growing interest in history, culture and monuments throughout the world. The State Russian Museum has developed a special four-year programme in aesthetics for students of technical universities. The first two years are entitled 'The development of Russian art'. The course takes place in the museum. Each lecture is followed by a concert which creates a special ambience relating to a particular historic or cultural event. The course also includes visits to restoration workshops where students meet the conservationists. In the third and fourth years the students' acquired knowledge is put into practice: from passive listeners they are converted into guides and lecturers who also participate in various other aspects of the museum's work (Stolyarov 1991: 4–9).

The Museum of Theatre and Music in St Petersburg has developed evening programmes specifically for students. One is called 'Games for mature children'. This uses amateur theatre productions, and the invited speakers are amateur actors and producers popular among students. Another programme is 'Twenty years later'. This is specially designated for students of theatrical schools and gives them the opportunity to meet professional actors and producers. There is a third programme in which actors and producers of new plays meet with students after the opening night. Experience has shown that programmes such as those described above have been very successful, both at national and at local level, in enhancing students' education.

From the late nineteenth century onwards there has been a strong tradition of educating students through the active involvement of museums. A number of museums maintain a very fruitful co-operation with local teachers on specific topics of the school curriculum.

A major group of adult visitors to museums are pensioners; consequently, many museums are developing educational programmes specifically for this sector of the population. The most encouraging development has been the growth of co-operative programmes with social workers in a number of regions. For example, in Zelenograd one programme includes not only museum visits but also excursions to the region which is rich in historic and cultural monuments.

In pensioners' clubs in Sergiev Posad there is a two-year programme of lectures, meetings with artists and poets, and visits to various museums. The programme is called 'In the realm of beauty'.

Russian museums are very experienced in playing an interactive role in society. They are good at identifying needs and designing programmes to meet these. Frequently they develop phased programmes with quite a long time-scale for completion. For example, the Museum of History and Ethnography of Shushenskoe (Eastern Siberia) identified for its purposes specific groups of visitors:

The first main group, 'Adults', has two sub-groups:
(a) working population (aged 18 to 55), which also includes students and professionals who can contribute to the museum's work;
(b) pensioners, which also includes invalids, people who have been detained for political reasons, and so on.

Two other main groups, 'Tourists' and 'Occasional visitors', are also divided further into two sub-groups. This classification is necessary for developing special programmes. For example, the following programmes operate in this museum:

'Museum and the Local Population', 'Museum and Private Collections', 'Museum and Students'. The priority programmes are 'Rebirth of Traditional Crafts' and 'Museum and the Tourist'

(Sukhova 1997: 54)

In contrast, in the Krasnoyarsk Cultural and Historic Centre the programme of adult education is called 'Communication, a non-traditional activity'. This centre operates on the site of the former branch of the Central Lenin Museum which was opened less than a decade ago in a beautiful building – but with an almost total absence of exhibits. Thus, the centre began its work not with a collection of static artefacts but with people representing different cultural and political movements. In this way the centre developed partnerships with a number of important groups, and today it consists primarily of clubs, societies etc. In this way the centre introduces folk arts, culture and rituals not only from the local area but from much further afield, such as, for example, the Chinese tea ceremony. One of the primary aims of the centre is to engage the active participation of the young people and to generate a creative atmosphere. Among their programmes is one entitled 'Paths and roads of Siberia'.

At present a number of museums in Russia have had an important role to play in developing new educational concepts. This involves developing a wide range of educational programmes suitable for students through to pensioners, taking into account specific features of each museum, such as geographical and physical space, resources and expertise. To fulfil this role it has been vital to develop partnerships with a variety of organisations and with the public at large.

References

Faizova, E V, *Lecturing bureau at the Arts Museum today*, State Hermitage, Science-educational work currently being undertaken at the Arts Museum: Reports and papers of the science conference, St Petersburg, 1996

Kossova, I M, *Museums in the cultural life of the region*, Moscow, 1989

—— *Cultural-educational activities*, papers from the Workshop on Museum Education, Department of Museum Studies, Moscow: Institute for Retraining of Workers in Art, Culture and Tourism, 1997

—— (ed.) *The museum, education, culture: integration processes*, papers from the Workshop on Museum Education, Department of Museum Studies, Moscow: Institute for Retraining of Workers in Art, Culture and Tourism, 1999

Nurutdinova, G G, *Student practical work*, Annual of the State Museum of the Tatarstar Republic. Kazan, part 1, 1995

Stolyarov, V A, *The socio-pedagogical significance of the problems of access to arts museums for young students at technical universities: museums and the rising generation*, St Petersburg, 1991

Sukhova, N A, *Regarding the question of educational concepts at the 'Shushenskoy' Museum and Nature Reserve for history and ethnography: cultural-educational activities of museums*, Moscow, 1997

12 Slovenia

Tatjana Dolzan-Eržen

In Slovenia, the museum is supposed to be working in many different fields –
collecting, documenting, caring for the objects, devising exhibitions,
researching, publishing and popularising cultural heritage; in short, functioning
as a centre for taking care of one aspect of our social life (which usually does not
make any money). It is particularly difficult to operate well if the staff of the
museum is small in number and the museum is not supported by some
well-established Museum Society or Museum Friends' Club that provides
unpaid volunteers to help: raising money is always a matter of great concern to
museum workers. Often we are caught in a vicious circle: not enough money –
not enough staff – no new projects.

I have been employed as a curator/ethnologist in a regional Gorenjski
museum in Kranj, in the north-west of Slovenia. As I enjoy working with
groups who share my interest in past times and artefacts, I lectured for more
than a year at the University of the Third Age, an organisation for adult
learning, dealing with the local history, art history and ethnology of our region.
Subsequently, I was invited to take part in an education course for mentors of
study circles and, being motivated to learn more about the subject, I successfully
passed the course and was qualified to run study circles in 1994.

The experience convinced me that the study circle approach enables
people to work and learn well together, and I decided to run a circle at the
University of the Third Age. I gathered together a group of 14 older people (11
women and three men). They had all completed at least secondary school
education, and several had graduated from university. What we had in common
was an interest in, and sense of, the cultural and historical values of our region,
and so we called our circle 'Let's discover our country'.

In Slovenia study circles had not been a traditional method of working
with adults. They were introduced some years ago at the University of the
Third Age. When such a Centre for Adult Learning was founded in 1990, one
of its main objectives was the formation of study circles, and the Ministry for
Education in Slovenia has been supporting their development. Workers at the
centre began to train mentors in 1993. While in that school year (1993/94) 36
study circles operated throughout the country, this number had risen to 200 in
the year 1996/97.

Methodologically, study circles in Slovenia are based on those in some
Western European countries and the USA, where at the end of the nineteenth
and beginning of the twentieth century people developed this special way of
promoting local or public initiatives. Study circles have been a means of
encouraging adults to learn foreign languages, to educate themselves to work

more efficiently in their jobs, or to enhance their qualifications. And they have also been a way of helping people put into practice an idea or a project for the benefit of their communities. The important difference between traditional courses, where people learn about specific matters, and study circles lies in the relationships among participants. The mentor of a circle is not a teacher who needs to bring knowledge to students. That would not be sufficiently encouraging for adults to work and learn because it might remind them too much of school. Members of a study circle are seen to be on an equal footing with their mentor, and able to take responsibility for their work and studies. They formulate a plan and decide on their aims as a group. The mentor's task is to help members with professional knowledge and to check that the work follows the accepted plan. Every study circle also needs a member to act as mediator and encourage good social relations among the participants. One of the points of this way of educating and collaborating is that 10 separate individuals, for example, will never be as successful as will a group of 10 people who work together.

One of the most important points for the function of study circles is its *raison d'être*. The group I gathered together accepted my suggestion that we should publish leaflets on cultural and historical sites in our region, since this fitted in with our common interest. Subsequently, we agreed to concentrate on the town of Kranj and its surroundings. We collected a number of suggestions as to which themes and sites to choose, and decided, by vote, to work on four themes: castles; the heritage of the painter Leopold Layer (1752–1828); constructions by well-known architects in Kranj; and traditional old crafts. We also decided that each theme should be covered in the form of a leaflet, and that all four leaflets should have the same design so as to make up a set.

Each theme was given to a team of three or four members of the circle. They themselves decided how to group, according to their affinities. Every team worked independently on choosing sites representative of their theme. During our meetings all aspects of the topic were discussed. I encouraged them, helped them with my own knowledge and organised access to the museum's photographic department. Each team prepared a short text as a historical review of the theme. When sites were selected, all members of the circle made excursions to those which we had not visited yet – castles, churches, houses, private collections of tools associated with traditional crafts. Two teams obtained photographs of the Gorenjski museum site (or from owners of the castles), and one used photographs taken by one of the team members. The main difficulty was photographing the works of the painter Leopold Layer, which were all part of church decorations. We were fortunate to meet a good photographer who was a collector of data about churches and willing to take photographs for us, on the understanding that he could subsequently use them for his own purposes.

When all texts and photographs had been assembled, I handed the material over to a professional designer to prepare it for printing. We chose a small local printing house well-known to one of our members, with whom we could negotiate for standard quality printing at a low price, as our budget was small. That said, we have been supported by the Ministry of Education of Slovenia. Normally the grant was sufficient for paying the mentor and some small expenses for materials; but our group, which was still included in the programme of the University of the Third Age, decided to pay the mentor and expenses from their own pockets in order to save money for our publications. The rest of the money we obtained from the community of the town of Kranj, after some weeks of persistent lobbying of the mayor. We also collected a smaller sum of money by appealing to potential sponsors.

It was our wish to present the publications to the public in the form of a small exhibition. At the Gorenjski museum we received permission to use one of its galleries. In addition, the director of the museum was ready to support us. The exhibition was planned by the same designer who helped us with the publications. Most of the preparatory work was undertaken by members of the circle themselves: this was something novel and exciting because none of them had ever been involved in this type of activity. We presented each site of the themes by displaying photographs, texts and literature. The exhibition was enhanced by objects from old craft collections and canvases of the painter Layer which were borrowed from the Kranj parish art gallery.

On 31 May 1995, after four months of hard work, the exhibition 'Let's discover our country' opened, and four leaflets were presented to the public. According to our budget and estimate of interest we had ordered 1,300 copies of each leaflet. Almost half were distributed to museum visitors at the exhibition. The rest were handed over to the Gorenjski museum, the Tourist Information Office of Kranj, and the two biggest hotels in the town for wider distribution.

After completing the project, all the circle members felt very proud to have taken part in it. We were congratulated on our work – contents, shape, design. In fact, we achieved something special – we had all gained a more active attitude towards matters we love, and we had done something to serve our community. None of the members of the study circle had previously had such an experience, and although they had been uncertain about the final outcome, they worked diligently to the end.

The entire edition of leaflets was distributed in less than a year. They were judged to be a very good form of promotion of local cultural heritage. 'Castles' was republished in a national newspaper as a suggestion for a family excursion. Members of the study circle looked forward to the autumn to start a new project: one suggestion was the possibility of researching a nearby village – Strazisce, home of almost half of the members.

The fact that a group of elderly people, educated but not professionals, succeeded in producing four well-regarded leaflets to promote local cultural heritage, gave us the enthusiasm to persevere with similar projects. In 1996/97 the museum ran two study circles – the original one, formally still part of the University of the Third Age, prepared a publication about the history and life in the village of Strazisce; and a new one, run by a fellow curator who had recently qualified to conduct circles, with participants of all ages and professions, which deals with the lineage of ancient families from the north-west region of Slovenia-Gorenjska. They intend to collect data concerning the origin, age and family relations of well-known inhabitants of that region.

The advantage of running study circles lies not only in practical outcomes. The museum is also engaging more closely with new people and a new public. It has been noticed that members of the circles and their families are faithful museum visitors. And members of another group involved with an art-history programme at the University of the Third Age have also become regular visitors. They are supporters of Gorenjski museum, even if we still do not have a Friends of the Museum Club. Most importantly, they are also ready to work voluntarily for the sake of the museum.

13 Cyprus

Loukia Loizou Hadjigavriel

In 1881, Luigi Palma di Cesnola, US consul in Cyprus, organised the first private museum on the island in his house and consulate in Larnaca. He was an amateur archaeologist and spent his time excavating all around the island and collecting relics from various ancient sites. It was a privilege and honour for European and US visitors to see his collection and admire these unique artefacts. The guided tours given by Cesnola to these 'visitors' may be considered as the first educational programmes for adults organised on the island. But one fact must not be overlooked: this private museum and the guided tours were exclusively for foreigners, not for the local people ('the natives', as Cesnola and other consuls used to call them). The Cesnola collection was gradually sold and shipped out of the island, to be dispersed among famous museums such as the British Museum, the Louvre, and especially the Metropolitan Museum of Art in New York.[1]

In 1888 the Cyprus Museum was established by the Colonial Government, and in 1905 a large building was specially constructed to house the magnificent antiquities of Cyprus. Although the museum was open to everybody it was, in a way, again destined for foreigners, bearing in mind that the locals had no motivation, nor, indeed, the curiosity to see 'the treasures': these 'treasures' were, after all, found everywhere around the island, and sometimes even prevented them from cultivating their land. The Cyprus Museum is still the largest museum on the island, under the administration of the Department of Antiquities.

The first Cypriot to open his own collection to the public was Demetris Pierides from Larnaca. He began his collection in 1839 and decided to show it to the public towards the end of the nineteenth century. He turned his own house into a museum, and certain privileged Cypriots were invited to view the collection and take tea in his gardens. This museum is still functioning today (Vassos 1985).

From the beginning of the twentieth century until 1960, when Cyprus became an independent republic, very few museums were established and none of them was organised to arrange temporary exhibitions, educational visits or other activities. Most were set up in order to exhibit archaeological material discovered in various excavations all over the island and were visited mostly by archaeologists studying Cypriot antiquities.

From the end of 1940 to the beginning of 1950 the curator of the Cyprus Museum organised some temporary exhibitions, including displays of contemporary art among the showcases packed with antiquities. Unfortunately, he was already old and soon retired; his successors did not follow his example until the 1980s when, for the first time, one room in the museum was refurbished for temporary exhibitions and lectures.

In 1984 the Municipality of Nicosia, with the sponsorship and support of the A G Leventis Foundation, established the first historical museum on the island, the Leventis Municipal Museum of Nicosia. From the beginning, the policy of this museum has been different from that of all other museums in Cyprus:

- It is a historical museum depicting the history of Nicosia, the capital city, from antiquity to the present day, thus covering the early Christian, Byzantine and especially the Frankish, Venetian, Ottoman and British periods that were not covered by most of the other 33 museums on the island. Exceptions were the 'Struggle Museum', dedicated to the EOKA struggle against British Imperialism in the 1950s, the Folk Art Museum dedicated mostly to rural life in Cyprus in the nineteenth century, and the Byzantine Museum of the Archbishopric of Cyprus.
- The museum is primarily dedicated to and intended for the people of Nicosia and generally for Cypriots. The main target of the museum is to present the history of the city to its citizens, and then to other visitors.
- The museum is housed in a nineteenth-century building which was specially restored and turned into a museum. Before its official opening and during restoration work, various events were organised in order to inform the public about the museum and its objectives in the cultural life of the city.
- The museum opened its doors in April 1989. Educational programmes featured among its priorities, and guided tours and workshops have been held regularly since the beginning.
- A series of temporary exhibitions are also organised in the museum every year.
- An active Association of the Friends of the Museum, which helped the museum to realise its targets, was established in 1986. It became the main sponsor of the educational programmes.

The Leventis Museum was, according to Kenneth Hudson, Director of the European Museum of the Year Award Committee, 'the first modern museum [in Cyprus] which provided a real opportunity to break out of the straitjacket of archaeology which ... [had] held back museological progress for far too long' (Hudson 1991).

Educational programmes in the Leventis Museum

Educational programmes were introduced as soon as the Leventis Museum opened to the public. They were aimed at the following groups:

1. schoolchildren at elementary schools and gymnasia;

- students at colleges and at the University of Cyprus;
- special groups, such as children with special needs, members of associations; and
- adults.

The programmes for groups (1)–(3) were established and have been surprisingly successful, with children of all ages visiting the Leventis Museum and working on special themes and projects related to the museum and the history of Nicosia.

Provision for adults

The museum's various activities such as lectures, guided tours, special exhibitions, the annual event for donors, and many other events may, and should, be considered as 'adults' educational programmes'. Parallel to all these events the museum tries to organise special educational programmes in which adults may participate. These programmes were to deal with subjects of special interest such as historical themes, among other activities, that can involve adults.

The first 'Educational programme for adults' began on an experimental basis in 1992. The programme was limited to 20–25 persons and was planned to take place once a week from 10.00 to 12.00 for a period of one month. Consequently, between March and April of that year a group of 20 women gathered in the museum every Thursday to follow a brief lecture and view photographs of the old city. The objective was to work on the identification of buildings and the families who lived in them, The programme was called 'Photographic details', and its target was primarily to introduce the modern history of the city and the large photographic collection of the end of the nineteenth and beginning of the twentieth centuries to participants. Ideally, the museum was trying at the same time to train volunteers to help with the cataloguing of this collection of photographs.

The programme was partially successful for the following reasons:

1. the museum gained new Friends, as all adults who participated in the programmes became members of the Association of the Friends of the Museum;
2. all participants enjoyed the lectures and viewed the photographic material with great interest;
3. a number of participants donated objects and photographs to the museum.

However, the museum failed to provide the proper incentive or guidance to encourage the participants to work on the photographic material on a voluntary basis: instead of focusing their attention on a specific photograph, they saw the sessions mainly as an opportunity for social intercourse. Nevertheless, the museum has persevered and since 1992 has set up a number of other adult educational programmes. These events may be divided into the following categories:

1. tours and lectures combined with temporary exhibitions;
2. tours in the museum for special groups, by appointment;
3. thematic tours in the city, such as 'Medieval Nicosia: a tour of the medieval monuments', 'Traditional craftsmen', 'The Colonial period';
4. Thematic tours and excursions around the island; and
5. series of thematic lectures, such as 'Museums in Europe', 'Collections and collectors', 'Conservation'.

Five years after the establishment of educational programmes for adults the museum undertook an evaluation. Results may be summarised as follows:

- 90 per cent of the participants were women;
- 50 per cent of those who participated in the first educational programme also took part in the subsequent programmes;
- most of the participants used the events as an opportunity to meet their friends;
- the most popular events were walking tours and excursions;
- all participants are now Friends of the Museum.

The Leventis Municipal Museum is now starting its sixth year of educational programmes for adults. The target will again be to motivate adults towards voluntary work in the museum.

The programmes for adults offered before 1997 were free of charge, with all expenses covered by sponsors. Since 1997 these educational programmes have carried a fee which varies according to the theme. These fees give the museum a profit and contribute to the support of other projects undertaken by it.

Educational programmes for adults in other museums in Cyprus

The example of the Leventis Museum in organising educational programmes for children was followed by several other, mostly private, museums on the island. These museums did not, however, attempt to organise educational programmes for adults.

The only example apart from the Leventis Museum is that of the Nicosia Municipal Arts Centre. This Arts Centre, the so-called 'Power House', is housed in the old electricity power station of the city. In one sense, it is not a museum as it has no permanent collections, but it is considered to be a contemporary art museum because its target is to arrange and host a number of art exhibitions, either from Cyprus or from abroad. It was inaugurated in 1984 and since then has been organising two or three exhibitions per year. Within the various activities arranged by the Centre during such exhibitions are educational programmes exclusively for adults. They are usually run by an artist and include a guided tour of the exhibition and one or more lectures which focus on the artist(s). The events are very successful and the number of participants, mostly Cypriots, is high.

As indicated above, the Power House is the only other example. Up to the present, no other museum or art gallery on the island has prepared and offered educational programmes for adults. Cyprus is not, therefore, a good example for adult education provision in museums!

Nevertheless, one must take into consideration the fact that the Republic of Cyprus is only 38 years old and that during this short period the citizens have suffered greatly, due to intercommunal problems created by the division of their capital in 1963 and political upheavals leading to the division of their country in 1974. These events necessitated concentration on a number of projects for the development of the country's economy and industry, and especially the social development and well-being of its citizens. For a number of years a visit to a museum was not a priority. People considered museums to be for tourists, not for locals.

Today we are able to talk about cultural activities and visits to museums. And this is why in the Leventis Municipal Museum of Nicosia we decided to focus our attention on organising educational programmes for children so that in the future they will be well prepared to become our adult collaborators.

Note

1 Alexander Palma di Cesnola, *Lawrence-Cesnola collection, Cyprus antiquities, excavated by Major Alexander Palma di Cesnola, member of the Biblical Archaeological Society [etc],* *1876–1879.* This is a special photograph album, printed and bound by W Holmes & Son, London, 1881. The album measures 37.5 cm x 28 cm and contains 100 plates depicting the Cesnola collection. It was donated to the Museum by Lellos Demetriades, Mayor of Nicosia.

References

Hudson, K, *European Museum of the Year Award 1991,* Helsinki: EMYA, 1991, pp. 61
Vassos, K, *Ancient Cypriot art in the Pierides Foundation Museum,* Athens: Pierides Foundation, 1985, pp.13–15

14   Italy

Three separate contributions, by Edi Fanti, Lida Branchesi, and Paolo Orefice & Gianni Maria Filippi

Introduction

In Italy, potential links between the adult education system and museums in general have not yet been well developed, structured or formalised. Educational activities aimed at adult visitors are all too frequently left to the inspiration and initiative of museum staff or groups of museums acting together at local level. There is no national policy in this regard, and it follows that there is no precise, well-co-ordinated national development programme.

The education departments of museums, where they exist, are mainly concerned with activities for children; indeed, there is a well-established relationship between museums and schools, from primary level upwards. The perceived main purpose of museums, however, continues to be the protection and preservation of the Italian cultural heritage, and it is only now that links with the adult education world are beginning to be organised into a coherent structure able to respond to local needs.

The most significant advances in adult education came about after World War II in an attempt to reduce illiteracy. The 1970s also saw a burgeoning of '150-hours' courses which gave workers the opportunity to make use of 150 paid hours to complete their formal education.

Based on the positive experiences of these courses, local centres for permanent education have recently been set up under the auspices of the Department for Education. These aim to improve access to both formal and informal education, not simply through activities at school, but also by bringing together local authorities, trade unions, associations and other interested parties in an area which may wish to be involved in adult education programmes. The reason that Italy has failed to develop a firm national policy with respect to the adult education sector is undoubtedly attributable to the unique historic, cultural and social conditions which characterise our country.

Italy's political unification and consequent establishment as a single nation took place only about 100 years ago (1861), which is why certain sectors are still defining themselves politically, socially and culturally, and lack previous traditions or coherent policies on which to draw. The adult education system and the museum service are under the control of several Italian central government departments for legislative, administrative and bureaucratic matters, yet they are also subject to regional, provincial and local political decisions. A further historical fact which may help to explain the difficulties in the relationship between the two sectors is the emergence in 1970 of the 20

Italian regions as political and administrative forces. Once again it is a historical date which serves to remind us that it takes time for recently established regional organisations to define and consolidate newly created decentralised roles. Another factor which contributes to the general situation of delay is the economic, social and cultural imbalance in the country, characterised by a wealthy northern region with its large industries, a central swathe with small and average-sized businesses, and a southern area mainly known for its agriculture.

Italy has witnessed, and continues to witness, a number of museum-oriented initiatives which have implications for adult education. Areas of attention include heritage, culture and the environment.

Edi Fanti

The following account discusses some recent and major developments with particular reference to the work of a newly established National Commission of Heritage and Culture.

Some important innovations

The National Commission for Museum and Territory Education

In 1990, the then president of ICOM suggested that the right to heritage was something which each country's political and educational culture must guarantee (Konare 1990). Although Italy is a country with many museums and heritage sites throughout its territory, museum and heritage education has not always been adequately supported at a political, financial, administrative and, I would say, scientific-academic level.[1]

In fact, there have been many initiatives and activities over the last few years which could be mentioned for their cultural level and innovative aspects – some of them even have an international reputation. This is borne out by the production of some material and published reviews (Gelao 1983; Guarducci 1988; Panzeri 1990, 1992, 1995); some are also available on-line.[2] However, the lack of any education departments in many museums, of any permanent specially trained staff, of specific financing and of appropriate structures has not allowed, except in rare cases, the setting up of a permanent education service with continuously running differentiated programmes targeting various age groups.

The reasons for this situation are, above all, due to basic unresolved political issues in Italy (Dalai 1999): there are difficulties in co-ordination and information between state institutions and local agencies. Communication has traditionally been poor between the three institutional parties which should programme every form of heritage education promotion. Their task is the safeguarding and conservation agencies on the one hand, and schools and universities – together with their respective ministries – on the other.

New signs have emerged in recent years. Since the time I took part in the Second International Conference on Adult Education and the Arts in 1993 at Wadham College, Oxford, on the theme 'Museum and adult education' (Elias *et al*, 1995), there have been many innovations in the field of museum education in Italy. Among these, the most important has been the setting-up of a National Commission for Museum and Territory Education by the Italian Ministero dei Beni e delle Attivita Culturali (Ministry of Heritage and Culture). This has highlighted the will to put heritage education at the centre of the Ministry's institutional activities and thus place it on equal footing with the direct safeguarding of heritage itself. The Commission, set up in 1995, is chaired by Marisa Dalai Emiliani, Professor of History of Modern Art at 'La Sapienza' University of Rome, and has members from the Ministry of Heritage and Culture, the Ministry of Education, the Ministry for Universities, from the European Centre for Education (CEDE), and directors of state or locally run museums.

Museum and territory

Why museum and territory? In Italy, these two terms are closely connected and sometimes inseparable. Italian museums mostly refer to the geographical territory in which they are located – it is their context, and they preserve its history and artefacts. Sometimes a territory is a museum in itself. Above all, small and medium-sized museums are closely linked to their urban context and geographical surroundings. In order to protect the heritage works of their territory, museums have had to house many of these on their own premises, from religious works to those of material civilisations, thereby removing them from from their original locations. However, the territory itself – with all its various layers of history starting from prehistoric and archaeological remains – should be considered a real kind of extended museum for people to get to know, respect, preserve, and also 'use' in the education field. This consideration has become cultural policy since the 1970s and has often been at the centre of much heated debate (Emiliani 1974, 1985).

From an educational perspective, the close link between museum and territory enabled the relationship between artefacts and locations to be kept alive. Removing artefacts from any one location and putting them elsewhere means not only decontextualising them but, in some way, removing their meaning. Moreover, museum and territory, as such, offer invaluable resources for education in Italy, for all age groups and communities. Heritage works that are often less well known need to be valued, 'adopted' and taken care of, making the most of their educational potential and thereby arousing widespread public awareness.

In a broader context, the distinction between museum and territory allows the Commission to recover that unity in method and orientation which characterises the Italian peripheral system[3] and thus sends out a clear signal to indicate the need for networking between the various museums in Italy, be they state, regional, provincial, public, diocesan or private museums.

Towards an Italian education service system

During the years the Commission has been running (1995–98), it has drafted a project for devising a general organisational model on a national scale. This is a composite Italian system of education services for museums and territories – both at state and local level – which will, it is hoped, be networked and co-ordinated by a centre to be set up at the Ministry of Heritage and Culture.

The Commission's working materials have been published in a volume (*Verso un sistema dei Servizi educativi per il museo e il territorio*, 1999), gathering together the many materials produced and the results obtained from the various studies. In order to draft the project, there was a need to undertake two kinds of investigations: one at national and the other at international level.

A study was thus made of the experiences gained in Italy through initiatives of state and local preservation organisations and also of school institutions. Research was also undertaken through meetings and seminars with those in charge of education departments. At the same time, an international study was carried out on the organisation of educational services for heritage in other European countries and on the activities of relevant international organisations (Branchesi 1999).

On this historical and documentary basis, the Commission's proposal gained some political responses and the first opportunities for implementation. One of these is the Framing Agreement (March 1998) between the Ministry of Heritage and Culture and the Ministry of Education, which established innovative regulations for experimental educational activities jointly designed by schools, through school autonomy,[4] and by the education services of the *Soprintendenze*.[5] The provisions laid down are in line with the most advanced international directives, also expressed by the recent Council of Europe Recommendation (no. 5, 1998) concerning the pedagogy of heritage.

A Centre for Museum and Territory Education Service was also set up by law in 1998, with co-ordination, orientation, monitoring, counselling, information, experimentation and documentation functions. The Centre has just commenced its activities: it is certainly a historic opportunity for developing museum education in Italy, and many educational projects, through school–museum agreements, have already been started.

Adults – museum – education: some considerations

What are the problems faced with particular reference to adult education? Those who are familiar with the situation in Italian museums know that over the last few years many initiatives have been introduced to make better use of museums. These include extending opening times and providing for evening visiting times; setting up 'additional services' such as catering areas, bookshops, publishing facilities – services provided by private enterprise through calls for tenders and introduced by law (with some controversy) in 1993; as well as the use of new interactive and multimedia technologies. All these innovations make museum visits more attractive, especially for adults.

However, such important opportunities also involve some risks. As the Commission's chairwoman notes (Dalai 1999), the focus of debate has in the last decade moved – and not only in Italy – on to the economics of culture, ways to find resources, and marketing and management. An alarming sign of this is the theme chosen by ICOM for the 1997 world conference, 'Museums under profitability pressure': the focus is more on increasing the number of visitors than on cultural quality control and the educational value of initiatives.

The Commission has tried to distinguish between the 'additional services' activity, to which guided visits are normally entrusted, and the educational-scientific activity of education services; between cultural tourism initiatives, so widespread in Italy and normally entrusted to tourist guides, and adult education, as part of lifelong education.

It has also focused on initiatives for categories with 'particular' needs requiring in-depth specialist skills. There are some very advanced examples that can be identified for these categories of people, such as the well-known initiative carried out with visually impaired adults by the Turin Egyptian Museum, which is now included in the European project *European cities within reach: travel and culture for visually-impaired people* (D'Amicone 1999), or the initiative with mentally disabled people carried out by the education department of the Uffizi in Florence with the co-operation of physicians in that particular field (Trenti Antonelli 1998).

Many are now pointing to the fact that in a multi-ethnic society such as ours, museums often find themselves facing a great challenge at the educational level. These are issues which directly involve anthropological museums, defined as 'the threshold separating identity from otherness' (Lattanzi 1999). There is an interesting inter-cultural education project for adults on this, co-ordinated by Professor Tullio Tentori, which has been planned jointly by the Pigorini Anthropological Museum in Rome, the Italian Prime Minister's Office and the National Museum of Folk Arts and Traditions. The project envisages the implementation of inter-cultural education courses in museums for people working in jobs that specifically deal with the immigration issue – something that is particularly felt today in Italy, as elsewhere – and its social and cultural implications. Students of police academies, employment agency workers, medical staff and teachers are members of this course for adults which has a double purpose – namely, a vocational training aspect and an educational one.

Museums have taken many initiatives for adults with such dual functions: for example, the school workshops in the public museums of Genoa aimed both at professional development and personal enrichment. The theory–practical course on the foundations of sculpture, held at the Sant' Agostino Ligurian Architecture and Sculpture Museum, has a similar function.

Laboratory work is especially envisaged for contemporary art museums, such as the Pecci Museum in Prato. Here the Education Department has developed laboratory activities for adults in order to test interactions between language forms and the employment of useful techniques and materials for education, artistic expression and personal communication, as well as considered interpretations of the works on display in the permanent collection.

The Commission has paid particular attention to reflections on professional profiles that are necessary for the development of the museum and territory education system (Fusco 1999). Without going into the current lively debate in France on the value and role of 'cultural mediation' and the new kind of professionalism this implies (Caillet 1995), I feel that the issue in Italy is particularly sensitive, also in view of the relationship between the public and private sectors. Naturally, however, if teacher–museum staff interaction and co-operation can meet educational and cultural needs within the educational opportunities that museums can offer adults, while also considering the needs of different public users, then cultural mediation may in certain cases be able to meet better the aim of bringing together pleasure, culture, education and training.

Days devoted to museum education

A further sign of obvious renewed interest in museum education comes from the fact that in the last four years, one of the days in Heritage Week has always been set aside for education. The Commission presented its first works in 1995; a national seminar was held in 1996 with the well-known directors of the education departments to discuss the project; the year 1998 saw the presentation of the Framing Agreement between the two ministries; the first national experiments began; and an international round-table meeting was held which saw the participation of the Council of Europe, ICOM/CECA and ICCROM as well as British, French, German and Spanish representatives, who met to present their models and discuss the Italian project. Apart from the presentation of the *Commission Proceedings*, the year 1999 saw the proposal and debating of educational projects deriving from the Framing Agreement, the development of the pilot projects, and some particular case studies, such as that for visually impaired people at the Cagliari Archaeological Museum.

Lida Branchesi

Notes

1 Despite a degree course in heritage preservation and art history departments in universities, Italy lacks any real courses in museological and museographic subjects.

2 See, in particular, the databank of the *Centro di didattica museale* (museum education centre) of the Third University of Rome. This centre was set up in 1994 based on a project by Emma Nardi, who is in charge.
3 The Italian state heritage system is divided into *Soprintendenze* (superintendencies). These are peripheral territorial units charged with the preservation of archaeological, architectural, landscape, historical or artistic works. They are responsible for those museums in their sphere as regards territory or type.
4 Schools' organisational and educational autonomy, established by law in 1997, was experimentally implemented and will come into full force in the year 2000.
5 See note 3.

References

Branchesi, L, 'Per un confronto con l'Europa: modelli organizzativi e linee di tendenza', in *Verso un sistema dei servizi educativi per il museo e il territorio*, Rome: Ministero per i beni e le attivite culturali, 1999, pp. 231–90

Caillet, E, *A l'approche du musee, la mediation culturelle*, Lyon: Presses Universitaires de Lyon, 1995

Dalai, M, 'Difficolta e traguardi di un percorso', in *Verso un sistema dei servizi educativi per il museo e il territorio*, Rome: Ministero per i beni e le attivite culturali, 1999, pp. xiii–xx

D'Amicone, E, 'Le attivita educative del Museo Egizio di Torino', in *Verso un sistema italiano dei servizi educativi per il museo e il territorio*, Rome: Ministero per i beni e le attivite culturali, 1999, pp. 89–101

Elias, W *et al.* (eds), *Truth without facts: selected papers from the first three international conferences on adult education and the arts*, Brussels: VUB Press, 1995

Emiliani, A, *Dal museo al territorio: scritti vari 1967–1974*, Bologna: Alfa, 1974

—— *Il museo alla sua terza eta. Dal territorio al museo*, Bologna: Nuova Alfa Editoriale, 1985

Fusco, A, 'Professionalita museologiche, educative, turistiche a confronto', in *Verso un sistema dei servizi educativi per il museo e il territorio*, Rome: Ministero peri beni e le attivite culturali, 1999, pp. 71–6

Gelao, C, *Didattica dei musei in Italia, 1960–1981*, Molfetta: Mezzina, 1983

Guarducci, M L, *Musei e didattica. Esperienze e dibattiti in Italia dal dopoguerra ad oggi*, Firenze: Barocci, 1988

Konare, A O, 'Les activités de sensibilisation hors du cadre scolaire', in *Les jeunes et le patrimoine architectural*, Travaux réunis à l'issue du colloque organisé à l'Unesco en 1989 pour Jeunesse & Patrimoine International, Liège: Mardaga, 1990, pp. 47–52

Lattanzi, V, 'La didattica dei beni demo-etno-antropologici: l'esperienza del museo "Pigorini"', in *Verso un sistema dei servizi educativi per il museo e il territorio*, Rome: Ministero peri beni e le attivite culturali, 1999 pp. 107–15

Panzeri, P, *Didattica museale in Italia. Rassegna di Bibliografia I*, Rome: Fratelli Palombi Editori, 1990 —— *Didattica museale in Italia. Rassegna di bibliografia II*, Rome: Fratelli Palombi Editori, 1992

—— 'Didattica del museo e del territorio: 1991–1995', *Bollettino d'arte del Ministero per i beni e le attivita culturali* no. 91, 1995

Trenti Antonelli, M G, 'Le puissance de l'art: une expérience avec de jeunes malades psychiques pour sortir de l'isolement', in *Le patrimoine culturel et sa péedadagogie: un facteur de tolérance, de civisme et d'intégration sociale*: Actes-Seminaire, Brussels 1995, Brussels: Editions du Conseil de l'Europe, 1998

Verso un sistema dei servizi educativi per il museo e il territorio. Materiali di lavoro della commissione ministeriale, Rome: Ministero per i beni e le attivita culturali, 1999

Continuing changes linked to museums and the education of adults can be illustrated by the case study described below. This project, still in its early stages, considers the conceptual foundations upon which a recent experiment relating to adults has been developed.

The *Locus* Project

Background

The Veneto region (Venice) occupies a position of prime importance at national and international level in terms of the richness of its cultural heritage with respect to its environment, art, history, science and anthropological and cultural traditions. An unrivalled number of tourists, both Italian and foreign, are attracted to its heritage which is unique in the world. The field of museum education and its related infrastructure must therefore be considered to have priority status within the region. It is gradually emerging from international literature, from the insight of culturally aware international organisations such as UNESCO, and from the collective experience of the more industrialised countries such as the USA, Canada and Germany, that the buildings which house our cultural and environmental heritage can no longer be viewed simply or predominantly as places to preserve and mount cultural and environmental displays for the public. This function has been superseded in time by the arrival of a hi-tech society which demands that even the most basic information is transmitted by means of mass-communication techniques which can guarantee swift and direct delivery.

It is a paradox that highly sophisticated levels of mass communication are regularly adopted to instil and reinforce concepts concerning social and cultural conditioning, whilst those used to transmit the complex nature of beautiful and even sublime levels of achievement go no further than simply displaying the exhibit in question. This leads us to pose the question: if we exclude the museum staff and the real *aficionados*, how much does the average visitor, ranging from the most to the least culturally aware, benefit from their visit to a museum, an exhibition or a site of cultural or environmental interest? How many precious artefacts have we managed to make accessible to the public at large? To what extent have we succeeded in enabling visitors to go beyond a superficial sense of wonder at a certain work of art or a scientific discovery, or have they merely wondered instead at their own lack of comprehension of it and gone away with their preconceived cognitive and perceptive stereotypes still intact?

From these questions have arisen the need, and hence a proposal, to carry out a piece of action research within the museum service to augment its ability to provide culture and education. One area of enquiry is the implicit and explicit educational need of visitors and another is an examination of the integrated provision which the museum service can offer to improve the aesthetic, historical, cultural, scientific and environmental education of the general public.

This piece of action research limits itself to researching two areas: educational need and educational provision. It seeks new ways of operating in terms of structural solutions, methodological procedures and technical and educational resources. The working model is transferable and, hence, adaptable to correspondingly similar situations, given necessary modifications.

The research focuses on the topic of high-level provision of museum education for adult visitors. For this, dual modelling is required: that of analysing their educational needs and that of trialling the proposed adult education methodology on a suitable cross-section of visitors. Both aims, although interdependent, have specific operating procedures, set out in the stages outlined below.

Stage 1: background research

The operational side: definition and interaction

In operational terms there were two interconnected areas of concern: firstly, we needed to detail and develop the ideas behind the project; and secondly, we needed to ensure that the research team felt fully involved. The project had been initiated by the person in charge of science who, at the request of IRRSAE (Regional Institute for Educational Research, Experimentation and Training, Department for Education, Veneto Region) presented the idea for the project: an examination of the current state of museum education and the need to improve its provision. An operational chart was then drawn up to show how the project could be structured. This was discussed at IRRSAE and adapted as necessary to the specific requirements of the Veneto region. From this came the final structure of the working project, set out both in diagrammatic form and descriptive style.

The second aim was realised by ensuring active participation as a working method. This is of critical importance for a collaborative research project at both theoretical and strategic levels. Within a research group there exists the potential for individual creativity, but inter-personal relationships and the unexplored nature of new areas may create difficulties. A good sense of team spirit allows the individuals concerned to develop their expertise and share their skills in the best possible way. A research group can be neither creative nor productive if it does not have that spirit of solidarity within itself, born out of collective support for the project aims and working patterns.

The initial project plans were developed into a working plan through a series of consultation exercises with members of the Veneto museum staff group, whose contributions were welcomed.

Literature search on museum education

Possible sources worthy of consultation were identified, and an initial national and international bibliography was compiled. It was noted that literature on museum education is more fully developed abroad than in Italy: our country concentrates more on integrating museums with the school sector, providing support with materials for some of their educational activities.

The International Council of Museums (ICOM), based in Paris, proved to be a very rich source of information concerning studies and experiments in museum education. On the international level particular use was made of the studies by the psychologist Dufresne-Tasse of the University of Montreal, a specialist in the field of the behaviour of adults in museums (one of her suggested educational activities, the *game of concepts*, was later incorporated in the *Locus* project). Overall, the first literature search resulted in the discovery of a wide area of contributions which the *Locus* team studied and later integrated into the project at theoretical, methodological and technical levels.

Identification of museums in the Veneto area interested in participating in the Locus project, and definition of their collaboration

Our research into museum education in the specified region had several results: it allowed us to review the situation in Veneto museums, to find out the current state of museum education for adults, to initiate links with these museums, and to set up a regional support network with them.

The available resources also allowed us to build a map of the Veneto museums. Firstly, a typological grid of museums was drawn up, divided into public and private buildings. The museums which were publicly owned were then subdivided into national or local concerns and classified according to their content: art, history, culture and science. This typology was not intended to be exhaustive but to serve the interests of the project, and we recognise that different typological classifications are possible according to one's perspective. We were then able to see the typological distribution within each of the provinces of the Veneto. In this way we constructed an overview of the possible participants in our project.

On the operational level it was the organisations which had had previous experience of educational projects that tended to be most interested in the *Locus* project (museums, local authorities and associations); they were usually small or medium-sized operations. It seemed that the *Locus* project was seen as an opportunity to revitalise the museum service in a more general way.

For this first stage of the project the network collaborated in putting together some joint reflections on 'The museum for permanent education'. Contributions were taken from inside and outside the region to focus on the theme of museum education on theoretical, methodological and technical levels. Again, this was not intended to be exhaustive.

It was recognised that museum education has its own place and specific professional needs. It also has a cultural role to play in a society in which the world of information technology is expanding at a rate which is inversely proportional to the ability of the general public to select, interpret and intelligently master the information it requires. Faced with this requirement for 'messages of a high educational standard', including 'messages' from museum exhibits, it is important that museum staff develop and maintain high professional standards in order to communicate on a cultural level with the public and within the context of lifelong learning.

In Italy in general there is only a weak, localised commitment to policies which aim at developing higher standards of museum education. This reflects the ineffectiveness of our national and regional policies in protecting and maintaining Italy's cultural and environmental heritage, which is one of the richest in the world.

Stage 2 : analysing the need

In order to ensure a successful outcome to a project which aims to assess the educational needs of visitors to museums, we must first pose certain questions concerning the relationship between environment and knowledge. There is a very close relationship between representational systems of learning about the environment which surrounds us and their configuration. Human beings do not possess an innate body of knowledge, but have the ability to formulate, expand and adapt it – in fact, to work it out for themselves, through their own personal constructs, as a basis from which they can enrich their lives. If all mankind has such cognitive potential, it is obvious that its expression depends on the content of each individual's experiences. Hence it is the quality of this content shaping our daily lives which is of fundamental importance and allows us to achieve our full cognitive potential.

It also follows that the more one's representational cognitive system is developed and co-ordinated, the more one is able to derive meaning from stimuli which surround us. To return to the concept of quality within the content of our experiences, one can, with some justification, maintain that the richer and more varied the stimuli offered by the environment, the more one can expand one's ability to interpret the environment and hence realise the true potential of the human condition. One's relationship with a stimulating environment creates a sense of belonging in a unique way to a natural order and encourages self-expression and cultural depth. This is certainly a precious source of learning, which serves to extend and qualify one's cognitive representational system and which leads to positive effects on the life of the individual and also on the environment itself. The converse is also true: those who live in an impoverished environment and are deprived of opportunities to explore external stimuli undoubtedly have fewer resources at their disposal with which to nourish and extend a representational system of the environment.

The importance of offering worthwhile stimuli to draw on can be seen.

Historical, man-made achievements of the highest quality must occupy a privileged position in this regard. They represent the collective cultural heritage in the fields of art, science, technology and other contributions made by the creative spirit of independent races, small groups or individuals. This rich heritage is under the gaze of everyone in a country like Italy, where the very surroundings overflow with cultural exhibits which provide stimuli of the highest quality. Museums are privileged places in which such exhibits are accumulated and displayed: from this perspective they are authentic 'gems of knowledge' which are priceless not only in economic terms but also in terms of the immense opportunities which they provide for people to explore their environments.

It is at this point that the central problem of the *Locus* project emerges, and in particular the aim of this second phase: should the educational concepts of our cultural and environmental heritage remain implicit and therefore difficult to assimilate, or should they be made explicit, for the benefit of a wider audience?

It must be said that even if, as has been stated, there exists a close link between environmental stimuli and cognitive representation, this relationship is not automatic or mechanical, but happens through a series of 'mediators' who encourage this cycle of osmosis from one to the other. A cultural or natural history exhibit contains within itself cognitive stimuli of the highest quality. An individual looking at it may not have sufficiently highly developed cognitive categories to interpret the stimuli and therefore remains unable to access the information and extend their cognitive representational system. Conversely, an individual who already enjoys a highly specialised cognitive learning set in one particular area, such as an art expert or a biologist, is well able to enjoy at the highest level even seemingly insignificant exhibits, such as a painting of little value or an ordinary flower.

These two extremes demonstrate how important the 'mediators' are. They hold a unique position as educational facilitators, and as thus may be defined as educators. It is important to be concerned both with how to 'explain' a cultural or natural history exhibit to facilitate maximum access to the heritage which it stores, and with the 'threshold level' of knowledge of the individual who enters into a relationship with the exhibit.

If the 'explanation' is lacking and the 'threshold level' is low, such relationship does not take place, or rather it takes place at levels which are completely inappropriate, resulting in ineffective or, at worst, counter-productive processing. Individuals may eventually become alienated, not only from one particular exhibit but also from all others. They may lose confidence in their ability to understand them and, in extreme cases, may stop visiting museums and exhibitions altogether.

If the 'explanation' is suitable and the 'threshold level' is low, the ensuing relationship will develop from an initial superficial stage to increasingly deeper levels of understanding; in this case the cognitive 'threshold level' does not remain impenetrable but will gradually rise. There then begins a positive feedback process: if the 'threshold level' improves, one's interpretation of the exhibit improves, and hence one's interpretation of the environment. The information contained within the 'explanation' gradually becomes more understandable and accessible in terms of quality and quantity, and finally the 'threshold level' rises: the process of interaction between stimuli and knowledge may then begin again at higher levels in a never-ending upward spiral.

If the 'explanation' is good and the 'threshold level' is high, we engage in an ideal situation. The relationship becomes one of rich abundance, culminating in a deep sense of well-being for the individual. He or she will succeed in engaging with the cultural or natural history exhibit in a deeper and more subtle way and, arguably, will relish the challenges offered by the acquisition of his new knowledge. They will feel ever more bonded to the exhibit, which in turn is more cared for, protected and valued.

Thus, within the context of the *Locus* project, in order to assess the educational needs of the visitor at this stage, we must try and understand, at least in a rudimentary way, the situation regarding the 'explanation' of the exhibit in the museum and the cognitive 'threshold level' of the individual.

The words 'explanation' and 'threshold level' should be understood as offering a way of justifying the need to provide high-quality education rather than a way of arriving at significant statistical data. Certainly the intention is to present an initial snapshot of the situation within museums of the Veneto from an observational point of view. But of greater scientific importance, and therefore operational significance, is the methodological aspect of the definition of training needs.

Hence, in drawing up the survey as a technical instrument in the way discussed above, and in anticipating its usage, we have mostly been concerned with two aspects: to see what kind of cognitive 'explanation' was offered in the museums, and what the 'threshold level' of the visitors was. Both had to be explored indirectly and it was important, given the limitations and the characteristics of the research as described above, to discuss them in introductory and simplified terms.

Questionnaire design

The following was the final structure of the questionnaire which was first trialled by groups of adults taking part in museum activities within the Local Authority of Venice.

It was designed to cover seven different areas. The first three items – (1) The visitor; (2) Reasons for visiting/Expectations; (3) Existing knowledge – and the sixth – (6) Effects of the visit – focused on elements which were important to gain an understanding of the cognitive 'threshold level' of the visitor. The fourth, fifth and seventh – (4) The route; (5) Communication; (7) Improvements to learning materials – focused more on the cognitive 'explanation'. The aim was not to gain comment on it *per se*, but to ask questions about the interaction between factual knowledge about the museum exhibit and the visitor's cognitive system. The 'explanation' (which comes under 'educational activities offered') is observed from the point of view of educational need, and hence from the perspective which the visitor has. It is an important distinction which the questionnaire must highlight so as not to provide false results: we are concerned with 'explanation' observed from the point of view of the visitor's 'threshold level'. It is a question of method of analysis but also of principle, since the educational activities offered (that is, the 'explanation') must be finely tuned to the educational requirements. It must correspond as closely as possible to the visitor's perspective if it is to set up that osmotic cycle of positive stimuli which, as mentioned earlier, can be invoked between the 'explanation' and the 'threshold level'. An 'explanation' which is not tailor-made for the visitor may be perfect in itself but may ultimately fail to communicate and therefore be ineffective on an educational level.

The items which focus on the 'threshold level' offer information concerning the 'situation on entry', although it must be borne in mind that the questionnaire is completed after the visit to the museum. By combining the data available on the different types of visitor (1), on their reasons for visiting the museum (2) and on their specific knowledge (3), it is possible to build up an initial methodological 'identikit' of the educational needs of the visitors in terms of the elements which constitute their 'threshold level' of knowledge on entry. The item on the effects of the visit (6) allows us to shed light on their 'threshold level' on exit and hence, indirectly, on whether the 'educational explanation' has been successfully received.

It is, however, by combining the information from items (3) and (6) that we can find out about any internal changes which may have happened to the 'threshold level' of pre-existing and post-visit knowledge.

The items which focus more heavily on 'explanation' and visitors' response to it allow us not only to view its effect on the visitors' 'threshold level', but also to gather useful information on any problems and eventually to formulate ideas on different ways of delivering educational activities. The visitors' reactions to the route and to modes of communication, and their suggestions as to improvements to learning materials, can be profitably considered individually or in combination. These make for a significant database which will provide a sound methodological and technical basis for any museum which aims to establish a rewarding relationship between the museum exhibits and their visitors' cognitive representational systems.

This type of result which is essentially the main aim of the second stage of the project on the level of needs analysis, is also useful for the development of stages 3 and 4 of the *Locus* project. These concern the teaching proposals and testing out materials. Such feedback allows us to gain concrete data and, above all, suggests ways of improving the educational provision for adults in museums in the Veneto area.

Stage 3: the teaching proposals

At this stage of the project one can formulate the general outlines for educational provision, on the basis of the theory and the methodology adopted and also along the lines of the general ideas which had been discussed and agreed with the museum organisers.

The teaching proposals may be hypothetically viewed as a *micro-experimental model in non-formal adult education for museum visitors*. They refer to specific regions, in this case the Veneto region, and may be defined as providing a model of adult education activities suitable for gaining insight into the cultural and environmental heritage, in the sense discussed earlier, of improving one's cognitive representational system of the environment. The aim of museum education may be considered to focus on two levels: one of *teaching proposals* and the other the *learning response*. From the point of view of proposals we were eager to produce an 'educational experiment' concerning museum exhibits which would offer a key for interpreting the exhibit to the visitor. We recognise that it is not enough simply to present cultural or natural history exhibits in an educational, but also informative, way or by producing a technical or specialised explanation of the object. It is, instead, important to offer a suitable 'trail' to the visitor who may not be an expert in 'the subject' or who may have a rather fragmented cognitive 'threshold level'.

It follows that the proposals, although focusing on the exhibits in the museums, are strongly orientated towards the individual who approaches them. In this way the proposals bear the visitor in mind and prepare the visitor's 'response'.

The second aspect is as important as the first. The visitor's involvement and participation are vital, otherwise we cannot speak of a learning activity, even if we speak about non-formal education. The individual's active participation in the many possible expressions of learning (perceptive, emotional, imaginary, cognitive) is an indispensable condition of the learning process of the individual, changing their initial cognitive 'threshold level'. We cannot speak of a learning activity if we limit ourselves to setting up only the activity without regard for how it is received. This is to ensure the extension of the individual's learning set, enabling them to change their initial cognitive 'threshold level'. Rather than just offering knowledge (although this has its place), it is important to create the conditions suitable for individuals to improve their learning set, so that they interpret the cultural exhibit in their own way and assimilate information which may be new for them and specific to particular disciplinary viewpoints. Only in this way can they succeed in not being alienated when looking at a cognitive stimulus from our cultural heritage, and they will manage to approach it not in a stereotyped and limited way but by establishing a symbiotic relationship of knowledge with the exhibits.

The question therefore now moves from the level of the aim to that of *method*. This must also be considered from two angles: how to present the learning materials and how to ensure a response. Below are some operational criteria which are then technically defined during the specific operational stages. Above all, one must adopt a 'selective approach' towards the cultural exhibits, not an indiscriminate one: the individual is not invited to read every display which the museum offers, but rather to concentrate on a particular theme. This then does not take the form of a 'descriptive approach' which is widely adopted in museums and which limits itself to providing and highlighting a set of information, but is presented more in terms of an 'interpretative approach': the 'key points', or several linked 'key points', are highlighted, and in this way the themes are developed, contextualised and made available for interpretation. They can be viewed from different angles which are firmly based within the cultural exhibit itself; aspects may, for example, be historical, cultural, psychological, disciplinary or technical. One must not limit oneself, as happens in many museums, to a mono-linear approach, such as the disciplinary one, which frequently serves to isolate and cause misinterpretation of the exhibit if opportunities are not created to examine the different factors which have come together in creating the object. In short, one can say that the selective and interpretative approach defines 'what to read' and 'how to read it'. In this way it gives a series of operational procedures as to the technical choices to be adopted in specific cases.

The educational proposals can be divided methodologically into three areas:

1. *the processing:* The themes can be sorted into a logical sequence according to the key point(s) to be read and in relation to the museum exhibits which are available. These must then be chosen to correspond with the chosen topic and, where the originals are not in the museum, they can be integrated with any reproductions of museum objects which are considered fundamental to the understanding of the topic. In this way the possible modes of learning are defined with reference to the type of learning that one wishes to achieve – namely, the 'learning skills' discussed earlier.

2. *the preparation:* We focus on the educational resources which the organiser of museum education has at their disposal and on the resources which are available to the adult visitor. As a general principle one could say that on a methodological level, multimedia and interactive criteria are important as they permit communication of the internal messages of the museum exhibits on a multiplicity of levels and hence encourage the movement of information and knowledge in two directions: of the museum exhibit and the museum educator towards the individual visitor, and vice versa.

3. *the presentation:* This is where the actual educational activity is presented through multimedia and participatory techniques outlined above, following a logical sequence. A presentation prepares the visitor for the intended visit and then accompanies them throughout their stay in the museum. It first introduces the visitor to what there is to see and how to look at museum exhibits, and then gives them first-hand experience of interpreting museum exhibits through the thematic display which unfolds.

This method encourages a response in the learner as it is not only selective and interpretative, but encourages, above all, the visitor's involvement which as has been stated, must be understood in the sense of turning the visitor from a passive receptor into an active protagonist. Frequently they are not even receptors but merely passive individuals who stay outside the range of cognitive stimuli. Their involvement must be understood in terms of the activation of the learning process in order to raise their cognitive 'threshold level'.

Paolo Orefice and Gianni Maria Filippi

The case study above concludes by referring to the adult visitor as 'an active protagonist' rather than a 'passive receptor'. This important distinction is illustrative of a developing emphasis on adult learners as 'variables' in a museum context rather than 'givens', incapable of growth or development.

15 Malta

Carmel Borg and Peter Mayo

Recent developments in Maltese adult education

Adult education is being given prominence in the discourse on education in Malta (a nation state which consists of an archipelago of islands, the largest one being Malta and the other substantially inhabited one being Gozo). It has, during the last decade, begun to be accorded its long overdue recognition, at least as far as public declarations go, by those entrusted with the task of improving Malta's educational infrastructure (Mayo and Wain, forthcoming). The recently launched draft document for a New National Curriculum also gives prominence to adult education, as it encourages the reconceptualisation of schools as community learning centres catering to the interests and needs of community members of all ages.

There have been several developments in the area of adult education over the past decade. We now have women's programmes, a University of the Third Age, a prison education programme, parent education programmes and a Night Institute for Further Technical Education. At the conceptual level, there seems to have been an overdue shift in thinking regarding the range of adult continuing education provision. A recently published compendium of writings on adult learning in Malta (Baldacchino and Mayo 1997) broadens the dimensions of the area to incorporate such fields as cultural studies, women's studies, environmental education, workers' education, religious education, peace education and youth studies.

Museum education: an underdeveloped field

Despite these developments, museum education remains considerably underdeveloped within the context of adult education in Malta. It is one of the areas which are not dealt with in the above-mentioned compendium (Baldacchino and Mayo 1997) and it does not feature in the Draft New National Curriculum document, even though both publications emphasise the importance of alternative sites of educational practice. There seems, to date, to be very little effort channelled in the direction of producing personnel specialised in museum pedagogy. This is an area which hitherto has remained untapped by the University of Malta's Faculty of Education in its diploma courses, master's degree components and first degree course units, intended to cater to the formation of adult educators. This is not unique to the Maltese experience, with Anderson (1995) arguing, with respect to UK museums, that 'the current internal neglect by most institutions of appropriate staff training in basic educational theory and practice is a telling metaphor for the external neglect of appropriate public adult education services in museums' (1995 pp. 30).

It would be fair to remark, however, that there have been studies, published in one of the faculty's journals (Buhagiar 1983), and other efforts (the production of such study aids as work cards, the writing of student dissertations and the submission of proposals by faculty members) intended to enhance the role of museums as centres of learning for schoolchildren and adolescents. There is little, however, in the way of rendering museums centres of learning for adults or, more comprehensively, centres of lifelong learning.

Eurocentric colonial legacy

And yet there are sufficient museums and archaeological sites on the two main islands in the Maltese archipelago to warrant a considerable investment in this area. Situated in the centre of the Mediterranean, Malta was contested, throughout the centuries, by various powers vying for supremacy in the region and elsewhere. They sought to avail themselves of the archipelago's strategic location. One finds, in Malta, a concentration of important historic relics attesting to the impact of different cultures on the islands. The language spoken by the inhabitants (a Semitic language with a romance script) and the place-names testify to over 300 years of Arab rule. The main islands, Malta and Gozo, also contain one of the greatest concentrations of megalithic remains, over a given area of land, to be found anywhere in the world. Despite the country's historic links with the Phoenician, Arab and Punic worlds, Malta's most affirmed cultural connections have been predominantly Western European, with strong Roman Catholic overtones. This is reflected in much of the country's 'artistic heritage' (that which is extant) that testifies to an unmistakably Eurocentric colonial legacy.

The aforementioned and simplified historical scenario naturally provides the backdrop to one's appreciation of the various museums scattered throughout Malta and Gozo. These include approximately 18 state-run museums and archaeological sites open to the public, including places of historic interest which are run on the lines of a conventional museum, such as the newly refurbished Hypogeum, and the Tarxien and Ggantija Neolithic temples. There are also many Church museums, among which the Cathedral Museum at the former capital city of Mdina, eight parish museums (including the one connected to the late-Baroque Sanctuary at Zabbar) should be mentioned, as well as a small number of museums run by religious orders (Azzopardi 1995: 135,136) and private museums. These are open to visitors by appointment and include museums run on commercial lines, such as the Gozo Heritage Museum and the Mdina Dungeons.

Multi-functional educators

Despite the presence of such a diversity of museums and the fact that the state museums have, over the last 11 years, consistently fallen under the Ministry of Education, there has been a general lack of policy concerning the link between educational institutions and museums. Such a policy is urgent, given that certain museums are conceived of as centres of education, the most notable being the Church museums where the emphasis is on the role the cultural and religious heritage play in catechesis. There seems to be a lack of planned educational initiatives in connection with museums. Group visits by schoolchildren and adult learners occur on an *ad hoc* basis. This is in keeping with trends manifested elsewhere in relation to small museums:

> In smaller and less complex institutions, it is still likely that many of the museum staff will be involved in adult education, but often in a reactive rather than a proactive way. When asked to work with a group, perhaps to give a talk, or to contribute to a course, generally the response will be positive. However, little may be done to initiate an active approach to work with adults.
>
> (Hooper-Greenhill 1995: 52)

Groups that frequent museums in Malta include foreign visitors on guided tours, the elderly (often in connection with the University of the Third Age, local councils and international Elderhostel programmes consisting of a series of lectures complemented by 'on-site' visits, young adults in connection with parish youth centres and women undergoing adult education access programmes. The Culture Division within the Ministry of Education has been organising, since the mid-1970s, a highly popular and often oversubscribed programme of guided tours to places of historical and cultural interest in Malta, including museums and archaeologiocal sites.

These tours, which are held in Maltese, are open to members of the general public who join the programme against payment of a nominal fee. The number of applicants is often in excess of 1,600, the set limit in recent years. The participants in the programme, which consists of 10 guided tours per year, are therefore split into different groups. Similar tours are organised by other cultural societies, including the Vittoriosa Historical and Cultural Society which, since its inception in 1954, has been organising cultural outings to museums and other places of historical interest, often on weekdays (this renders the programme appealing to pensioners and women who work solely as homemakers). Tours such as these, but most especially those organised by the Culture Division, call for the use of personnel with pedagogical experience, both in terms of working with young learners and with adults.

The micro-state condition of the islands, with the challenge of scale that it poses, makes it difficult for the country to be able to afford all the specialisms it requires. There is a tendency therefore for people to assume multi-functional roles (cf. Farrugia and Attard 1989). This certainly applies to the situation concerning small-scale museums where 'adult education will be one of the many tasks undertaken, and decisions will have to be made in relation to competing calls on limited time and resources' (Hooper-Greenhill 1995: 53). As with independent and local authority museums in the United Kingdom, we can come across a situation where one person carries out the roles of curator and educator simultaneously (1995: 51).

The situation concerning a multi-functional approach to work applies more generally to the field of education and more specifically to adult education in Malta (Baldacchino and Mayo 1996). We (the authors) often come across educators who 'double up' in their work, being schoolteachers during the working day and adult educators during the evening, summer months or weekends. The introduction of a cluster of course units in adult education, in our teacher-preparation programme (leading to the BEdHons degree), is intended to enable educators to fulfil their multi-functional teaching roles well. It is also intended to prevent them from replicating with adults methods employed in schools with children (ibid.). Programmes intended to render museums centres of lifelong learning, catering to people of different ages and often groups with members of varying ages, require educators in possession of these multi-functional skills.

Museum education as cultural politics

The faculty programme for the formation of educators reflects a particular ethos. It is concerned with the formation of educators as reflective practitioners who are sensitive to the relationship between *education and power* and therefore the *politics of knowledge*. Both authors of this chapter belong to a group of faculty members whose work is inspired by writers in the area of *critical pedagogy*, an approach which entails that schooling is perceived as being 'always implicated in relations of power, social practices and the favouring of forms of knowledge that support a specific vision of past, present and future' (McLaren 1994: 168, 169). In this respect, we conceive of the curriculum as a *site of contestation*. The curriculum is strongly connected with a process wherein different cultures are engaged in a contest for legitimacy. Established curricula accord *legitimacy* to different kinds of knowledge at the expense of others. They establish what the leading American curriculum specialist Michael W. Apple calls 'Official Knowledge' (Apple 1993). In our view, museums have a similar role. Like established curricula, they too give legitimacy to particular forms of cultural production, creating 'official knowledge'. Like curricula, they are caught up in the politics of knowledge and *representation*. The museum constitutes (to adapt and modify Dennis Lawton's words) a 'selection from the cultures of society'. We feel that it is pertinent for us to ask: in whose interest has the selection been made? Whose voices and cultural preferences (what Pierre Bourdieu calls *cultural arbitrary*) does the museum represent?

We would argue, therefore, that any programme concerned with the preparation of museum educators should help foster sensitivity to issues regarding voice and representation. The marginalisation of cultures in our society has generally not been challenged in museums. Museums in Malta are still viewed as depositories of neutral knowledge. As a result, they continue to reproduce a view of the past and present 'regimes of truth'.[1] In contrast, museum educators, who adopt a critical pedagogical stance, disturb the romantic and harmonious political and cultural state of affairs, and render problematic that which at face value appears to be 'beautiful' and 'interesting'.

Any critical focus on, say, the National Museum of Fine Arts would enable the critical museum educator concerned to render problematic the Western eurocentric bias of most of the works on display. It would also seek to make the educator sensitive to the way women are represented, in a collection consisting almost entirely of works by men. For example, of the 265 paintings listed by Espinosa Rodriguez (1984) in his study concerning the paintings at the National Museum of Fine Arts, there is not a single work attributed to a woman artist.

The 1995 exhibition catalogue 'Woman in Maltese Art *c.* 1600–1995', with its two perceptive essays on the subject by Rosa Lapira and Isabelle Borg, would be a useful tool for any educator using the museum as a site of critical educational practice. The catalogue, which focuses on both the so-called highbrow and the popular, also highlights other aspects of the 'politics of representation' in our art museums. Lapira (1995: 3) refers to the tendency, in the early part of the century, to romanticise country people, depicting them in poor clothes but with radiant faces. This is a situation which, judging from some of the socially committed literature of the period, such as Gwann Mamo's *Ulied in-nanna Venut fl-Amerika* (Grandmother Venut's children in America), bore no resemblance to the harsh reality faced by the downtrodden class of peasants at the time, a point underlined by Bartolo (1993: iii).

A critical focus on such artistic centres as that of St John's Co-Cathedral in Valletta, a place of worship which can also be considered a museum in its own right, would entail the problematising of the manner in which the traditional 'Other' in the southern European context – the 'Saracen' – has been represented in works of art commissioned by a colonial military religious order (the Sovereign Order of St John, known as the Knights of Malta). These works contained images relating to the Order's war against the Ottoman Empire. What effect can such representation of the Muslim 'Other' have on present-day racial politics in Malta with regard to Arabs, in a context characterised by (1) geographical proximity to the Arab world, (2) the presence in Malta of an Arab (mainly Libyan) community and (3) an evident eagerness by political and opinion leaders to assert a European identity? In problematising these forms of representation, the critical educator can help transform the site in question from a colonising into a de-colonising learning space. In this regard, the task might well involve, as Peter McLaren and Ricky Lee Allen, echoing Patti Lather, have suggested, the creation of 'a space that is both decolonised and opened to the colonised' (McLaren and Allen 1998: 229).

Similar questions can be posed in relation to other museums and archaeological sites. In posing these questions, the critical adult educator would be conceiving of the museum as a site of *cultural politics*. This is a site where one poses questions concerning dominant and subaltern cultures, remembered and forgotten/repressed histories, boldly projected and marginalised images, heard and silenced voices, besides questions regarding who represents whom and on what basis (Jordan and Weedon 1995: 4).

Many of the items on display in Maltese museums testify to a strong colonial presence on the island, the most notable being that of the British garrison and the representatives of the European aristocracy – namely, the Sovereign Order of St John. They are mainly valuable items which the colonisers had commissioned and bequeathed to posterity during a period of settlement in Malta. While none of the exhibits at the Malta and Gozo museums resembles the 'booty' associated with Western European colonialism at its most rapacious – unlike several items on display at, say, the Louvre or the British Museum – they do tell us much about identity construction in a colonial context. It can be argued, certainly in the case of the Sovereign Order of St John's legacy, that the ethos of European aristocracy is presented as the mark of *distinction*, in Bourdieu's terms.

But what about indigenous popular cultural production? We feel that, although there is a token presence of this culture in some of the major museums, it is fairer to say that it is much more in evidence in parish museums. The Zabbar Sanctuary Museum is a case in point. There, one can find items relating to Grand Master Alof de Wignacourt and a painting attributed to the acclaimed Mattia Preti. But these and other items are displayed alongside a large collection of *ex voto* paintings (Borg 1995: 11), forms of popular devotional 'naïve' art which shed some light on the social and economic history of the island. They attest to a socio-economic situation which compelled many Maltese men to expose themselves, for the greater part of their working lives, to the vagaries of the sea. Other items to be found in a parish museum relate to the history of the village community. The critical adult educator can avail themselves of such a museum to focus on the role of popular culture in identity formation. The *ex voto* paintings at Zabbar offer this educator the opportunity to provide an unromanticised view of popular culture, by drawing out the contradictions that characterise its 'common sense', the term being used here in the manner intended by Antonio Gramsci; Isabelle Borg provides examples of these contradictions with respect to the gender issue (Borg 1995).

The focus on exhibits reflecting communal life, in a museum like the one at Zabbar, makes it difficult to engage in a process of selection and omission in order to make optimum use of limited space and therefore provide a better display. For we regard a good display as necessary for any museum to serve as a pedagogical site, and it has been argued that parish museums have been found wanting in this regard (Azzopardi 1995: 132). The removal of exhibits, to enhance the display, can cause friction between museum curators/volunteers and some members of the community. For community members, who are closely related to the donors of the exhibits in question, can be living and operating in close proximity to people engaged in the running of the parish museum. The 'management of intimacy' factor (Baldacchino and Mayo 1996: 26) comes into play and compels the museum personnel to tread with extra caution when removing objects from display in museums often situated in small communities. One must bear in mind here that many parish activities depend, for their realisation, on the voluntary commitment of community members.

As far as popular culture is concerned, we have witnessed the demise of the National Folklore Museum at Vittoriosa. One eagerly awaits, however, the establishment of the promised ethnographic museum, even though one can avail oneself in this context of a number of museums on Gozo; namely, the Xaghra Windmill Museum, the Gozo Folklore Museum (inside the Citadel, Victoria), the new Folklore Museum at Gharb and the Karmni Grima Museum, also at Gharb. But it is not only within the context of popular and 'highbrow' forms of cultural production that one can engage in a critical education. Exhibits relating to the larger eco-system also offer interesting possibilities in this regard. And yet, the Natural History Museum at Mdina strikes us as lacking an ecological political trust, of the kind to be found, for example, at the highly interactive and educational Natural History Museum in South Kensington, London, where the viewer is confronted by powerful statements on such issues as 'the plight of the rain forest', or the Victorian penchant for collages of stuffed birds. The involvement of ecological groups in the running of the Mdina Museum can help give the display the critical educational edge that it lacks. The same can apply to the Natural History Museum at the Citadel, Rabat.

Accessibility

A critical educational approach must also take account of the issue of accessibility in terms of facilities available, the social interrelationships involved and the choice of cultural production on display.

Within a critical pedagogical framework, curators and educators perceive their relationship with potential users of museums differently. In sharp contrast with the present practice of transmitting knowledge, where curators and guides alike adopt a 'pedagogy of answers' (Freire, in Freire and Faundez 1992: 40), critical pedagogues encourage people to take the risk of 'inventing and re-inventing' knowledge and experience. The pedagogy of answers tends to de-legitimise and devalue the experience of the user, and as a consequence, any sense of equality in the exchange between the curator/guide/teacher and visitor/student is lost. On the other hand, the critical pedagogical approach, based on respect for the knowledge and experiences of all participants, transforms the educational process into what Freire (in Freire and Faundez 1992: 55) calls 'something that is viable, and not as something ready-made'. The challenge here is how to transform the power of popular resistance towards museums into active participation, solidarity and justice. Access in this sense becomes an issue of democratising national public spaces which still seem to be popularly perceived as 'elitist' in nature. This is a perception that starkly contrasts with the enthusiasm for artistic endeavours registered at parish levels, as attested by Canon John Azzopardi, Curator of the Cathedral Museum, Mdina, and the St Paul's Collegiate Museum, Rabat:

> A visit to our churches, especially on feast days, reveals a wealth of paintings, statues, silver-plate, rich liturgical vestments and other objects, ranging from 17th and 18th centuries down to our times. Their commission was provoked by the deep faith of our people including the poorer classes ... even though at times certain artistic commissions were motivated by rivalry and an exaggerated parochialism.
>
> (1995: 131)

Another missed opportunity for greater popular access is the dearth of initiatives taken by local museums in the field of *oral history*. While subordinated individuals/groups often live on the periphery of society, their 'culture of silence', to use Freire's term, is often marked by a rich oral tradition. The critical pedagogical museum can provide public access to these individuals/groups by documenting their oral history. This political stance empowers subordinated groups to access museums by reclaiming lost history. As a result, potential users are provided with an opportunity to rediscover history and re-invent the present.

One notices the almost complete absence of information technology in our museums, despite the fact that it is fast becoming the basis of human communication in our country. Communication is still not seen as a right and as an essential component of the education process within museums. This fact continues to privilege the access of the functionally literate, mainly in one language (English), and articulate members of society. The use of audiophones, of the kind already available elsewhere in the Maltese archipelago, is recommended in this context. If one were to take the National Maritime Museum as an example, one could point out that this museum is situated in an area, the Inner Harbour Area, traditionally characterised by high levels of functional illiteracy. Audiophones can also capture the narratives of people from the area, who are former coxswains, boatswains and so forth, in an attempt to render 'oral history' a significant feature of the museum.

Physical access is perhaps the most basic requirement for participating in the cultural politics of the museum. Unfortunately, most of the museums in Malta were neither built purposely as museums nor built in the era when physical accessibility constituted an important socio-architectural issue. For example, there are no elevators in any of the museums in Malta and Gozo, despite the fact that there are 'old' houses in old cities like Valletta which enjoy such facilities.

Language issues are also relevant to any discussion concerning accessibility. In a society where the population communicates mainly in Maltese, opting for English as the language of the museum is not only exclusionary but also anti-pedagogical. This is the situation obtaining at the National Museum of Fine Arts, where all labelling is in English. In addition, the literature about the museum is produced in this foreign language (perhaps the small size of the Maltese market has much to do with this), consolidating the impression that museums are exclusive sites. The linguistic situation described above is not that obtaining in all museums. In fact, the excellent display at the National Archaeological Museum is instructive in the way both the Maltese and English languages are used effectively. However, referring to Maltese museums in general, the fact that Maltese is not widely considered as the language of artistic consumption confirms Gramsci's argument that there is a close relationship between linguistic stratification and social hierarchy (Gardiner 1992).

An accessible museum is essentially an inclusive museum. It builds on an appreciation of: the potential of every member of the community to contribute towards the definition and development of Maltese culture; the principles of solidarity and affirmation of difference; the different learning patterns; and an adoption of an unconditional positive regard towards each user/learner.

Outreach

Outreach is often understood as the transportation of the museum to the community. The loan of artefacts to national exhibitions is common practice. Exhibitions organised by the Fondazzjoni Patrimonju Malti,[2] captured in attractively published books in English, present a case in point. We also have religious exhibitions centring on themes which draw exhibits from private and public collections (Azzopardi 1995). However, travelling exhibitions and the loan of artefacts as resources, presentations and temporary exhibitions within parishes are rare. Moreover, while some museums are endowed with excellent research facilities, such as the Cathedral Museum and the National Museum of Archaeology, centres equipped with technology and resources for use by educators in their communities are still a missing feature of our museums. Hence it is difficult for anyone to transport a museum to a closed community such as that represented by the inmates at the Corradino Prisons where there is the right infrastructure for such an activity and an elaborate adult education programme which has been provided since 1996 (Giordmaina and Vella 1996).

The Catholic Church is most active in the process of transforming its sites, mainly parish churches, into centres of adult learning. Apart from the existing parish museums, there is a drive towards conservation and preservation beyond the main museum. Borg (1994: 98) argues that:

> a substantial part of Malta's Christian heritage is due to the intimate relations that existed between the vital experience of the Christian message of our ancestors and its direct impact on one of the riches with which nature has endowed these islands, the conclusion seems to be all too obvious. This richness constitutes a substantial prolongation of our museum ... and indeed proposes for the consideration of all participants at this Symposium that it is highly opportune to have our Diocesan and Cathedral museums involved in the preservation of this extensive heritage within each Diocese, at least, through a detailed documentation to be available within them. Such documentation, moreover, will help scholars in their research and thereby also promote further interest in the vast Christian heritage of each nation and region.

A living museum would constitute another important form of outreach. The Maritime Museum can provide a perfect example of the potential which living museums have as outreach centres. Situated in the Grand Harbour area, this museum, a former bakery of the British armed forces, is surrounded by communities which have traditionally existed because of the activity connected to the harbour. Hundreds of people still live out of the area.

The Docks, private workshops, private collectors of maritime memorabilia, regatta (traditional Maltese rowing contest) clubs and workshops, to mention but a few potential sites, can serve as extensions to the museum. Through such an initiative, community members would actively participate in the making of culture. While visitors interact with the living experiences of community members, the latter maximise participation by assuming the role of protagonists rather than 'props' in a museum. In the process, intellectual curiosity, co-operative relations, communication and research skills will develop as each site transforms itself into an educational centre (McLaren 1995, 1997). Built on the discourse and knowledge of daily life, such an outreach activity would constitute an authentic and personalised experience which would render and identify the community members as 'subjects' rather than 'objects' of the learning process within a museum that is, once again, conceived of as a site of cultural politics.

Acknowledgements

We are indebted to the following persons (listed in alphabetical order) for granting us in-depth interviews in connection with the preparation of this chapter: the Rev. Canon John Azzopardi, Curator of the Cathedral Museum, Mdina and the Museum of the Collegiate Church of St Paul (Wignacourt College), Rabat; Mr Carmel Bonavia, from the Zabbar Sanctuary Museum; Mr Dominic Cutajar, Curator of the National Museum of Fine Arts, Valletta; Mr Antonio Espinosa Rodriguez, Curator of the National Maritime Museum, Vittoriosa; Mr Tony Pace, Acting Director of Museums.

Notes

1 Foucault (1980: 131)) explains 'regime of truth' as follows:

> Each society has its regime of truth, its 'general politics' of truth: that is, the types of discourse which it accepts and makes function as true; the mechanisms and instances which enable one to distinguish true and false statements, the means by which each is sanctioned; the techniques and procedures accorded value in the acquisition of truth; the status of those who are charged with saying what counts as true.

2 The aims of the Foundation were described in one of its publications as follows:

> Fondazzjoni Patrimonju Malti was established in January 1992 by a group of volunteers on the initiative of the Minister of Arts with the principal aim of exhibiting treasures from private and institutional collections not normally accessible to the public. It also assists research into the culture and historic heritage of Malta. It produces publications, catalogues, books, documents and other material related to the aims of the Foundation.

References

Anderson, D, 'Gradgrind driving Queen Mab's chariot: what museums have (and have not) learnt from adult education', in A Chadwick, and A Stannett (eds), *Museums and the education of adults*, Leicester: NIACE, 1995, pp. 11–33

Apple, M W, *Official knowledge. democratic education in a conservative age*, New York/London: Routledge, 1993

Azzopardi, J, 'Ecclesiastical museums in Malta, with special reference to the Cathedral Museum', in *Cathedral and diocesan museums: crossroads of faith and culture*, 1995, Proceedings of International Symposium under the patronage of the Pontifical Commission for the Cultural Heritage of the Church, Malta, 27–29 January 1994

Baldacchino, G and Mayo, P, 'Adult and continuing education in small and island states: the case of Malta', *Convergence*, 29(2), pp. 22–34

Baldacchino, G and Mayo, P (eds), *Beyond schooling: adult education in Malta*, Malta: Mireva, 1997

Bartolo, E, 'Jghinna Nifhmu Mnejn Gejjin' (Help us understand our roots'), in G Mamo, *Ulied in-nanna Vnut fl-Amerika (Grandmother Venut's children in America)*, Malta: Sensiela Kotba Socjalisti (Socialist Books Service) 1993

Borg, I, 'Definitive images: the role of women in Malta seen through the people's art', in *Woman in Maltese art c.1600–1995*, Malta: Commission for the Advancement of Women, 1995

Borg, V, 'Christian heritage and Malta's stone', in *Cathedral and Diocesan Museums: Cossroads of faith and culture,* 1994, Proceedings of International Symposium under the patronage of the Pontifical Commission for the Cultural Heritage of the Church, Malta, 27–29 January 1994

Buhagiar, M, 'Some tentative suggestions for a children's museum', *Education (Malta)*, 1(2), 1983, pp. 17–22

Espinosa Rodriguez, A, 'The provenance of the paintings on permanent display at the National Museum of Fine Arts', in *Proceedings of History Week 1983*, Malta: The Historical Society, 1984

Farrugia, C and Attard, P, *The multifunctional administrator*, London: Commonwealth Secretariat, 1989

Foucault, M, 'Truth and power', in C Gordon (ed.), *Power/knowledge: selected interviews and other writings 1972–1977*, New York: Pantheon Books, 1980

Freire, P and Faundez, A, *Learning to question: a pedagogy of liberation*, New York: Continuum, 1992

Gardiner, M, *The dialogue of critique: M M Bakhtin and the theory of ideology*, London/New York: Routledge, 1992

Giordmaina, J and Vella, A, *An educational programme for Corradino Correctional Facility*, unpublished proposal to Minister of Social Policy, Faculty of Education, University of Malta, Department of Foundations in Education, 9 April 1996

Hooper-Greenhill, E, 'A museum educator's perspective', in A. Chadwick and A Stannett (eds), *Museums and the education of adults*, Leicester: NIACE, 1995, pp. 49–64

Jordan, G and Weedon, C, *Culture politics, class, gender, race and the postmodern world*, Oxford (UK)/Cambridge (USA): Blackwell, 1995

Lapira, R, 'In search of heroines', in *Woman in Maltese art c1600–1995*, Malta: Commission for the Advancement of Women, 1995

McLaren, P, *Life in Schools: an introduction to critical pedagogy in the foundations of education* (2nd edn), New York/London: Longman, 1994

—— *Critical pedagogy and predatory culture*, London/New York: Routledge, 1995

—— *Revolutionary multiculturalism: pedagogies of dissent for the new Millenium*, Boulder, CO: Westview Press, 1997

McLaren, P and Allen, R L, *Review of* Paulston, R (ed.), *Social cartography: mapping ways of seeing social and educational change*, in *Comparative Education Review*, 42(2), 1998, pp. 225–8

Mayo, P and Wain, K, 'Malta', in P Jarvis, P and A Stannett, A (eds), *Perspectives on adult education and training in Europe* (2nd edn), Leicester: NIACE, forthcoming

16 Portugal

Ana Duarte

The adult public and museums

The museum is not an exclusive place for a single type of public but a place for several types. People have diverse competences and seek in museum spaces different emotions and aspects of knowledge, according to their individual needs.

Usually, the educational services of a museum are targeted towards the school community, but this focus has been changing over time. In Portugal, the *Museu Nacional de Arte Antiga,* Lisbon's National Museum of Ancient Art, was, through its director Dr Joao Couto, a pioneer in educational activities with schoolchildren in small groups; and by the beginning of the 1970s, the *Associacao Portuguesa de Museologia* (APOM) addressed the importance of education in museums at one of their annual meetings. In a perspective of non-formal education, we now see in certain Portuguese museums some random applications of the reflections and interchange of experiences gained at such meetings, as also at the international meetings of ICOM/CECA. Although these programmes were intended to complement the school curriculum, they, in fact, reached only a limited number of specially selected teenagers and young children.

It was with the dawn of the Revolution in April 1974 that Portuguese museums felt that the changes wrought in the society had to be reflected in their institutions at the level of themes, museography and communication. Educational or cultural animation services form part of the last-named – that is, communication.

These changes that have been taking place in Portuguese museums since April 1974 until the present day are manifested in two ways: firstly, the transformation of ways of communicating with the public both in state-managed and municipality-managed museums; secondly, the rapid growth of local museums, private and public associations and a number of institutions introduced to the country from north to south, which concentrate on preserving its heritage and cultural identity.

There are 600 museums in Portugal, of which 29 are under the management of the *Instituto Portugues de Museus* (IPM), and about 200 under municipal management. Approximately 10 museums belong to the *Instituto Portugues do Patrimonio Arquitectonico* (IPPAR – Portuguese Institute of Architectonic Heritage). The rest are scattered and managed by a number of authorities. The largest concentration of museological units is around Lisbon and Oporto, and it is in these locations that the concept of *various* museum publics – not *a* public – has been defined more precisely, as well as the determination to create a museum educational service not confined to the school community but extended to the adult public of very diverse origins.

We have chosen the following examples which illustrate the work developed by two Portuguese museums in areas with different characteristics: firstly, the city of Setubal, with 120,000 citizens; and secondly, the parish of Ribeira de Cha on the island of S Miguel in the Azores, with 438 inhabitants. The former is an urban multi-cultural area divided into primary, secondary and tertiary sectors. Over the past seven centuries the dominant service has been a council which once belonged to what was called the 'industrial belt' of Lisbon. It is still considered to be a multi-cultural council because it has, since the late nineteenth century, taken in migrants from all regions to work in the fishing, canning and metallurgy industries, as well as (since April 1974) immigrants from the former Portuguese colonies in Africa. The other area is a rural parish, long-established, whose economy is based on agriculture and livestock, and many of whose younger members have been emigrating to Bermuda, Canada and the United States since the late nineteenth century.

Museum of Work Michel Giacometti, Setubal: ethnography and industrial archaeology (municipal management)

This museum was inaugurated on 18 March 1995, after the closing of the last canned sardine factory, It has a permanent exhibition of agricultural and other rural implements, collected by Michel Giacometti with pre-university students during a campaign of the so-called Civic Service, just after the April 1974 Revolution. Another permanent exhibition is dedicated to the canning industry, one of the largest commercial enterprises in Setubal.

The displays are installed in an old factory unit, thereby evoking memories of the industrial identities connected with this space through the evidence of people associated with it over many years of work.

Through sharply focused fieldwork we have tried to elicit from the community living near the museum (a traditional quarter for fishermen and factory workers) a set of notions about the concept of the museum and what its function should be. It is through working with the population that a museum and a community can become social partners, much like other organisations or groups interested in local development.

The idea of innovation may be initiated by the museum and presented to the population, and should then be internalised by the latter. It must provide a meaningful objective. The museum has to be created from 'inside' the community, not from the 'outside', so that it becomes part of 'common sense'; and the knowledge of this 'common sense' is the public knowledge shared with others in normal everyday life. A survey of the whole local population when the museum was opened revealed that almost everyone recognised it as an important means of progress. (Many of them had not visited the museum at that point.)

Real social and economic development suggests a cultural progression. Thus the idea of an integral museum emerging from the community suggests that it should also be managed and developed by its members. The community museum only exists through its collective and individual participants, who are responsible for its structure and animation. Where this does not happen, the community museum is a mere abstraction.

Over time, museums have been instruments of power propagating ideas and concepts of life and the universe, in an attempt to shape citizens and educate the people. Communication has been one-way, with museums being comparable to places of worship. At the end of this millennium, different attitudes and types of dialogue are clearly emerging in our country, in common with other museums throughout the world. According to the Swedish museologist Per Uno Agren (1995):

> There are to-day two museologic traditions, co-existing side by side: the traditional museums, created and supported by official bodies, and the local museums, based on people's initiatives. A considerable reciprocal influence – one can almost say an osmosis – can be observed between the museums from the bottom and the museums from the top.

Although the Museum of Work Michel Giacometti belongs to a state organism and can be seen as a traditional museum in its structure, it benefits from the fact that its programmers and technicians have visited many different museums, especially in northern Europe. From their experiences came the commitment to make this institution an essential place for citizenship and sociability, allowing the reconstitution of cultural foundations not chained to the past. For these activities to be successful we had to take into account the living and learning conditions of the groups, as evidenced by their circumstances and social activities. The quarter and the museum have been placed in the perspective of the city's own structure and fluctuating times of production and consumption.

We have tried to create elements from the past to illustrate the relationship of local history to global history. As Setubal is a place that has continuously attracted people from all over the country, several connections were attempted in designing the exhibitions. Thus, objects from different cultures or different epochs were displayed together in such a way that local residents and visitors could understand the cultural changes over the years, and the inter-cultural contacts established through such changes. Culture and identity have never been static concepts, and thus, 'the words and the material symbols are static, but their meanings are constantly shifting' (Agren 1995).

To reach these goals with the adult population we used a variety of strategies, depending on the social and professional groups to which people belonged. A number of these strategies are described below.

1. *The barber's chair*, an exhibition which interpreted the transformations undergone through time by local shops and barbers/hairdressers, and gathered relevant objects and witnesses. A brochure on the theme was published.

    As a complement to this exhibition, we carried out a project of living history on the theme of *A dancing matinée in the 1920/30s* at the musical society *Capricho Setubalense*, a centenary workers' institution in Setubal. The historic reconstruction saw the participation of 1,500 teachers and pupils across several age ranges, who had their hair dressed by the local barbers and hairdressers who had already co-operated in the museum's exhibition.

2. An exhibition on the theme *Taverns – places of meeting and loneliness*, in collaboration with a local cultural association. The recreation at the museum of a space of conviviality for fishermen and working people enabled contact with this social group who participated with us in the collection of witnesses and objects. A brochure was published, and several nights of *fado vadio* (traditional singing in urban and seaside areas) took place. At many of these occasions former sailors and fishermen joined in the singing.

3. *Commerce and traders in Sebutal*, an exhibition designed in collaboration with Setubal's Trade Association and the Trade Workers' Union. This allowed us to trace all commercial houses between 50 and 100 years old. With the recreation of an old shop, the museum was able to perform several animations with the school community. It also published a brochure.

    To complement this activity, the council's leisure services organised a *chita* (cheap coloured cotton cloth) dress contest, recreating a traditional party of young women workers. As they were making their evening gowns in *chita*, they were fulfilling their dream of being Cinderella for one night, and finding relief from the tedium of their daily work.

4. An exhibition *Doctors, hospitals and nurses in Setubal Municipality*, developed in collaboration with S Bernardo's Hospital. It allowed the museum to make an inventory of old medical instruments and helped to create a small display room for these memorabilia at the hospital itself. One brochure was published.

5. *Working in the household*: a reconstruction of a traditional quarter of Sebutal where one could follow the evolution (1900–90) of the façades of houses. Inside the small buildings the development of household utensils could be traced through the displays.

    In co-operation with Setubal's Professional Theatre Group we have created several animations for the women visiting the exhibition. These activities demonstrate some issues of equal opportunities between men and women, such as the burden of work usually borne by Portuguese women, as compared with those in some other European countries – for example, working outside the home but still having full responsibility for the family.

6. An exhibition, *From the market to the can*. With this project we mainly targeted the workers in the canning industry. By means of collecting together numerous witnesses in this sector which has been deeply embedded in Setubal's society over the past 150 years, we were able to publish a brochure. The information thus obtained was extremely important for the museum, which, as already mentioned, is located in an old canned-fish factory. The relationship established between the school and the working communities was greatly strengthened, as there were still many children and teenagers whose direct forebears used to work in this industry.

The exhibition facilitated the collection of numerous objects and documents essential for a study of this activity. Many of these were donated by factories and the Canning Industry Union, which ceased activity in Sebutal after the closing down of the last factory.

7. It was within the African community which had chosen Setubal as its new home after the independence process of the Portuguese colonies that we worked with literacy groups on the project *The toy of my childhood*. Both men and women had the opportunity to create small objects and to talk mainly about their childhood in and memories of a distant home country, and about their sense of identity. The objects were exhibited and, with the closure of the exhibition, incorporated into an educational case. This is still available to schools in the Setubal locality, so that 'the other' civilisation component can have its own space and develop its own identity. As a complement, a group of women from Cabo Verde gave a performance of drum-beat and African dancing at the Museum of Work Michel Giacometti in partnership with a female choir composed of rural workers in southern Portugal.

These exchanges gave visibility and value to cultural differences before audiences who showed their enthusiasm by attending in large numbers.

With such activities we have enabled the adult public to take part according to its degrees of interest, and put them in direct contact with the school community, thus forging a close museum–school–community relationship.

The exhibitions with the diverse interactions as described above, and the gathering of information, confirm that

The memories from the past can also change with time, but even when they don't change, they are surely selected, from a set potentially infinite of possible memories, by their relevance to the individuals who are remembering, by their contribution to the building of identity and personal relationships. This is true to the individuals that are evoking their personal experience when they remember episodes from the reserve of memories preserved collectively.

(Fentress and Wickham 1980)

The witnesses from the social groups contributing to the museum exhibitions were a fundamental factor in its firm grounding and brought to us diversified publics. They made the museum into a space of desire, a space of Eros; they provided indispensable dialogues with the public and the community; they effected the communication – a fact which is the core of museological activity and an immediate means for acquiring a knowledge of the objects and of the history that provides the context. As a consequence, it is the population who make the museum a favoured place for leisure and learning.

Ribeira Cha's Rural and Ethnographic Museum: S Miguel, Azores (private management)[1]

The religious life of this parish is an extremely important factor in the establishment of the museum, which reflects the daily life of the population, its traditions and beliefs, at personal and working levels. As the museum is an extension of the church (the museum director and the parish priest were one and the same person), the two are closely linked, each benefiting the other.

These links between church and museum have led to a close association between religious feasts and museum activities. The museum became an institutional point of reference in the community, it achieved legitimacy and found a place in its religious life. The parish priest reached the top of the community's hierarchy: to them, he was the embodiment of authority, of central structure; to central structure, he was the embodiment of the community. In this way he was able to obtain benefits for both the community and the museum.

The establishment of the museum was one of the important components in the construction of the community's collective memory. It has expanded in terms of space as well as in the size of collections. Its objects were collected as long ago as the building of the new church: the museum and the church were born at the same time and have been surviving side by side.

In the museum there are three sets of objects which can be placed in the world of Eros and are part of the memories of almost all the interviewees from the community who say that they know the museum – some because they remember the objects from their social context (members of the first generation who gave the objects to the museum), and others because they had this memory passed on by their forebears. The objects concerned are the old religious artefacts which used to inhabit a space that, for the community, was not only a sacred space but also a place for leisure, conviviality and support of traditions through the ceremonies which it promoted. On the other hand, the building of the new church is a mark in the evolution of the parish. Both men and women appreciate the religious artefacts, while agricultural tools receive more attention from the men, who are mostly farmers. Everybody, however, young and old, knows their function and how to use them.

The third set of objects evoking memories is the wheat-watch. Once its context is re-created, the watch-houses of the 'plague' (birds trying to eat the seeds during the first week of planting) bring personal memories to a large number of women. These objects are displayed in the open. They lead to reminiscences, sometimes painful, and to new dialogues, as the women whose experiences included using these objects have many different ways of talking about them and valuing the past. It was noticeable, for example, that their displeasure increased when they remembered the 'watching' period on their employers' land, as compared with watching on their own family land.

The community's co-operation was essential for the development of this institution, and the parish women's voluntary collaboration is remarkable. Their active participation was seen during the Craftsmanship and Gastronomy Festivals which were organised by the museum, gathering people from the entire island, who would come to taste their 'grandmother's cooking'. Ribeira Cha's oldest women were cooking, for several weekends in a row, all the traditional food of the parish and the island, and they would also take the opportunity to sell their craft objects, such as corn dollies and straw hats.

> We would make chickpeas on coal and with frying pans, cabbage soup, olive oil soup, baked beans, octopus, beef and chicken, pumpkin, sweet potato, *massa sovada* and sweet rice, yeast cake and yams. During the food fairs we would do all this because we wanted to co-operate with the Museum in keeping the traditions, and we worked very hard.

> We used to make chickpeas, pork chops in garlic, corn bread, baked beans. It would be like that all Saturday from morning till midnight. That was how we got the money to build the Agriculture Museum. We were very happy.

Holding to the idea that whatever comes from this parish and this island is what is best for the other islands or even the mainland, and fostering this belief to attain a certain goal – to get funding for maintaining the proper and original identity of the Museum of Ribeira Cha – these women managed to turn the eyes of the island to their parish through the authentic and pleasant means of eating well – that is, eating, as in times past, healthy food unlike that of any other place – and at the same time buying the products 'made by the old ones and also used by them' in an attempt to devise new consumption patterns from old traditions, at a time when so many quick and significant changes have taken place, such as 'fast food' and mass production.

As these festivals took place at times of large immigrant visits (August), they also promoted socialisation and the renewal of behaviour and value systems, as well as a sense of identification with the community to which they belong and the institutions that represent, express or symbolise it – in this case the church and the museum, as promoters and defenders of traditional gastronomy and craftsmanship.

In both museums (Setubal and the Azores), the adult public joined in and took an active part. The objects which belonged to the museums and were used in the thematic exhibitions described above, became part of their collections in the domain of Eros, as they were placed at the service of an active collective memory bank. They provoked new dialogues to be added to those which took place when the objects were used within the community where they were first conceived or applied.

Note

1 This account is based on the author's field research for a master's degree between 1992 and 1994.

References

Agren, P U, Paper presented at meeting of *Museums and Education*, Setubal, 1995
Fentress, J and Wickham, C, *Social Memory*, Lisbon, 1980

17   Austria

Gabriele Rath

This chapter is based on the findings of a recent survey on educational programmes in Austrian museums which was prompted by an enquiry by the International Council of Museums (ICOM). As the last survey, dated 1982,[1] did not reflect the changes which had since occurred in the educational field in Austrian museums, there was no up-to-date information at hand to respond to the enquiry, and this was the stimulus for setting up a project group to pave the way for a new study.[2] The aim was to provide all parties concerned – namely, museum managers, employees involved in educational work, persons with political and administrative responsibility as well as the public itself – with the information required to exchange experiences, expand existing facilities, raise levels of professional qualification and optimise communication with visitors.

Statistical survey

Austria has a very high density of museums compared with other European countries. It is, in fact, a country of museums. One-third of all local authorities have at least one museum. Of course, this also means that the majority of the museums are located in smaller towns, 50 per cent of them in communities with fewer than 3,000 inhabitants. Almost all major museums are in large towns, but this does not mean that the most active and resourceful museums are only to be found in major centres. In Austria, a large part of museum work is carried out by volunteers. Only a third of the museums have salaried employees, and only every seventh museum has at least one employee with an academic qualification. Small museums are almost exclusively run on a voluntary basis. State or local authority museums often have professional museum managements.

Eighty-two per cent of museums are devoted to cultural history, a significantly higher proportion than in other European countries. Compared with other countries, however, there are relatively fewer art galleries and museums of science and technology. Collections concentrate on the fields of history (85 per cent) and local ethnology and folk art (62 per cent). A remarkably high proportion of art museums and museums of applied arts are involved in educational activities; 60 per cent of this group of museums belong to the category of active and very active museums.

Between 1970 and 1995 the number of museums in Austria more than doubled. This is a significantly greater increase than in other European countries. In the first half of the 1990s this trend has gained momentum. A relatively large number of science and technology museums have been founded since the 1970s. On the other hand, the increase in art galleries over the same period of time is low by comparison with other European countries. While the expansion of the large and medium-sized museum foundations came to an end as early as the 1920s, since the 1960s there has been a boom in the establishment of small museums. Many of these recent foundations are private or company museums. This has confirmed a trend away from public museums which has manifested itself since the 1960s with the foundation of museums by registered societies or charities. With very few exceptions, large museums are located in large cities. Increasingly, medium-sized museums are to be found in the provincial (Länder) capitals. Overall, however, the location of a museum does not determine its size relative to staff and visitor numbers. And the size of a museum does not necessarily guarantee a higher level of educational activity.

Over half of the museums in Austria do not have regular opening times – some are open in the summer months, others have varying opening times. Even in very active museums, evening opening hours are not standard. The pricing of tickets tends to be within reasonable limits. In Austria, noticeably fewer museums have free admission than in Germany.

The significance of visitor research for planning purposes has not yet been recognised by Austrian museums. Very few maintain differentiated statistics on visitors. It has to be assumed that the decision makers have hardly any detailed information on museum visitors. The present study also showed that the majority of museums (two-thirds) did not register more than 5,000 visitors per year. Visitor numbers are divided between museums of cultural history, art, science and natural history in proportion to the number of museums in each category.

The educational work of museums

The educational aims most frequently mentioned by museum directors in response to our enquiry are those which can be categorised as 'cognitive transmission of knowledge' with respect to the various collections. The second most frequent aim listed is the transmission of values: in other words, the preservation of cultural traditions is the keynote of educational work. In very active museums a shift of focus in favour of a critical approach to museum collections with reference to topical issues can be observed. One of the most likely reasons for this development is probably the fact that these museums are located in urban environments where the transmission of traditional values is less important. The educational concepts set out by museum workers in the interviews demonstrated, above all, that those with specific qualifications and training in education present more differentiated reflections on the principles of concrete practice.

Personal provision of programmes has top priority among the tasks which the museums as well as the workers themselves allocate to the educational field. One of the reasons is simply reality – personal contact with visitors is, in fact, the primary activity of the workers – but there is also an inadequate knowledge of the actual scope of educational work. This lack of knowledge leads to certain self-imposed limitations in what is offered to the visitor.

As the museums have hardly any differentiated information on visitors' motivation and interests, what is on offer to specific target groups is equally undifferentiated. Only a third of the museums indicate that they have developed programmes designed to address specific target groups. Whereas half of the museums see themselves as particularly interesting for pupils, less than half of these museums actually offer their own educational programmes for schools. Most of those offers target pupils at elementary or secondary schools. Very few programmes address nursery schoolchildren or students in vocational training. Programmes for teachers, who play an important role as multipliers, are also a neglected area within the educational work of museums. The relatively strong emphasis on schools as a target group, however, does not at all mean that museums abandon the specific opportunities and possibilities of informal learning which the museum offers. Only the need to find adequate forms of educational work relating to pupils has prompted many museums to begin to differentiate what they offer in terms of target groups. The demands which schools make on museums today have often become the driving force for the development of educational programmes at museums. In Austria, museums do not offer syllabus-orientated programmes. This should not be seen as a disadvantage. In other countries – for example, the United States, where educational work in the museums used to be adapted to the requirements of the school syllabus – this is being reviewed. It has been recognised that the informal framework of a museum is a special asset, so there is now a move away from a strictly syllabus- and classroom-orientated approach. Austrian museums can look back on many years of educational work in museums in the course of which distinctive forms of informal learning have developed.

According to the information provided by the museums, it can be assumed that the proportion of pupils relative to the overall number of visitors in Austrian museums corresponds to the European average. Although this group is often considered to be the primary target of museums' educational efforts, it represents only 10 per cent of the total number of visitors. Museums offering particular activities in the educational field tend to attract a larger number of visitors. The museums attracting a larger number of pupils are also in this group.

The majority of children visiting museums, however, do not come with their school class but with adults or other children. Holiday and leisure schemes for children which require a large number of staff are mainly provided by large and medium-sized museums. So-called 'family programmes' are often available at small and very small museums because they require less supervision. By comparison with the situation in other countries, however, the available children and adult schemes are not nearly as well developed as they could be. Among adult groups, only pensioners are addressed as a specific target. Groups with special requirements such as disabled people and ethnic minorities are almost completely ignored. In general, it is evident that the role of adult education in museums is, at best, secondary.

Austrian museums are actively committed to exhibitions. Over half of the museums organise special exhibitions. Also about half of the museums have reviewed and rearranged their displays at least once since their foundation. With regard to the provision of text namely, labels, explanatory material or overviews – the standard of Austrian museums is comparable to the German standard. Conventional information systems dominate; the introduction of other means of communication such as audio-visual media or, in particular, interactive computer systems, is slow.

In the various stages between the planning and completion of an exhibition educational experts are rarely consulted. Only 22 museums state that experts trained in museum education are involved in all stages of a project. A remarkably large number of museums, nevertheless, would like to consult education experts during individual stages of an exhibition project, especially in the development of a concept and in the practical realisation of an exhibition. Most museums currently co-operating with experts in museum education in the preparation of exhibitions are among those characterised as being active or very active.

Among the interviewees, many volunteer workers interacting with the public are also the managers of the museums and in charge of the work on exhibitions. It still seems to be unusual to entrust freelance museum education workers with such tasks although this is the group with the largest number of trained specialists. Many employees in the educational field do not necessarily see exhibition work as an essential educational activity.

Almost all Austrian museums offer guided tours, but a third do so only on request. According to the information supplied by the museums, the most frequently practised type of guided tour is the lecture-style tour. Only a little over 50 per cent of the museums claim to offer a 'question-and-answer' style tour, at least as an option. Guides usually conduct the tours with a high degree of personal commitment. Only a sixth of museums offer more interactive forms of personal presentation. These involve a broad range of activities, carried out with widely varying intentions and professional competence, and with widely varying degrees of success. Work with groups, which can be time consuming and requires extra staff, is on offer in all types and sizes of museums. Most of these programmes are developed for school classes, and unfortunately other target groups have only limited access to them.

Over 50 per cent of the museums make use of their existing space to accommodate events. A few committed institutes and personalities stand out because of the interesting supporting programmes around exhibitions which they have developed, or who see their work as one part of the activity of a regional cultural centre. With the exception of cases where those in charge of education at the same time bear responsibility for a museum's overall activities, very few educationalists are the initiators of such events. In general, it has to be noted that while there is much commitment, creativity and pioneering spirit, there is as yet no sufficiently innovative conception of personal educational work. This is due not only to a lack of experience and knowledge of possible theoretical and practical approaches on the part of the individual active mediators between museum and public, but also to the absence of a relevant framework in the museums themselves.

Some Austrian museums offer service facilities which are open to the public. These are either educational facilities in addition to the collection on display or the exhibition (such as a library, a studio or a cinema), or service facilities such as a café or a bookshop. The availability of the facilities the museum has to offer is also reflected in their accessibility to all groups of visitors. Less than 20 per cent of the museums claim to be able to guarantee full accessibility. The buildings, many of which are historic, would have to be adapted to allow or facilitate access not only for disabled and elderly people but also for adults with small children. About 40 per cent of the museums provide seats in permanent displays and special exhibitions. Only a sixth of the museums provide café or restaurant facilities; 25 per cent have additional rooms for events, 12.5 per cent make room available for educational work with groups at the museum.

Museum work is public relations work: visitors spread the word as to what they have seen and experienced at the museum and, preferably, encourage others to visit. In many museums the conventional media of public relations work predominate. In most cases, though, the museum as a whole is advertised rather than individual events. Guided tours are almost never publicised. Only very active museums, which offer many events, develop their own distinctive publicity. Those in charge of educational work rarely regard this activity as part of their work.

The framework of educational activities

Compared with Switzerland, Germany, the United Kingdom and the Netherlands, Austria has by far the lowest density of education posts in museums. There is only one post in 18 museums, whereas in Switzerland the figure is one in 9, in Germany one in 6, and in the United Kingdom one per 3. Only a quarter of the existing posts in Austria are exclusively devoted to educational work. In most cases these employees are also in charge of public relations. In the 1990s there was an increase of tenures in the field of educational work. Similarly, the establishment of permanent posts in the field of educational work increased considerably during the 1990s. The institutionalisation of museum educational work is a comparatively recent development in Austria. Without the large number of volunteer workers, educational work would be restricted to large and some medium-sized museums. Professional centres offering educational work for an association of smaller and very small museums almost do not exist. Such centres would help to achieve international standards in terms of the variety and quality of educational work, they would relieve the strain on volunteer and freelance workers in museums and provide the continuity needed to promote the existing activities successfully. Currently, a great deal of innovative potential is wasted because of a lack of continuity.

Most of the volunteers, who are also the directors of the museums in which they work, are men over 45 years of age. This work is usually perceived as a contribution to the community. Women, on the other hand, tend to work in the area of education in part- or full-time employment, as employees or freelancers. About half of those working in education – whether as volunteers, freelancers or employees – have some general training. About 10 per cent have completed a postgraduate course specifically designed for museum education. Such courses have been made available in Austria since the 1990s. They are attended by existing employees, and especially by freelancers; that is, they are mainly of interest to those who regard museum educational work as their profession. But the proportion of education experts among the museum employees is relatively low.

With the exception of volunteers, those working in museum education feel that their role is a marginal one. The majority perceive their position in museums as isolated, lacking in influence and insufficiently appreciated. Also, museums offer no career opportunities to those working in the educational field. Accordingly, identification with the institution where they work is not of a kind that productive co-operation would demand. Most freelancers feel that they are not an integral part of the staff of the museums where they work. They often see themselves in the role of a person who is called in from outside and is easily replaceable.

Austrian museums have not yet fully appreciated the concept of a number of experts with specific competences complementing each other to work out jointly what constitutes a museum. Even high-quality educational programmes will not survive in the long run if educational work and those in charge of it continue to receive such little recognition.

If educational provision is granted a greater structural influence it will also be easier to perceive it as a task for all people involved in museum work, regardless of their function. This is not only confirmed by the interviews with those volunteers who represent, as it were, all functions in one, but is also reflected in the (admittedly few) examples of museum managements putting educational work at the centre of the museum concept. The employees in charge of educational activities rightly claim that educational provision can only be achieved if all the individual museum departments co-operate and if the relevant workers are represented in the decision-making bodies. Co-operation between educational workers and decision makers in the museums is, in fact, shaped by the fact that the educational programmes on offer are merely perceived as 'extras'. The emplyees concerned with this field often only deal with the co-ordination, but not with the planning, of events and programmes. There are a few existing institutionalised forms of co-operation between museum managements and/or curators and workers in charge of education, and almost nothing involving freelancers.

The lack of material security on the part of the freelancers is another problem which makes it difficult to establish a basis of continuity and experience in the educational field. The frequent changes of staff put a strain on the more experienced employees who are continually having to train new staff. Centralised museum services would not only offer smaller museums the opportunity to draw on professional support in the educational field, but they would also improve the income of freelancers and thereby facilitate a continuous long-term co-operation with the museums. Also, the demand for a simultaneous supervision of work could be met in a more satisfactory way.

(*translated from German by Esther Kinsky*)

This chapter is the slightly shortened version of an abstract published in Rath, Gabriele (1999), *Museen für BesucherInnen: eine Studie, published by Büro für Kulturvermittlung, Institut für Kulturwissenschaft, Vienna.*

Notes

1 Hildebrand, H and Klein-Wisenberg, L (1982), *(...das lebende museum...): Umfrage zur Bildungsarbeit in österreichischen Museen*, Vienna: unpublished manuscript
2 The members of the project group were: Regina Doppelbauer, Heiderose Hildebrand, Hartwig Gebetsroiter, Magda Kron, Walter Stach and Gabriele Stoger. The author conducted the study between 1994 and 1997 by order of the Institut für Kulturwissenschaft, with Renate Goebl being the project leader. A detailed final report was presented in 1997.

18 France

Jean Galard

The educational role of museums has always been affirmed as being one of their main *raisons d'être*, often the most important. In France, the founding texts of the 'Museum des arts', which opened to the public in 1793 in the Louvre Palace, are very explicit. The 'Commission du Museum', entrusted with the preparation of this opening, expressed itself clearly, on 17 June 1793, on the two objectives of the government: 'l'instruction publique et l'adoucissement des moeurs par le spectacle enchanteur des chefs-d'oeuvre' (public instruction and the appeasement of morals through the contemplation of masterpieces) (Guiffrey and Tuetey 1909). The text does not state whether this 'instruction' is aimed especially at children and young people. Everything suggests, on the contrary, that it was adults who were concerned: the museum was to be a place of instruction for those called, in this period of the French Revolution, the 'citizens'.

Why is it that when one refers to the educational mission of museums, one still thinks essentially of the activities designed for children? It seems that the initial objective has been much diminished or even forgotten. It is, none the less, a constant theme reaffirmed right through the nineteenth century. Is it an abstract word, an intention without effect? The link between the museum and adult education was proclaimed very early on; but one is under the impression that it is only recently that real efforts have been made to realise it (Dufresne-Tassé *et al.* 1998).

During the first years of museums in France − that is, at the end of the eighteenth and the beginning of the nineteenth centuries − their educational role was experienced mainly by the artists themselves. It was they who found, thanks to the works of the great masters of the past, examples which enabled them to perfect their talents. However, very early on, numerous written documents testify that the main function of the museum was conceived as something broader. For example, an article of 1795 of 'La Décade philosophique et littéraire' (no. 28) (Galard 1993: 139−41) requests that the works, until then shown somewhat haphazardly, be presented in a way both useful for young artists and 'la grande généralité du public', that they should be presented chronologically and by author. The same article further says: 'It is also for the use of the public, and to facilitate its instruction, that we propose to write at the bottom of each painting its subject and the name of the painter.' An inscription under each work prevents the possibility that 'the people take back with them false ideas after promenade in the museum'. In 1801, Jean-Baptiste Pujoulx (*Paris à la fin du XVIIIe siècle*) wanted the '*livret*' (hand-list), which already existed in the Louvre, to be at a price more accessible to the less fortunate so that 'this type of instruction penetrates all the classes of society''. In fact, this *livret*, like those that were to follow, had two shortcomings: not only was it too expensive for the 'personnes les moins aisées', as Pujoulx says, but it was rather perfunctory and, compared with today's standards, it was far from giving the explanations which the majority of the public needed (Galard 1993: 141–2).

From the middle of the nineteenth century, the museums widened the range of their collections, and the instruction they were expected to provide for adults seems to have been extended. Existing art museums already provided models for artists. The new applied arts museums were to show exemplary works to craftsmen and workers. Britain was the originator of this movement, so characteristic of the second half of the century. Shortly after the Great Exhibition, held in London in 1851, the South Kensington Museum opened – the first museum of 'arts applied to industry'. The principle of a place where the improvement of industrial production could be extolled was soon imported into France. At Lyons, capital of silk production, the Chambre de Commerce decided, in 1856, to create a 'Musée d'Art et d'Industrie'. In Paris, the Union Centrale des Beaux-Arts appliqués à l'Industrie was founded in 1864. In 1905, the museum which it runs was installed in the Pavillon de Marsan of the Louvre Palace. The end of the nineteenth century is thus marked by this intention of putting the museums at the service of the learning of techniques and trades. But it is difficult to find documents that show how this apprenticeship was actually practised. There was, in France, no equivalent of the Henry Cole System which, in Great Britain, aimed at instituting a close integration of the national network of the Schools of Science and Art with the South Kensington Museum. It is for this reason that one does not notice, in France either, at the end of the nineteenth nor at the beginning of the twentieth century, the break which happened 'when the development of the formal education systems in Britain had made museums seem redundant as instruments of public education, and the curatorial functions of museums had become increasingly separated from their educational functions' (Anderson 1995: 16,20).

How can we explain this gap, in France, for more than two centuries, between the didactic intention (concretised by the effective creation of museums) and the teaching in fact offered to adults of which we can only find embryonic traces? The explanation could be that for many years it was considered sufficient merely to expose people to objects so that knowledge could be transmitted. Nineteenth-century ideology distinguished learning through words from learning through objects. The policy of instruction promoted, on the one hand, learning through teaching and discourse, and on the other, learning through the eye and by example. An apprenticeship based on perception was considered to be appropriate to complete an apprenticeship based on discourse. This ideology has not completely disappeared, as one still opposes the teaching at school, where language is predominant, to the visit to a museum which is addressed to personal sensibility. But it has now become generally admitted that an exhibited object needs an oral accompaniment not only to be understood but also to be felt.

In the twentieth century, museums have progressively experienced the obligation to furnish commentaries on the objects shown. What were known as 'lecture-promenades' took place in the Louvre and in other national museums from 1920 onwards. They were targeted towards adults. Printed guides became real introductions to the history of art (L. Hourticq in 1921, Paul Vitry in 1922). The radio was used in 1933 to help adults prepare for their visits to museums. From 1936 to 1938, museums were conceived, by both the government and the workers' trade unions, as a means of developing 'popular education'.

World War II broke this impetus. The period of reconstruction which followed had other priorities. When the matter of 'cultural policy' began to be raised explicitly, from 1959, an essential divergence appeared at the forefront of the stage. On the one hand, the Ministry of Cultural Affairs (entrusted to André Malraux) upheld professional artists and wanted to favour direct contact of the people with the greatest masterpieces of universal culture. On the other, the Associations of Popular Education defended the principles of tuition, mediation and pedagogy, as well as the encouragement of artistic activities by amateurs (Urfalino 1996). Today this conflict is partly forgotten. But consequences remain, which help us to understand why in France the provision of adult education by museums lag somewhat. In fact, both positions which were in confrontation excluded the possibility of an educational action for adults in museums. The 'ministerial' position claimed that access to all masterpieces was favoured but that this contact should be direct, 'sensible' (calling upon the senses), that is to say without the intervention of mediators and educators. The Associations of Popular Education affirmed the necessity for mediation and apprenticeship, but situated its field of action more in local reality, in everyday surroundings rather than within the museums. Between the professional artist and the 'animateur de milieu' (local activity leader), the museum educator could not find a place.

If professional museum educators have now found a role (at first very modest), this stems first of all from the establishment of relations with schools. From the beginning of the 1970s, the educational departments of the museums have benefited from a strong involvement by the Ministry of National Education, which has consented to assign some of its teachers to the museums, so that they may receive groups of schoolchildren and work on common projects with their teaching colleagues. The debate remains open as to the type of relationship which can be established between the knowledge that is dispensed in school and the experience that can be acquired in museums. Is the visit to a museum merely complementary to a school activity? If the museum does not restrict itself to the simple illustration of a course, what can it offer specifically? The exact nature of what the museum can bring, compared with 'normal' teaching, is quite difficult to define, particularly in countries like

France where History of Art does not figure in the curriculum of secondary schools (*L'Ecole* 1995). Another delicate question should be asked, that of knowing the effects of school visits to museums on the ulterior attitude of the adults who benefited (or suffered!) from them when they were children. The only reliable statistics that we have indicate that the frequentation of museums by adults is strongly linked with the number of years spent in school: the rate of visits of adults increases from 13 per cent among those who have no diploma to 52 per cent among those who continued their studies beyond the baccalauréat examination (taken at the end of secondary school). As far as our subject, adult education, is concerned, it should be noted that there has been no halt over the last 20 years in collaboration between the staff of museums and teachers. Of the 3,000 museums with different statutes and of different sizes that exist in France, 850 have Education and Cultural Departments which produce pedagogical support materials and lead operations in concert with teachers. This type of action can undoubtedly be classified under the title 'adult training' as these teachers are the first (and sometimes the foremost) beneficiaries of the actions prepared for their pupils.

Having learnt how to work with teachers, museums spread their activities to specialised educators or 'activity-leaders'; that is, towards adults in charge of children, adolescents or young adults outside the national school system. In recent years the Service Culturel du Musée du Louvre has devoted special efforts to the training of adults in positions in Popular Education Associations, and in organisations responsible for municipal policies. The Ministry of Culture has, for its part, tightened its links with Popular Education Associations, such as the Fédération Nationale Léo Lagrange. Created in 1950 to continue the work undertaken by Léo Lagrange (Secretary of State for Sports ands Leisure 1936–38), this federation brings together local associations, thus constituting a network organised on a regional basis with different sectors of activity. Its objective is overall responsibility for the apprenticeship of citizenship. It has 100,000 members and contacts with 300,000 users of its services and activities. It employs 600 professional activity-leaders and indirectly mobilises 2,000 salaried people of affiliated associations. The Musée du Louvre taps into a privileged field of action with such a federation and with similar organisations, as it is in a position to develop training programmes. Indeed, an important problem confronts activity-leaders of popular education desirous of encouraging cultural practices: it is precisely that of their own qualifications. The museum can offer them guidelines, methods and suggestions which will help them to equip themselves to introduce cultural themes to those people who feel that they are not familiar with them. Among the most recent initiatives of the Musée du Louvre in this respect is the work undertaken with the organisations concerned with literacy skills among those who have recently immigrated. For these people, regular visits to the museum can be experienced as a sign (or a hope) of integration.

Long and patient research should be carried out with people suffering from a variety of disabilities. The Musée du Louvre began by making an effort to render its space accessible to visitors with restricted mobility. Those with physical handicaps can from now on circulate in the whole of the palace. They are, moreover, admitted in groups on Tuesdays, closing day to the general public, for lecture-visits. Blind and partially sighted people have a permanent 'tactile space'; and for the deaf and those with hearing difficulties, an original operation was devised in 1990: rather than train guide-lecturers, the Cultural Department of the museum undertook to train about 10 deaf people in the History of Art, following a three-year course. In this way, deaf visitors can benefit from explanations given by individuals who not only share their cultural background but also their physical predicament.

The museum acts as an education centre for numerous adults who use the works published by the Cultural Department in partnership with the Réunion des Musées Nationaux (ranging from the most general to the highly specialised), or who come to follow the lecture-visits and workshop activities. The lecture-visits vary from those that concern a collection, a theme or an artist, to those that concentrate, for one hour, on one single work, and others which are organised in planned cycles. As for the workshops, some of the 20 or so themes intended for adults are: (1) principles of museography and exhibition design; (2) how to organise an exhibition; (3) introduction to hieroglyphic and cuneiform scripts; (4) ancient painting techniques; (5) pastel techniques; (6) mosaic techniques; (7) how to film a work of art; (8) architecture of mosques. In an auditorium seating 420, lecture cycles on the history of art and archaeology are organised regularly; renowned international specialists come to share their most recent researches with an informed public.

For many adults, the role of the museum can be likened to that of an organisation of '*rattrapage*' (remedial courses), for those who have not had the opportunity of receiving adequate school or university training, or who have discovered later in life their interest in fields such as history, archaeology or history of art. For all these the museum plays its role not only *in situ* but at a distance: audio-visual techniques constitute an essential means by which museums are enabled to extend education. The condition for effective diffusion by this means lies in co-production. Partnerships with, for example, television channels, publishers of video-cassettes, permit both an increase in the volume of production and the guarantee that such production will be exploited on a large scale.

The potential for the development of adult education by museums appears considerable for several reasons: firstly, because there is not only an increase in leisure time but also an increase in the demand for training (Lorriaux 1998); secondly, because the museum can constitute, as mentioned above, an organisation of 'remedial teaching' and professional life can be characterised by a number of changes in orientation; thirdly, because, faced with an expansion of demand (explicit or latent), museums are increasingly disposed to take into account the needs and desires of their visitors, real or potential.

For different motives — economic, ideological, political — museums reveal themselves as more and more attentive to their adult public. This phenomenon has gone so far as to worry some authors, such as Françoise Choay (1992), who consider that museums and historic monuments have become 'cultural products' destined to be 'consumed':

> The metamorphosis of utility value into economic value has been realised thanks to what may be called Cultural Engineering (*l'ingéniérie culturelle*) — vast public and private enterprises in whose service work an army of activity-leaders, communicators, development agents, engineers, cultural mediators. Their task consists of exploiting the monuments by all possible means in order to multiply, indefinitely, the number of visitors.

Faced with this legitimate fear, the remedy consists of proposing authentic aids to the visit, such as are hoped for by many visitors. It is the duty of the museum to install within its walls, in a spirit of education, elements of information, resource centres for knowledge. The intervention of 'cultural mediators', in order to transmit knowledge, is more necessary than ever today, because of a fairly recent phenomenon. Within a few decades we have witnessed the dislocation of a general classical culture which was common to all cultivated elites. This does not mean that the younger generation has a poorer culture. It means simply that culture has become more varied. We have acquired a sharper conscience that there is a history and geography of cultures. Hence there is an increased need for the iconographical deciphering of works, for the knowledge of their context, for the understanding of their initial significance. This contribution of knowledge is most often indispensable for emotional appreciation. The sight of a decapitated head is not felt in the same way if we know it is that of John the Baptist, Goliath or Holophernes.

In any case, the transmission of knowledge by museums follows a different route from that employed by schools, to such an extent that one hesitates even to speak of 'education'. In French museums, the departments devoted to the transmission of knowledge prefer the title of 'Service Culturel' to that of 'Service Educatif'. An educational project, strictly speaking, implies an ordered process, a gradual unfolding, a progressive development; it supposes an overall design. The museum, on the other hand, acts in a sporadic way. Visits are irregular, if not occasional. It is capricious. It proceeds through proximity and not systematically. Moreover, gaps in collections preclude any hope for systematic knowledge. It has often been said that the museum, in its present function, is less educational than hedonist. It is also hedonist in other ways, apart from its collections: one can no longer imagine a museum without comfortable rest areas, without a restaurant, without musical programmes. It is a space of conviviality whose image is promoted by communication campaigns and whose seduction is expected to overflow to the collections themselves. It is also hedonist by its museographical layout and arrangement, which propose works for pleasure and enjoyment.

However, this enjoyment, in such circumstances, presupposes a practised eye, an informed perception. Cultural communication consists in producing the means of seeing better, of understanding better, of feeling more intensely. Several features distinguish it from communication in a 'normal' educational situation: it proposes diverse thematic 'inputs' and not the complete unfolding of a programme; it is available for those who desire to benefit from it, and discrete for those who prefer to do without it. These characteristics make it potentially infinite, and it can always be supplemented. Time is no longer counted (as it is in the school process). Space is no longer congested. Documentation is held in reserve; it does not invade the walls, does not compete with the works. It can be changed according to the different publics for whom it is destined and can notably be multi-lingual. It can be called upon according to need.

These are, typically, the qualities of the computerised documentary bases and, more generally, of the interactive multimedia tool. Today's museum fulfils its educational mission for adults or, in other terms, its cultural mission, by adding to the traditional interventions the production of CD-ROMs, DVD-ROMs, the creation and progressive enrichment of sites on the Internet.

Many fear that 'virtual' visits, this semblance of a museum, might discourage people from visiting real museums. But to use modern technology is to gamble that the image of the museum will induce the person to visit the museum itself one day. It has been noted that the image of works reproduced in art books has increased the frequentation of museums rather than the contrary. There is no real desire to see if the eye has been neither prepared nor warned. There is no real desire to understand and to search if the visitor has not been stimulated to prolong their reflection on the works of art outside the walls which contain them. The cultural responsibility of the museum could be thus defined: beyond formal education, the museum should also furnish optional aids which will render each person able to continue their self-education indefinitely.

Interactive technologies challenge the educational and cultural departments of museums to renew their methods and to increase and widen their audiences (*Patrimoine* 1998). The use of modern technology is potentially very powerful. But it is only a tool which will remain useless if the information conveyed has not been determined very precisely. Unfortunately, reflection on the different types of discourse that can be held on works of art is as yet very scant. This theme has scarcely been the subject of serious discussion between curators (who hold the initial scholarship) and the pedagogues, or mediators, who have the responsibility of addressing the public. Discussion on the material to propose to adults has for a long time been blocked by the idea that educational departments are essentially concerned with children. Because of this, adult education in museums has taken the form, for many years, of an adaptation or an extension of what was done for children. Today, the opposite phenomenon seems to impose itself. Producers of interactive cultural tools (CD-ROM, DVD-ROM, web sites) who have previously worked with adults in cultural departments or outside (notably for documentary films) and who have become used to the states of mind and needs of adults, are coming to interest themselves in the school world and to elaborate the contents of educational sites. To ask oneself what could or should be adult education provision by museums, is to ask the question of what, in the twenty-first, will be, both for adults and for children, the act of learning, the teacher–taught relationship, the organisation (or fragmentation) of learning, the sharing of personal initiative, and the place given to seduction in the laborious process of acquiring knowledge.

References

Anderson, D, in A Chadwick and A Stannett (eds), *Museums and the education of adults*, Leicester: NIACE, 1995, pp. 16, 20; *see also* M Conforti in E Pommier (ed.), *Histoire de l'histoire de l'art*, vol.2, Paris: Klincksieck, 1997

Choay, F, *L'allégorie du patrimoine*, Paris: Le Seuil, 1992

Dufresne-Tassé, C *et al*, 'Musée et communauté; importance d'un leadership muséal en matière d'éducation de l'adulte', *ICOM Education* 16, 1998

L'Ecole, le musée: Croisement des savoirs? Actes du colloque des 22,23,24 mars 1994, Lille: Palais des Beaux-Arts, 1995.

Galard, J (ed.), *Visiteurs du Louvre, un florilège*, Paris: Réunion des Musées Nationaux, 1993

Guiffrey, J and Tuetey, A (eds), *La Commission du Museum et la création du Musée du Louvre*, Paris, 1909. (This work reproduces the official texts which planned and defined the first national museum in France.) *See also* Poulot, D, *Musée, nation, patrimoine 1789–1815*, Paris: Gallimard, 1996 (on the function originally attributed to museums). *See also* Cabanne, P (1997), *Le nouveau guide des musées de France*, Paris: Larousse, *and Guide Tocqueville des musées de France 1997* , Genève: Minerva, 1997

Lorriaux, J-P, *La formation de A à Z*, Paris: Retz, 1998

Patrimoine et multimédia: le rôle du conservateur, Actes du colloque des 23,24,25 octobre 1996, Paris: La Documentation française, 1998; *see also* ICHIM 97, Fourth International Conference on Hypermedia and Interactivity in Museums, Paris, 3,4,5 September 1997

http:/www.archimuse.com/mw 991.

Urfalino, P, *L'invention de la politique culturelle*, Paris: La Documentation française, 1996

19 Germany

Dorothee Dennert and Helena von Wersebe

The Haus der Geschichte der Bundesrepublik Deutschland (Museum of Contemporary History of the Federal Republic of Germany) in Bonn opened in June 1994. It covers German history from 1945 to the present day and has, since opening, already attracted more than 3 million visitors to its permanent exhibition and more than 1 million people to major temporary exhibitions.

The following is a case study in training and staff development practised in this museum.

A typical Saturday

On Saturday, 12 March 1998, 10 groups were scheduled for a tour through the permanent exhibition of the Haus der Geschichte. Eight of these groups were composed of adult visitors, totalling some 200 persons. The groups comprised:

- former senior managing directors of the 16 state offices of the Association for the German Construction Industry, organised by the Association's Bonn office;
- a senior citizens' sports group with visitors from the region;
- a group of German and international guests on the occasion of a 50th birthday celebration;
- adult students from a neighbouring *Land* completing their high-school qualification;
- a mixed group from the constituency of an East German parliamentary deputy;
- Lions Club members from the region;
- members of a sports club from the city of Bonn and from the city of Xanten; and
- a group of Russian repatriates (ethnic Germans) who have settled in Germany.

What does this snapshot of a typical Saturday in the Haus der Geschichte with an average of 2,000 visits tell us about our adult visitors, and what does this, in turn, imply for Docent (teacher or lecturer) training and development?

Paradoxically, the unifying characteristic of the above-mentioned groups is precisely their diversity: these groups reflect a heterogeneity of educational background, geographic origin, familiarity with German history and language, ages, motivation for visiting the museum, and probably much more. This tells us that it is not enough simply to focus on 'the' adult visitor as opposed to 'the' non-adult visitor, but that museums need to identify a diversity of adult audiences, and train *Docents* to respond flexibly and individually to specific audience needs.

Secondly, it is noteworthy that many of the adult groups who chose to visit the Haus der Geschichte over that weekend did so during their leisure time. These visits were not 'official' or work-related events, but voluntary activities motivated by a desire to follow both learning and leisure pursuits. Those working with adult visitors in museums must therefore understand and respond to the complex mix of motivations and expectations that bring adult visitors to a museum.

Getting to know your adult visitors

Only ongoing exhibit evaluations and systematic visitor surveys provide the kind of detailed and representative data that will enable museums to go beyond a 'snapshot' understanding of their visitors. Visitor research provides accurate information about the socio-demographic background, length of stay, motives for visiting as well as a great deal of other information about audiences. In addition to visitor surveys, a systematic analysis of group reservations data can provide further information about organised groups as opposed to non-group visitors.

Since opening, the Haus der Geschichte has conducted a number of representative surveys on a regular basis to find out more about visitors to the permanent exhibition and to temporary displays. The museum has also conducted surveys of non-visitors, trying to discover what are possible barriers to visiting museums (Schäfer, 1997, 1998). Finally, the Office of Visitor Services compiles and analyses general museum attendance statistics as well as data about organised tour groups, generated by a computer-based reservation system (Dennert and Wersebe 1996). Based on these sources of information, we can state the following about our visitors:

- The percentage of 30–60-year-old people who visit the permanent exhibition accords with their percentage of the general population; the 20–29-year-olds are slightly over-represented, and the number of over-60-year-olds, as well as the under-20-year-olds, are slightly under-represented in comparison with the general average of the population. In contrast to single visitors, the last two age groups listed are over-represented in guided tours.
- Roughly 70 per cent of all those who visit the museum come as individuals or as a part of informal groups; 30 per cent of visitors receive a guided tour through the exhibition. During 1998 some 117,000 persons participated in more than 5,700 tours.
- The large majority (70 per cent) of all groups receiving a guided tour are

composed of adult visitors; school-age children account for the remaining
30 per cent of guided tour participants.

- Visitors who participate in a guided tour tend to have a lower level of
formal education. This reflects not only the high percentage of school
groups but also the high percentage of visitors over 60 years old.

- Adult visitors are more reserved in their use of and response to audio-visual
stations and interactive mechanical tools, such as flip-charts or information
drawers.

- While 12 per cent of total visitors admitted to not using audio-visual
means, 24 per cent of those over 60 years old responded that they did not
use such resources.

- Many of our visitors (40 per cent) go to museums two or three times a year;
30 per cent of group visitors say that they visit museums at most only once
a year.

Implications for *Docent* training and development

The key characteristic of adult audiences is their diversity. Also, in the case of
the Haus der Geschichte in particular, it appears that among adult audiences we
attract a relatively high percentage of non-typical museum-goers – that is, the
'everyday' visitor as opposed to the museum 'elite'. Thus the primary goal for
Docent training and development is to sensitise *Docents* to this diversity and
provide training which can enable them to deal flexibly with a variety of
groups.

Selection

Ideally, the *Docent* staff should reflect the diversity of the target audiences it
serves. Thus, in addition to the large pool of students which typically composes
the core of our *Docent* staff, we encourage, for instance, applications from retired
professionals and carers looking for work outside the home. Applicants
generally have a university education (or are students) in the social sciences.

Our experience at the Haus der Geschichte has shown that it is helpful to
have a two-phase interview process and to conduct the application interviews
in a group setting. The initial group interview is designed to gauge the
applicant's motivation, understanding of the museum's mission and general
communication skills. The second group interview focuses on exhibit content
and design as well as historical background. We have found that the two-phase
group interview process provides us with a much better picture of the
candidates – and them with a clearer picture of us – thus enhancing our hiring
decisions.

This two-step group interview process has resulted in several benefits.
Firstly, applicants have the opportunity to become acquainted with their future

colleagues; by the time training sessions begin, candidates have already established a basic level of group cohesion, thus improving group communication and learning outcomes. Secondly, during the interview process we have already signalled what the important issues are, in essence providing a preview of the main training topics to come. Finally, the information gained about the candidates not only as individuals but also as a group helps us to adapt the standard training curriculum to meet their specific needs.

Training

Docent trainees attend a two-day seminar comprising presentations by curatorial staff, discussions and video training. The Museum Educator and the Co-ordinator of Visitor Services jointly lead the seminar, and both also present training units. Training content focuses on three main areas: museums as a site for learning from objects; the specific content and design of the permanent exhibition; and communication with groups. Some key points for training *Docents* to work with adult visitors are as follows:

- Design tours for a specific audience: know the target group, its background and motivation for the visit by group members.
- Be aware of the multiple roles that a *Docent* guide plays: educator, leader, host, public relations representative and interpreter/conduit (Pond 1993). The last three of these are especially important when dealing with adult visitors.
- Use video training to help guides evaluate verbal and non-verbal communication skills.
- Remember that the museum experience for most adults is a leisure-time activity: use informal learning approaches. For example, encourage visitor activity by making your tour enquiry- and discussion-based; allow time for visitors to experiment with hands-on exhibits and audio-visual stations; be flexible about the tour route – follow pathways established by the visitors.
- Museum learning is lifelong learning. The goal of the tour is not to provide as much information in as short a time as possible, but to make the museum visit an important building block in a life filled with a variety of continuous learning opportunities.
- Tap into the font of personal experience. Adult visitors, having 'experienced history' themselves, are 'experts' in their own right; do not relegate them to the role of student. Begin at the level of personal experience and then help the visitor to expand beyond it to a broader level of understanding.

A key facet in our training materials is the list of 'interpretation modules', about 15 elements, including the museum mission statement, organisational structure, architecture, exhibition design, recurring thematic elements and pedagogical structure, that form the basis of every tour. These modules are used flexibly, depending upon the target group being addressed.

Evaluation

After the new *Docents* have conducted several tours, the Co-ordinator of Visitor Services conducts a feedback session with each *Docent*, based upon self-assessment. In a second stage, the Museum Educator, Co-ordinator of Visitor Services or a curator observes the *Docent* for a complete group tour and conducts an evaluation focusing on both content and communication skills. The Haus der Geschichte has developed a detailed, three-page checklist to help the *Docent* to assess themselves with regard to eight main areas: historical background, interpretation modules, general communication skills, specific museum interpretation skills, tour organisation, working in a team, familiarity with the museum and its activities, and further training.

Further training

The Haus der Geschichte provides further training on an ongoing basis, including lectures, workshops, lunchtime meetings and special tours through the exhibition. Both museum staff and invited guests conduct these training sessions. In addition to providing further information about the exhibits, training gives *Docents* the opportunity of meeting each other and sharing experiences and ideas.

The core of further training offers are tours by curatorial staff on specific topics. At present the focus is on 'Reunited Germany: the history of the Soviet Zone, the GDR and the German question'. This topic was chosen in response to *Docent* feedback, which indicated that there was a need – almost 10 years after reunification and four years after the museum had opened – to look anew at this question. In previous years we highlighted the topic 'Bringing objects to life'. In that training unit curators presented their collection areas over a series of weeks, and the sequence ended with a two-day workshop.

Additional offers of training focus on non-verbal communication skills, current information about museum activities, working with disabled visitors, and informal learning in museums. As a next step we are planning to create small working groups, composed of three to five Docents, which will have the task of focusing on the special needs of selected adult groups. The working groups will be a forum for collecting experiences, developing training materials and planning new programmes.

The German perspective

The particular experiences at the Haus der Geschichte with adult visitors and training *Docents* for adult education reflect the situation of a single museum. A brief look at the state of museum education in Germany and at an important

European project points to a growing awareness of this issue.

The best source of empirical information about the state of museum education in Germany is the Institut für Museumskunde, which sends survey questionnaires to all museums in Germany every year. In 1987, 1992, 1993 and 1997 these surveys included questions concerning museum education (Hagedorn-Saupe and Noschka-Roos 1994). The 1997 results were due for publication during 1998. Museums were asked to categorise and describe various aspects of their museum education organisation and offers.

From 1987 to 1993 a trend towards both a quantitative increase in the number of different programmes as well as a qualitative increase in the different types of education programmes that museums offer was noted. Not surprisingly, guided tours, the standard offer of many museums, were the most frequently mentioned; however, the frequency declined from 86 per cent in 1987 to 75 per cent in 1993. Conversely, there was an increase of other kinds of programmes, such as seminars, workshops and lectures, from 14 per cent in 1987 to 25 per cent in 1993.

Further, the findings indicated a trend towards increasing diversification of museum education programmes. In 1987 only 8.4 per cent of museums offered four or more different types of programmes. This proportion grew to 33 per cent in 1997. Museums offering only one programme (generally a guided tour) decreased from one-half of all respondents to one-quarter in 1993. Thus both the number and the types of programmes are expanding, and there is every hope that adult audiences are benefiting from this increased diversification.

Museum educators were also asked to identify their primary target audiences. In their replies, multiple answers were permitted. In 1987, 50 per cent of museums named schoolchildren; 20 per cent named seniors; 7 per cent named disabled visitors; 5 per cent foreigners, and 30 per cent the non-specific category 'other'. Indeed, 20 per cent of museums named only schoolchildren – to the exclusion of other groups – as their target audience. Clearly, there is a bias in museum education initiatives towards children and young visitors. An interim survey in 1992 showed a small drop in the focus on schoolchildren to 40 per cent.

The 1993 survey results suggest that museum educators are beginning to take a closer look at the diversity of target audiences: not only was the category 'schoolchildren' divided into three sub-groups (children, young visitors, school groups), but there was also a further differentiation of adult visitors: tourists (32 per cent) and Friends of the museum (20 per cent). The frequency of the target audience 'other' (students, specialists, adults (*sic*), teachers) decreased from 18 per cent in 1987 to 9 per cent in 1993. These results reflect an increasing awareness of target audiences in general, but also of adult audiences in particular.

Finally, there appears to be a growing awareness of adult audiences as reflected in the increasing diversification of co-operating partners that museum educators are seeking. Although schools were the most frequently named partner in all surveys, there was an increase of 42 per cent in the number of other groups that were mentioned in the 1993 survey: clubs, associations and churches – 40 per cent; traditional adult education programmes (*Volkshochschule*) – 20 per cent; universities – 29 per cent; and 'other' adult education programmes – 15 per cent. This is certainly a reflection of the attempts to reach a wider range of adult audiences.

Strategies for adult education and the training of *Docents*

These reflections are based on the following strategies which have been successful at the Haus der Geschichte in dealing with adult educators, the training of *Docents* and the provision of programmes.

Identify partners for pilot projects

Identify motivated individuals who are willing to experiment with new projects. Usually, these individuals will already be familiar with your institution; they may be 'repeat customers'. The aim of a pilot project should be to create a programme that you can easily replicate for other audiences. Ideally, your partner will be in a position to repeat the pilot project on a larger scale or publish the results.

The Humanistische Union, an independent foundation for adult and civic education, together with the Haus der Geschichte, organised a one-day seminar exploring the theme of personal biographies in connection with exhibit objects. A summary and analysis of the project was published (Behrens–Cobet 1997).

Train adult educators to use the museum

All too often, adult educators do not know how to utilise a display or objects for their learning purposes. Firstly, they need to be educated about learning in museums in general: an exhibition is not a seminar room. Secondly, they need to be guided in how the specific museum provides material for an abstract lesson. Twenty adult educators from the traditional *Volkshochschulen* who work nationwide with ethnic German repatriates have participated in a two-day teacher training workshop at the Haus der Geschichte. A primary focus throughout the workshop was dealing with site-specific and object-specific learning opportunities in the museum.

Share information with *Docents*

Given the diversity of adult audiences, it is necessary to provide *Docents* with as much information about a particular group as possible, so that the *Docent* can respond flexibly.

Understand the adult visitor

Identify the complex 'motivation mix' inherent in adult education as an element of lifelong learning. Adult visitors often plan their educational outings, such as seminars or lecture series, with leisure and social expectations in mind; conversely, social outings, such as office trips, birthdays, club and association events, are expected to have an educational aspect.

Know your visitor statistics

The more empirical information you have about adult visitors, both as members of a group tour or as individual visitors, the more focused *Docent* training for this target audience can be. A computer reservation system which provides statistical information, and visitor surveys, are two valuable instruments in this respect.

Develop adequate information materials

We have found that information materials developed for young visitors and teachers can often be used, or easily adapted, for the adult visitor. For instance, our theme-based education packs for secondary schools include material which can easily be used for adult seminars and workshops. A series of activity programmes geared to younger visitors often provide a non-threatening, relaxed way for older visitors to explore the exhibition.

Do not neglect the non-group adult visitor

It is important not to forget that the majority of adult visitors come individually or in small groups and not as an organised group. Thus general museum information must be attractive for them, such as publications about the exhibits, CD-ROM, object-related activity programmes as well as other programming, including events.

Conclusion

Adult visitors are a mainstay of museum audiences, and museums need to respond to the diversity and complexity of this target audience. Training *Docents* to respond to the needs of adult visitors is an essential task of museum education. The experience of the Haus der Geschichte shows that a multi-layered approach to this task, including visitor evaluation, a highly focused *Docent* application and training process, ongoing evaluation, further training opportunities, and co-operation with adult education programmes is necessary for success.

References

Behrens-Cobet, H, 'Zeitreise als Bildungsangebot: Seminare im Haus der Geschichte', *Ausserschulische Bildung: Materialien zur politischen Jugend- und Erwachsenenbildung,* vol.3, 1997, pp.385–6

Dennert, D and Wersebe, H von, 'Museumspädagogik und Besucherdienst in einem besuchsorientierten Museum', in *Museen und ihre Besucher, Herausforderungen in der Zukunft:* International Symposium, November 1995, Haus der Geschichte, ed. Haus der Geschichte der Bundesrepublik Deutschland, Bonn, 1996, pp.194–208

Hagedorn-Saupe, M and Noschka-Roos, A (1994), *Museumspädagogik in Zahlen, Erhebungsjahr 1993,* Materialien aus dem Institut für Museumskunde, no.41, Berlin; see also *Erhebungsjahr 1988,* no. 27

Pond, K, *The professional guide: the dynamics of tour guiding,* New York: Van Nostrand Reinhold, 1993

Schäfer, H, 'Non-visitor research: an important addition to the unknown', in *Visitor Research and Practice,* vol. 9: Selected papers from the 1996 Visitor Studies Conference, ed. R. Loomis and M. Wells, 1997, pp.195–205. Jacksonville, 1997

—— (1998), *'Museen und ihre Besucher', in Deutsches Jahrbuch für Kulturmanagement,* vol.1, [1997] pp.29–53, Baden-Baden

20 Switzerland

Flavia Krogh Loser

Status and development of adult education and museum education

From the outset, it is important to realise that Switzerland consists of 26 separate cantons, each of which has its own constitution approved by the government. Both adult education and museum education fall within the remit of each canton. This does not, however, mean that cultural or educational matters are overseen by these cantonal governments on a day-to-day basis: the development of culture as well as of adult education is basically undertaken by the private sector. Only in cases where this has been made impossible by lack of resources or opportunities will the cantonal governments intercede.

In the light of this background it is not surprising that adult education and museum education have developed very slowly, based on little structure. The fact for example, that in 1991 Zurich, the most populous canton, counted more than 1,100 organisations of general adult education, (that is, excluding vocational training centres) is ample evidence of the confused state of current Swiss adult education.

None the less, adult education is popular: 1.9 million adults per annum (about 40 per cent of the population) attend courses of all descriptions, seeking personal, social or career advancement. In 1996, 62 per cent of the courses were geared to the professional sector, 38 per cent to general further education. Of this lucrative market 80 per cent is covered by the private sector; the state's proportion of educational offerings is a mere 3 per cent (Gonon and Schlafli 1998: 28–9).

In Switzerland, the concept of adult education is based on seeing an individual as an integral being whose personal, social and occupational needs should all be served; it thus encompasses liberal education, personal growth and occupational competences.

In the German-speaking part of Switzerland, it is usual to speak of '*Weiterbildung*' (continuing professional education) and '*Erwachsenenbildung*' (adult education); the French-speaking part uses '*education permanente*'.

Generally speaking, adult education in Switzerland is seen as a kind of appendage to tertiary education (higher education/universities). However, there has been a gradual acceptance that it is an independent sector which may be defined as follows:

- further education is the continuation or resumption of organised learning after completion of the first phase of education in school, college and

profession, with the aim of renewing or enhancing the knowledge and experience gained or of acquiring new knowledge or expertise;
- further education is purposeful learning, ranging from self-study, with the help of specialist literature, to formal, institutionalised courses;
- further education may, thus, be offered in formal, non-formal or informal format at the work-place, in free time or through social or cultural activities.

By means of this integrated concept, the former division between professional and general further education no longer applies (Gonon and Schläfli 1998: 13).

Private and public sponsors of adult education

The principal sponsors throughout Switzerland are private organisations. They cater for further education and training within the commercial sector, as do trade unions. However, public institutions of business and vocational training also offer a variety of programmes. Additionally, there are distance learning and specialist schools working along private enterprise lines.

The state (cantons and central government) is represented mainly in adult education institutes, in postgraduate studies at universities, and in the organisation of further education colleges. It is also responsible for the further education of civil servants (for example, teacher training), which is organised regionally.

The largest non-profit-making private adult education institutions are the club-schools of the Migros Cooperative, the adult education institutes, the leisure centres of the cooperative and the educational establishments of the Protestant and Catholic Churches. Their programmes range from self-development courses, foreign languages, cultural and socio-political events to hobby-classes and complete vocational training courses, such as information technology.

The Swiss Workers' Educational Association and the Education Institute of the Christian-National Trades Union focus particularly on employees and trade-union members. For parents' education there is a strong network of local and regional parents' schools, financed partly by the community (via their education departments).

The Swiss Association for Adult Education (SVEB) oversees this confused situation: it manages an information and advice centre in Zurich; publishes, *inter alia*, the journal *Education permanente*; organises a course for employees; and maintains a statistical databank.

Museum education: development in three phases

There is no long tradition of museum education in Switzerland. Although the student uprisings of 1968 highlighted, among others, the topic of museum education, initiatives were timid and scant until the late 1980s. Developments which, in the 1970s, had been taken for granted in Germany, constituted real pioneering work in Switzerland, undertaken by a few dedicated people. The foundation of almost all posts of museum educators took place in this first phase. It was only in the late 1980s that the museums (most of which had not been privately endowed but had grown from scientific and public collections) began to feel the pressure of public demand.

Thanks to these endeavours, museum education could now be more easily integrated into the Swiss public domain. This new position, the second phase, effected the development of mediation work in museums, as evidenced by the rapidly increasing number of mediators since the end of the 1980s. In 1988, there were 80 such staff (of whom 10 people shared 4 full-time posts). In 1991, there were 200 (of whom 25 shared 12.75 full-time posts). In 1995, the number of mediators was still estimated to be 200, but the total of full posts had more than doubled: 59 persons shared 26.75 posts.

A third phase was introduced in 1993 with the foundation of a training course in museology at Basle University. The aim of this course is to impart museological and museographical knowledge; to further students' competence in systematic museum work; and to enhance their ability to make relevant decisions and act upon these in practice, in all aspects of a museum's activities. In the long term, it is hoped to achieve professionalisation of mediation work in museums and greater recognition in the political and public arenas.

Adult education in the museum: structural models

Mediation work in Swiss museums is organised in a range of different systems. Despite efforts of the Association of Professionals for Education and Mediation in Museums (MPS) to clarify the situation, the picture is confused.

The following are common models of the structure of museum education:

- Several large museums have, over the years, established their own education departments which are run by permanent staff and several freelance colleagues (cf. case study: Kunstmuseum Bern, below).
- Some museums employ part-time schoolteachers to be responsible for educational work with schools.
- Central school institutions, such as teachers' further education colleges and regional teachers' resource centres, sometimes have their own section, 'School and museum', which initiates museum educational activities in several museums in the region.
- Regional central institutes of museums take on the task of educational work, and some of them aim to establish independent education departments within these museums.
- Private association with broad financial backing: private enterprise, public funds, schools, private individuals (cf. case study: KUBIKO, below).

Adult education in the museum: practical approach

Although the notion of education and communication in museums for adults has theoretically been legitimised in the cultural and educational policy of Switzerland, there is little effectiveness in practice (Krogh Loser 1996: 122–37):

Of all museum visitors 81 per cent are adults, either single or in groups; 19 per cent are children and young people. However, twice as much is invested in educational activities for the young visitors as for adults. This is particularly evident in the opening hours and in what is on offer. Of the 64 museums which responded to the questionnaire 44 (there are 766 museums in Switzerland) do not provide evening openings – essential for working adults. Emphasis is on productive collaboration with schools. There is no close co-operation with adult education centres, nor are there any collaborative connections with Church or private adult education institutions. Museum education is, moreover, primarily perceived as imparting knowledge, especially with adults. While there is a steady increase in the use of educationally approved methods for children and young people, adults are generally faced only with conventional labelling of objects and, in the larger museums, audio-visual facilities. Above all, they are offered conducted tours (80 per cent of targeted museums).

On the basis of the empirical study quoted (Krogh Loser 1996), the situation may thus be summarised as follows: in theory, general museum education has been integrated into the institution museum. However, initiatives specifically for adults have only just begun. In practice, the educational form of collections and exhibitions, and the personal mediation (mainly through conventional conducted tours), are focused mainly on imparting knowledge, which does not satisfy the objective of developing the whole person.

However, more and more museums and institutions are experimenting with specific programmes for adults, and two examples are described below. It is often lack of financial or idealistic support, rather than of ideas or engagement, that may still be an obstacle.

Case studies

Tradition and experiment at the Kunstmuseum Bern

The Kunstmuseum Bern is in the enviable situation of having adequate finances and staff, and is almost the only museum in Switzerland that has a 50 per cent post for the organisation and delivery of adult educational programmes. Hence it is able to carry out many interesting experiments and offer unconventional ideas. Apart from the traditional guided tours (in German, French, Italian and English), the museum offers the following programmes.

Conversations

'*Art at midday*': a series of regular talks about one particular work of art for anyone who wishes to spend their lunch hour in this way. Talks are free, without prior booking. The museum café provides the opportunity of having a snack at the same time. The project is proving very successful: a core group of about 30 people participate every week with great enthusiasm.

'*Conversations with artists*': in several courses local artists share their knowledge of the museum's artefacts with the public, thus promoting a better understanding of the institution's tradition.

'*Conversations for senior citizens*': regular afternoon courses on selected themes encourage many older people to share their lifelong experiences.

Workshops

Workshops, by their very nature, are more time consuming for participants, but here, too, small groups of faithful enthusiasts have formed.

'*General workshops*': words can help to explain works of art and give them a deeper meaning. However, people's own creativity often enriches understanding significantly. The workshops offer a combination of practical work, lectures and conversations which together enhance the experience of looking at works of art.

'*Workshops for the whole family*': regular workshops are offered for educators and children aged 6–11, especially for temporary exhibitions. The sessions are particularly popular during school holidays. The programmes on offer enable parents and children to work and play together in activities such as quizzes, trails through exhibitions, painting, making collages, working with music in the studio. The special requirements for this targeted audience are fully met.

The museum provides the above for temporary exhibitions as well as for permanent displays. Furthermore, there are non-traditional tours, discussions and workshops in combination with other adult education institutions, such as the following:

Programmes conducted in collaboration with other adult education institutions

With regional teachers' continuing education centres

'*Introduction to temporary exhibitions*': usually one evening.

'*Teachers' continuing education courses*': about four evenings. In-depth discussions on the themes of current exhibitions and basic preparation for visits with schoolchildren.

The Kunstmuseum Bern also organises a regular programme of interactive conducted tours with specifically prepared contents for interested firms and companies.

With the Adult Education Centre in Bern:

'Discussion courses for a temporary exhibition': three evenings. Each evening focused on a different aspect of the theme of the exhibition, by means of lecture and discussion.

'Behind the pictures': three evenings. The aim of this course was to increase visitors' understanding of art by looking behind the scenes of the museum into artists' studios, the work of museum staff, art criticism, the media and so on.

'Adult education for the mentally disabled: Pablo Picasso – faces look at us': four evenings. 'We shall look at pictures but will also take part ourselves by working and creating with paint brush and paint, paper and scissors' (Prospectus).

The above three programmes have been offered only once, as there were very few participants. Perhaps this lack of interest stems from the long gestation period often needed for new initiatives to be realised: it can take two to three years for new projects to be established. This problem also applies to the following programmes which had been planned in co-operation with the Migros Club School in Bern but had to be dropped through lack of applicants:

'Art museum for potential visitors': five evenings. 'Have you ever wanted to visit the art museum? To talk with others about art? Would you like to find out more about the functions of the museum? We help to facilitate your entry into the museum and to a personal dialogue with art. Let us together discover the museum as a meeting place of works of art and people' (Prospectus).

'Adventure Kunstmuseum': five evenings. 'A workshop for all those who want to involve themselves actively with art. With the help of landscapes from different periods and styles we shall absorb atmospheric pictures and communicate our impressions to others. Creative and informal dealing with art inspires us to new experiments in looking at pictures' (Prospectus).

Similarly, programmes planned with 'Dante Alighieri', an association for promoting Italian language and culture, had to be dropped. These included:

'Discussion course in the Kunstmuseum': ten evenings. 'This course aims to combine information, exchange, conversation and the use of the Italian language. Works of art on different themes and from different periods give us the incentive to practise new and current vocabulary. But we also want to talk about the impact of the pictures so as to increase our ability to express ourselves in the foreign language. The objective is to use Italian as a foreign language in a new context and thereby promote holistic learning' (Prospectus).

KUBIKO: Centre for cultural education and communication (St Gallen): history of an ambitious project

The three cantons of St Gallen, Appenzell Ausserrhoden and Appenzell Innerrhoden (all situated between Zurich and Bodensee) together have about 60 museums (local museums, art museums, a cheese museum and so on); there are also many other exhibition venues such as private collections and galleries. Very few of these have a museum education service; those that do focus mainly on schools and are greatly over-stretched. KUBIKO aims to improve this situation and to promote and co-ordinate cultural exchanges throughout the region.

KUBIKO's mission is to connect with everyday realities experienced by the wide range of visitors so that the various societal groups may profit from such arrangements. Further, KUBIKO employs, above all, experiential and interactive methods of communication which will facilitate access to the exhibits by means of stimulating visitors' creative potential. The aim is to put onlookers in touch not only with the object but also with themselves.

Origins

It all began with an idea in November 1995. There followed definitions, research and analysis of the project. These initiatives led to a meeting in June 1996: for the first time in the history of museum education in east Switzerland representatives of education (such as schools), culture (like artists and art galleries), and politics (administrators of canton and community) from the three cantons listed above met together. A common interest in developing the project emerged. Institutions of art and culture clearly stated their needs for an organisation that would create a network for cultural exchanges.

Thus a project group was founded, and in November 1996 the association KUBIKO was established, with more than 100 members.

Over the past year the group has concentrated on basics, such as opening an office; conducting pilot tours and workshops for adults and children; publicity; promotional campaigns in educational organisations; establishing contacts with exhibitors and with other cultural networks; dealing with financial matters among others. From January 1998 KUBIKO was fully operational.

Funding

This required pioneering work. The association targeted a wide range of sponsors: apart from contributions from public funds and members, foundations, private enterprises and other institutions were asked for support. The envisaged means of financing ran parallel to the development of the project and was one of building blocks. This meant that even with low funds a few programmes could be put in place almost immediately.

One innovative aspect of the project was that museums and other exhibiting institutions did not have to pay for KUBIKO services, so as not to deplete their existing meagre funds even further. On the other hand, contributions were expected from adult education groups, which had to pay for conducted tours and courses.

First experiences

In spite of sparse funding, the following programmes were successfully piloted:

- art appreciation workshops for adults at a regional gymnasium;
- interactive conducted tours in an art gallery;
- interactive conducted tours for schools in the Kunstmuseum in St Gallen;
- art appreciation workshops for vocational trainees;
- further education for teachers (what is museum education?);
- conducted tours of a travelling exhibition which was organised by the canton.

Although these initiatives were not professionally evaluated, participants were clearly stimulated by the interactive style of these programmes.

The end

Unfortunately, KUBIKO did not survive. Despite earlier assurances of financial support by public and private institutions, such support did not – with very few exceptions – materialise. As membership fees alone could not finance the enterprise, it had to close at the end of 1998.

Training and staff development

Teaching in adult education in Switzerland is mainly a part-time or spare-time occupation. Only the largest adult education institutions employ full-time, suitably qualified staff. This applies also to the planning, administration and organisation of adult education.

Recently there has been greater demand for teachers who have not only specific subject qualifications but also competencies in adult education. The only academic institution offering such training is the University of Geneva, with a post-diploma supplementary course in adult education. At non-university level there is the Academy for Adult Education in Lucerne, with its accredited vocational course. Further, there are training opportunities at the Swiss Association for Adult Education (SVEB) and in organisations offering education to parents.

The picture in the field of museum education is similar. Currently about 25 full-time positions – that is, 100 per cent posts – have been established; these are distributed among about 60 persons. Museum educators, too, work mainly part-time, spare-time or even voluntarily. A modest special form of training/ further education in museum education is offered by the Association of

Professionals for Education and Mediation in Museums (MPS). As previously mentioned, a post-diploma course in museology was established at Basle University in 1993. Since summer 1999 a new group has been formed with the aim of initiating a course for cultural mediation and museum education (KUVERUM) throughout Switzerland. The organisation and contents of this course are supported by the Swiss Association for Museum Education, and a pilot run is scheduled for autumn 2000. KUVERUM consists of 20 modules which can be taken alongside employment. Practical work and a dissertation are compulsory. The course is targeted at people who either possess an educational qualification or have proven experience in museum work. Apart from museum education, the curriculum includes museology, project management and specific cultural themes. It is envisaged that lottery funds from the canton Aargau will contribute towards the financial outlay for preparatory work.

In autumn 1999, Basle University offered a new modular Certificated Course on Art and Profession which aims at integrating the needs of students within the economy. It hopes to strengthen the position of art in society and the economy, and includes topics such as art and culture as sectors of employment and the economy, and the needs for training and further education in the field of cultural management.

These new training opportunities are founded on private enterprise and offer hope for a gradual increasing professionalisation of museum educators in Switzerland.

One example of such increasing professionalisation is that of the training offered by the Henry Dunant Museum (Heiden/Appenzell Ausserrhoden). This small museum, in the place where the founder of the 'Red Cross' spent his last 20 years, was established at least 30 years ago. In 1998, it underwent total refurbishment, and ensured in its planning that an interactive programme for schoolchildren and adults was included. Accordingly, a group of local female guides were professionally trained, and an interactive conducted tour was devised. During the first six months, 10 per cent of all tours were fashioned in this way – a great achievement for a small museum outside an urban conglomoration. Since then, other small museums have shown interest in this educational concept for the training of interactive guides in exhibitions, and the idea has also spread to regional museums: an example of how in Switzerland the development of education for adults and museum education can be successful outside the public sector in small stages.

Potential for progress

Cultural mediation: private or public?

Cultural mediation is slow in gaining ground. It needs a strong lobby for support and development. A new 'article for culture' in the Swiss Constitution, which was meant to gain an official lobby for culture and hence, indirectly, for cultural mediation (with strictest regard for the principle of subsidiarity) – was vetoed in 1994 by the public and the cantons. The weak position of cultural matters could thus unfortunately not be strengthened. Any future development of culture in Switzerland, a matter for private enterprise, will also affect cultural mediation, and could thus open the way for museum education.

In any case, the poor economic situation does not augur well for cultural mediation. Current financial cuts are very evident in this field: museum education posts are cut or contracted on short-term basis only. Budgets are severely reduced.

However, despite this sobering state of affairs it should be emphasised that those art institutions which do offer adult education programmes show positive results: they have experienced the high qualitative aspects of cultural mediation with adults within their own walls.

Prospects for international collaboration

As cultural mediation is unlikely to progress rapidly in Switzerland in the foreseeable future, it will be all the more important to establish collaborative ventures throughout Europe, for the following reasons:

- Exchange between professionals enhances professional and personal development.
- The offers of cultural mediation might be improved.
- Research into cultural mediation could be initiated and developed.
- Cultural mediation might gain an ideal form of support internationally, even if not nationally, and this should in time lead to a greater awareness of its benefits to both government and public in Switzerland.

References

Gonon, P and Schläfli, A, *Weiterbildung in der Schweiz: Situation und Empfehlungen*, Report, Zurich: SVEB, 1998
Krogh Loser, F, *Treffpunkt Museum: Museumspädagogik mit Erwachsenen in der Schweiz*, Bern: Peter Lang, 1996

Bibliography

Bill, S H, 'Die Interessengemeinschaft der Museumspädagogik der Schweiz (IG MUPS)', in Arbeitskreis Museumspädagogik Norddeutschland (eds), *Vermittlung im Museum, Konzepte und Konkretes zur Aus- und Weiterbildung in der Museumspaedagogik*, Bonn: Denkbar/Lesbar, 1991a, pp. 53–4
—— (1991b), 'Wen für wen durch wen museumspädagogisch ausbilden? Ausbildungsbedürfnisse in der Schweiz', in Arbeitskreis Museumspädagogik Norddeutschland (eds), *op.cit.*, (1991b) pp. 90–1

—— 'Museumspädagogik in der Schweiz: ein kurzer Uberblick', in Weschenfeld, K and Zacharias, W (eds), *Handbuch der Museumspädagogik*, pp 389–90, Dusseldorf: Schwann-Bagel, 1992

Botschaft über einen Kulturforderungsartikel in der Bundesverfassung (Art. 27septies BV) vom 6. November 1991. (Drucksache 91.073 der Eidgenossischen Drucksachen- und Materialzentrale [EDMZ] Bern)

CECA Schweiz (1992), *Museumsarbeit in der Provinz: eine Fachtagung der Arbeitsgemeinschaft der deutschsprachigen Mitglieder der CECA im ICOM und der Interessengemeinschaft Museumspädagogik Schweiz, Solothurn, 4–8 November 1992,* Basle: Arbeitsgemeinschaft der deutschsprachigen Mitglieder der CECA im ICOM, c/o Museumspadägogik Basel, Steinevorstadt 53

Clottu, G, *Beitrage fuer eine Kulturpolitik in der Schweiz: Bericht der eidgenössischen Expertenkommission fur Fragen einer schweizerischen Kulturpolitik,* Bern, 1975

Erziehungsdirektion des Kantons Zürich, Pädagogische Dienststelle für Erwachsenenbildung (1991), *Erwachsenenbildung im Kanton Zurich. Institutionen und Organisationen der Allgemeinen Erwachsenenbildung* (2nd edn), Zurich: Erziehungsdirektion des Kantons Zürich

Interessengemeinschaft Museumspadagogik Schweiz, *Was ist Museumspädagogik?* [Informationsbroschure], 1990

—— *Feuer und Flamme: eine Kampagne der Interessengemeinschaft Museumspädagogik Schweiz* [Informationsbroschure], 1994

Lapaire, C, 'Des Musées pour mieux vivre?' in Alliance culturelle romande (eds), *Les musées de la Suisse romande,* 32, 1986 pp.11–14

Museumspädagogik Basel (ed.), *Alle zusammen sind mehr als eine Summe,* Basle: Museumspadagogik Basel, 1995

Rohrer, C and Sgier, I, *Erwachsenenbildungspolitik in der Schweiz: Strukture, Rechtsgrundlagen, Tendenzen: ein Forschungsbericht,* Zurich: SVEB Schweizerische Vereinigung fur Erwachsenenbildung, 1995

SVEB (Schweizerische Vereinigung für Erwachsenenbildung), *Entwicklungsplan der SVEB für die 90er Jahre,* Zurich: SVEB, 1990

Universitat Bern, Institut für Kunstgeschichte, Koordinationsstelle für Weiterbildung, *Zertifikatskurs Kunst und Beruf: ein neuer Studiengang und öffentliche Vorträge* (Informationsbroschure), 1999

Organisations

KUVERUM – Lehrgang Kulturvermittlung/Museumspadägogik,
c/o Franziska Durr Reinhard, Aargauer Kunsthaus, Aargauerplatz, CH-5001 Aargau

MGB – Migros-Genossenschafts-Bund,
Limmatstrasse 152, Postfach, CH-8005 Zürich

MPS/ASMCM – Verband der Fachleute für Bildung und Vermittlung im Museum,
Sekretariat: Museumspädagogik Schweiz, Postfach, CH-4018 Basel

SVEB – Schweizerische Vereinigung für Erwachsenenbildung,
Orlikonerstrasse 38, Postfach, CH-8057 Zürich

21 Belgium

Willem Elias

Introduction: cultural policy

In order to understand Belgium's cultural policy with respect to museums and adult education, its political structure should first be outlined. Indeed, the cultural policy is not the same in every part of the country. It has to a large degree been determined by the various state reforms in Belgium. After World War II, the idea of a cultural autonomy of communities gained ground. Since 1965, Belgium's Ministry of Culture has been divided. The 1970 state reform meant the end of the classical united state that Belgium had been since 1830, and the following territorial districts were added to the provincial and community districts: four language regions (Dutch, French, German and the bilingual region of Brussels); three communities (Flemish, French and the German-speaking community); and three districts (Flemish, Walloon and the Brussels district). The powers of the Brussels district have only been determined since the constitutional revision of 1988 and have become a 'federal' state, which will be the name of what had been the 'national' government.

The consequences of this are particularly important in Brussels. The capital was given a high degree of autonomy and no longer belongs to the Province of Brabant. In Brussels, various governments have, to a lesser or greater extent, power over cultural matters. Although culture has been a community matter since the cultural autonomy of 1970, a number of cultural institutions still depend on the federal government. Some institutions are indeed not divisible, as the situation would become too absurd or expensive. This certainly was the case for a number of museum collections. Most of these institutions now come under the Ministry of Science Policy, which has been divided into two departments: the Department of Federal Scientific Institutions (with, among others, the Museum for Fine Arts, the Museum for Art and History, the Film Museum, the Institute for Art Patrimony, and the Museum for Central Africa); and the Department of Cultural Matters (the *Koninklijke Muntschouwburg* [Royal Munt Theatre]), the National Orchestra of Belgium and the Fine Arts Palace (including, among others, Palace, Europalia, and the Association for Exhibitions).

The theme 'Museums and adult education' assumes research from the point of view, of 'adult education' and a 'permanent education' on the one hand, and from a museum sector point of view on the other. Each of the four domains described above has its own history. The museums once had a common history as the 'Belgian museums'. 'Adult education' in Flanders cannot be separated from the Flemish emancipation battle; that is, an attempt to turn an oppressed minority language into a valuable cultural language. 'Permanent education' has never known such language motivation.

This introduction to the political landscape of Belgium shows that we cannot give a Belgian answer to the theme, but that the Flemish and the French communities must be treated separately. Brussels, too, will be separate because Brussels is the place where the federal museums are situated. There is one common point, though; namely, that there is no structured and developed adult education provision in Belgian museums. Neither the adult education sector nor the museum sector shows any interest in this. The few isolated initiatives are therefore well worth mentioning in the context of this book.

Flanders

Adult education

In Flanders, the concept of adult education is part of what is called 'people's development' and may also relate to staff training. Furthermore, it is obvious that the relationship between adult education and museums is closely linked with the sector of cultural tourism.

As stated above, the Flemish emancipation battle has been an important factor in the policy development for 'adult education'. This results, *inter alia*, in the fact that oral culture has always been more important than visual culture. Museums, on the other hand, show the remains of material culture; language is only secondary here. In Flanders there is a disproportionate relationship with respect to subsidies between, for example, theatres and libraries (as keepers of the word) and museums (as places of visual objects). Adult education is hardly interested in image. Even within the confines of amateur art practice there is no place for the visual arts.

Adult education in Flanders is active in the following areas. Training takes place either via 'associations' that arrange programmes for their members, or via 'institutions' that have a more open offer. Recently, an attempt was made to stimulate the 'departments' to develop more educational means. A characteristic of the language is 'segregation', meaning that the variety of organisations is not based on the existing educational need but on the principle that every 'political or philosophical' section has its own organisations.

The following three work areas are particularly politically orientated: political education centres (only for the parties represented in the Flemish Council); archives and documentation centres (of these parties); and the 'umbrella organisations', federations uniting the adult education organisations per political ideology and undertaking preparatory governmental work. To increase the co-ordination in this domain, the Flemish government has founded the Flemish Centre for Adult Education. Furthermore, there is the 'amateur art practice' which is also strictly segregated, and the libraries and cultural centres which are less segregated. In this structure, there is no interest in the museum as a potential adult education institution. One exception is the organisation Amarant, which organises courses in history of art in the museums or elsewhere as a preparation for a museum visit. At the same time, it regularly organises museum visits abroad in the company of experts. Its target public is by no means a neglected group; indeed, it is orientated towards the middle classes and the bourgeoisie.

The Department of Culture comprises four departments, of which Adult Education and Libraries is one. Together with the Department of Youth Work, they particularly focus on the problem of participation in socio-cultural life. The Departments of Music, Literature and Theatre, and of Visual Arts and Museums are also divisions of this Department of Culture. Both aim at the production and upkeep of culture. The Department of Museums is not closely related to that of Adult Education. Although they now belong to the same administration, they have a different history and different purpose. No bridges have been built between the interests of the 'material object' and those of that specific sector of the community.

Until recently, the government has not given much financial support to the Flemish museums, but the situation is now changing. In 1979 the Department of Museums was put in charge of formulating a Museum Decree, which came into effect on 19 December 1996. By means of this regulation, the government intends to raise the quality of museum work by setting strict conditions for recognition and by encouraging good work through the granting of subsidies. Some reorganisation was needed. Flanders has more than 300 museums. The Flemish community itself is responsible for three museums; namely, the Royal Museum for Fine Arts in Antwerp, the Castle of Gaasbeek and the Museum of Modern Arts in Antwerp. With respect to the rest of the museums, government policy is restricted to the granting of subsidies, and, since 1981, it has collaborated with a Museums Advisory Council.

The Museum Decree covers four important objectives: firstly, a better restructuring of the museum scene; secondly, an enhancement of museum work by optimising the conservation and presentation of the collections; thirdly, increasing efforts to stimulate the participation of the public by giving the museum a more welcoming atmosphere, by developing good and well-considered educational work and by presenting interesting exhibitions. Furthermore, optimum co-operation between museums and other sectors of society are to be be encouraged. As in the Netherlands and the United Kingdom, one of the priorities will be the appointment of museum consultants, one of whom will be in charge of producing guidance and advice regarding 'public work', which also implies adult education. To create 'effective cultural educational guidance' with respect to public work, the staff will not only have to be educated in the arts but will also have to have an insight into the problems of educational work. The aesthetic model (work of art, transfer of knowledge to the 'ignorant' public) is an interesting vision, but other models exist in which the public is given a more mature role, which is a condition for using the word 'education'. The organisation responsible for qualified staff is the Flemish Museums Association, which acts as a mouthpiece of the government and studies museum themes, sometimes in specialised work groups (such as the Commission for Educational Work). It is also a member of ICOM (International Council of Museums).

Adult education research in Flanders

In 1999, research was undertaken with respect to adult education in one of the three museums that are fully controlled by the Flemish community – namely, the Royal Museum for Fine Arts in Antwerp. Simultaneously, information was collected about the situation in other Flemish museums. The customary way of imparting information is by using textual material and audio-visual aids. Textual material can vary from simple information in brochures to extensive information in a museum library. Firstly, general brochures exist which may contain information about the museum's collection and history. More extensive information may be found in museum guides or catalogues. *In situ*, there are text panels. Apart from such textual materials, new information techniques exist, such as CD-ROMs and computers. Interactive multimedia programs have been developed as a help for users to determine to which information they want to have access. Furthermore, traditional educational means still exist, such as guided tours, lectures and courses.

For this chapter, information obtained from 72 of the museums approached has been analysed. Of these museums 56 per cent provided us with a written reply to our questions about their educational resources for adults. Museums giving little or no response were additionally contacted by telephone (32 per cent). This information was added to the data contained in the *Museums Guide* published by the Ministry of the Flemish Community. Finally, a search on the Internet resulted in useful information for 47 per cent of the museums. It should be noted that only 24 per cent of these museums had their own home-page, while other Internet pages resembled a brochure with mainly practical information. The educational means were classified by means of a check-list. The proportion of the various educational measures as discussed above could thus be determined.

The educational methods which aim to increase the knowledge of the museums' content and, to a lesser degree, the form, are apparently well represented. These cognitive methods can be divided into oral communication, textual material and other visual means. With respect to oral communication, it is clear that passive guided tours in the museums (83 per cent) are still considered to be the best educational means. It is the quickest way to give visitors general information on a number of works in the collection. Other methods in this category, like courses and lectures, aim at studying certain themes in depth. It also appears that few museums (less than 15 per cent) give access to such means. An important source of (cognitive) education is textual material. Brochures (89 per cent) and catalogues (76 per cent) exemplify this. Other forms of textual information, such as folders and panels, are used far less (30 per cent). The final group of educational resources is audio-visual material. It is interesting to note that a more or less equal offer exists of various 'older' methods: slides/photographs, audio and video (each in about 35 per cent of the museums), while the computer is hardly used for educational purposes. Next to the cognitive approach to art education, research was carried out on an interactive approach. Studios and active guided tours can be found here. Only a few museums offer these means for individual adult visitors. Such people have little opportunity to access art actively, to be creative themselves in this domain. Finally, two-thirds of the museums have a library open to visitors.

To check whether the educational methods in the Flemish museums are soundly based, the research done by the museums was studied. Indeed, with respect to methods developed for a particular public, it is important to know that public as well as possible. Research at the Flemish museums resulted in the following figures: 36 per cent undertook some 'research'in the form of evaluation; 77 per cent of those museums restricted themselves to producing turnstile figures. Sometimes the public is analysed – for example, the numbers of foreigners, of regional visitors are counted, as well as those from other regions visiting the museum. Some museums analyse the educational level of their visitors, but none determines how the various categories of visitors actually look at art. Only in 23 per cent of the research done (or 8 per cent of the 72 museums) are the motivation of the visitors and the evaluation of the museum analysed. The lack of attention to these research aspects obstructs the evolution to improved educational methods.

Brussels and the Walloon provinces in Belgium, the *communauté française*

Brussels, together with the Walloon provinces in Belgium, is treated as the French community. Brussels is, as stated above, also the capital of Flanders and it is independent as the Brussels Capital Region. With respect to adult education, the Brussels Capital Region does not do very much, particularly in relation to museums, which are not stimulated by their communities. Brussels has many museums.

It should be noted that provinces, cities and towns all participate to a large extent in the financing of Belgian museums. The real Belgian museums – the 'federal' museums – are situated in Brussels and are subsidised by the federal government.

In Brussels the museums have a more or less French image. They are to be bilingual: their educational services are clearly divided into Dutch- and French-speaking services, and work separately. There is also one Flemish museum, the Archive and Museum of Flemish Life in Brussels. The guidebooks also show the French character of the museums. The *Guide des Musées* (Museum Guide) lists 73 of the 405 museums in Brussels (Watteyne 1997). The *Museumgids van Oostende tot Maaseik* (Museum Guide from Ostend to Maaseik) mentions 334 museums, of which 47 are located in Brussels (Verlinden 1997). A Brussels guide mentions 80 museums on Brussels territory – let us just emphasise that Belgium has a large number of museums!

The Department of Culture and Communication of the French community is differently structured from the Flemish. The Department of Permanent Education has as an objective the lifelong education of adults in general, and the 'social cultural promotion of workers' in particular. Furthermore, independent local organisations are subsidised. The department does not, however, promote adult museum work.

The French community has no special museum decree. It works according to the Royal Decree of 1958 in which education is not listed as a specific purpose; it only subsidises the publication of 'guidance books with educational aims and publicity brochures' (art. 2. 2a). The law facilitates subsidies without many regulations, not even with respect to what should be understood by 'museum'.

The French community has one museum of its own, the *Musée royal de Mariemont* (Royal Museum of Mariemont). Eight museums are partly dependent and the rest are subsidised. But here, too, adult education with respect to museums is not really promoted or structured, although the general means of information, mentioned above in the Flemish context, apply here also. Nor are we aware of any research. Nevertheless, there are some exceptions to this situation.

Some examples of good practice

Brussels

The Royal Museum for Art and History

This museum was the first to undertake educational work. In 1904, guided tours for the public were introduced; in 1922 an educational department was founded. The purpose was, in the context of democratising the culture, to make the museum accessible to every sector of the public – also to non-specialists. Attempts were made to let the works of art speak for themselves, to decode the messages, to learn to read the signs of the past.

The initiative *Dynamusée* was begun in 1971. It involved opening up studios in which adults could freely express their creativity and gain experience with respect to design and the use of materials (ceramics). Since 1970, thematic exhibitions have been organised within the framework of the Museum for Blind People, and since 1975, a special room has been set aside for this purpose. Blind people can touch a number of authentic works of art which are selected on the basis of their tactile properties. The museum has done pioneer work in this area, and many more museums are making use of its experience. With respect to methodology, an interesting form of 'indirect' adult education is that the education department tries to stimulate interest in certain objects by telling stories about them to children. As this is a real family event, adults will also learn, and questions will be asked by children which adults would not pose – for fear of appearing ignorant.

The Royal Museum for Fine Arts of Belgium

The interesting aspect of this museum is the particular approach to visual arts. Works of art are accompanied by contemporary texts that are read, or by contemporary music that is played on instruments depicted in a particular painting. There have also been experiments with dances, but in those cases it was the choreographer who chose the décor in the museum.

An interesting initiative for adults is the project *Museum met Klasse* (Museum with classroom), an excellent way of increasing accessibility for the public. The monthly magazine *Klasse* (Classroom) is freely distributed to all teachers by the Flemish community. Since 1969, the magazine *Klasse voor Ouders* (Classroom for Parents) has been published it is a magazine which relates closely to that for teachers but concentrates on themes with respect to the family as well as the classroom situation. Traditionally, the museum organises 'open houses for teachers'. This could be called a form of adult education because on those occasions teachers receive a model guided tour of the museum with additional didactic comments. In the beginning there was not much interest in this project. However, through co-operating with *Class* in 1995, interest grew rapidly, with more than 2,500 teachers taking part. For many of them, this was their first contact with a museum. Via *Class for Parents*, a Sunday programme was devised for the family: 10 educators explained 10 works of art. Each session lasted about 15 minutes and was adapted to the very varied audiences. This was repeated throughout the entire Sunday; everyone could set their own pace.

Since 1977, a *Klaas voor Jongeren* (Classroom for young people) has been organised and, using the above method, the project 'The secret of Picasso' was initiated. Young adults (up to 20 years of age) are given the opportunity during the summer months to discover the museum collection under professional guidance, either on their own or with friends.

The Royal Belgian Institute for Natural Sciences

Apart from the usual guided tours and courses, this museum also offers an extensive *'informatheek'* for interested amateurs. Although most initiatives are aimed at young people, adults, too, are closely involved in the projects. The museum pioneers work in the area of new channels of scientific information, such as multimedia and the Internet.

Flanders

Museum Sunday in south Antwerp

An example follows of co-operation among three museums in Antwerp – Royal Museum for Fine Arts, the Provincial Museum for Photography, Museum of Modern Art, which are located within a short distance of one another. Although they are very different, the idea arose in their education departments to link their collections in a specific way. They wanted to neutralise the artificial distance between old and modern art, between photographs and paintings, and at the same time effect collaboration with respect to content between the educational services of the three museums.

They therefore looked for a common theme that could be worked out by three guides, and a Sunday programme was devised. Each of the museums could be visited, each with a different focus, depending on the individual expertise of the guides. The project aims to reach interested adults with a notion of art who wish to obtain a deeper insight and break through the frontiers between the different disciplines. It began in the autumn of 1996, with the title, chosen by the guides, of 'About portraits'. In a second programme they look for 'Traces of the *fin de siècle*' (past and present).

The Museum of Modern Art

Several educational assistants organised a half or full day's workshops for adults in which the interaction with the participants and their own experiences are central. To reach this aim, various 'watch-and-do' tasks are included in the tour.

The Provincial Museum of Modern Art (Ostend): educational guidance to the exhibition from Ensor to Delvaux

In the course of this exhibition, a number of educational guidance possibilities were devised for the public, taking into account the different age groups, including adults. An educational work-book for young people and teachers was published for the various age groups and the respective teachers. It gives a short introduction in the form of a brief text on aesthetics, discusses two works of art per artist in detail and sets various tasks. The book has been a help for teachers and students in preparing visits to the exhibition with their class and in completing the set tasks during that visit or subsequently in class. In determining the tasks, special attention was given to the process of looking at a painting.

The Gallo Roman Museum (Tongres)

As from 1998, the Gallo Roman Museum intends to increase its educational offering to young people and adults, a group constituting over 40 per cent of the total number of visitors. The museum already co-operates with the Davids Fund, the Institute for Archaeological Heritage, and Amarant. On a regular basis, courses, workshops and lectures have been organised. Temporary exhibitions are being enriched with relevant varying programmes aimed at a young adult public. Adapted standard guided tours will be organised, lasting about 90 minutes, which will show additional replica objects and images. If requested, a particular period can be focused upon. This is possible since the museums have fully trained their guides for such standard guided tours.

The Gallo Roman Museum is hoping to organise a number of thematic guided tours for groups, such as 'Critical study of archaeological material and interpretations: is there an evolution in archaeology?'

The Museum for Industrial Archaeology and Textiles (Ghent)

This museum organises guided tours in the town in which, as well as focusing on heritage, additional explanations are given with respect to the social history of this textile-focused town.

The Museum 'Doctor Guislain' (Ghent)

The museum treats the history of psychiatry. It also organises a 'fitness walk' in Ghent, with special attention paid to places where, among others, mentally ill people are taken, such as hospitals, guest houses, churches, orphanages. In other words, its theme is social history from a different perspective.

People's education

Amarant Study and Exhibition Centre

This is the only association within the decree of people's education focusing entirely on art education for adults, and organising this frequently within museums. Amarant's areas of specialisation are visual arts, philosophy and drama. In these domains, Amarant undertakes research into historic as well as current developments. The objectives of the organisation are to offer information, to handle and order different levels of knowledge (both learning to learn and increasing knowledge are possible at Amarant), and to enhance insights about visual art, philosophy and drama and their history. Amarant thus develops a vast variety of initiatives from a recognition of the complexity and authenticity of the subjects. This is expressed in courses and lectures, in day excursions, accompanied visits to exhibitions and study tours.

Federation of Registered Flemish Cultural Centres

This federation co-ordinates the Flemish cultural centres. They sometimes co-operate with museums, as in the following example:

Le Musée du Petit Format

This 'museum on a small scale' was originally intended for children, but is also used for adult education. It comprises two cupboards with drawers and doors in which about 160 two- and three-dimensional pieces of art by Belgian and foreign artists are hidden. These cupboards are transported to a museum. There is also a game involved, which consists of an educational workbook, and for which training sessions are organised for the educational assistants.

Centre for Amateur Arts

The project *Kunstkader* (Art frame) aims to support the artistic work of mentally ill people. It also wants to raise sociological appreciation for such work. *Kunstkader* is a result of the KuMen project (art for the mentally ill) which was stimulated by the Toemeka Base Movement and which, since 1990, has been a project for cultural integration (Van Labeke 1995).

Guided tours and introductory visits adapted to the level of mentally ill people are the means for achieving this objective. A standard visit is organised as follows: in a particular institution assistants prepare a visit to, for example, the Ghent Bijloke Museum with a small group of about 8 to 10 patients. The assistants use the educational material supplied by the museum staff. Preparation, which takes about three hours, uses stories, pictures and drawings, and so on, with the aim of making the programme colourful and inspiring. Sometimes people are themselves asked to draw or paint, or to engage in role-play. Some days later, the Bijloke Museum is visited. The lively session lasts about two hours and links up with the preparatory work. All kinds of educational materials are used to make the guided tour as lively as possible. Furthermore, 'work and picture' books are used, the showpieces of the KuMen project. These are mainly produced by the museum staff themselves, supported by external experts. During the visit, they serve as workbooks; afterwards, they keep their value as picture books at home. About a fortnight later, the visitors come together again to discuss their experiences in the museum. The books are used again as work material.

The main problem for this project is the fact that the museum staff responsible for it work as volunteers, and thus cannot give the degree of commitment expected of a full-time worker.

The Walloon provinces in Belgium

In the Walloon provinces there are even fewer projects focused on adult education in museums. The Department of Permanent Education confirms that no specific initiatives are known in this respect however, the Department of Cultural Heritage, the umbrella organisation for museums, lists some good examples:

The Industrial Museum

This museum is concerned with preserving the technological, economic and social patrimony of the region around Charleroi. Here adults can learn how to forge metal by using traditional methods, for example.

Le Musée des Beaux Arts

A good example of co-operation between an association from the 'permanent education' sector and the museum is found in the Musée des Beaux Arts in Charleroi. Visits are organised in collaboration with *Femmes Prévoyantes Socialistes* exploratory. The target group is women, which determines the stance taken. The accent lies on artistic vocabulary, aesthetics, and on aesthetic ways of looking at art.

Le Musée de Louvain-la-Neuve (Catholic University of Louvain)

With a varied collection, this museum runs a number of programmes for adults, mainly in groups. There is also a special guided tour for blind people.

Le Muséum Préhistosite de Ramioul

This museum has installed educational workshops for children and for adults. A prehistoric project can be activated by working with silex, making ropes and so on. This takes place in a framework in which three historic houses have been reconstructed.

Training and staff development

Training is given by two museum associations (one Flemish, one French), both connected to ICOM. The training is focused on workshops for museum staff assistants and is also offered to museum attendants and volunteers. In Belgium, the latter is rather restricted with respect to museums, with the exception of the Friends of Museums associations. In co-operation with Platform for Volunteer Work, this topic is now receiving attention, and as from 1998, training was to be organised for museum attendants with, among others, a programme focusing on reception techniques and the development of communication skills.

In the framework of the above-mentioned KuMen project, training sessions are organised leading to a Certificate of Assistant Training Work with Mentally Disadvantaged People.

Conclusions

General

It is clear that in Belgium links between museums and adult education are rare. The two worlds have little or no contact. In the adult education area, the museum is hardly considered as an institution with educational possibilities. Indeed, the museum has an elitist history, while adult education is a result of a democratic movement for the benefit of the underprivileged. The museum world, from its perspective, gives a different meaning to 'education' from that understood by 'training' in the sector of social-cultural work. This is well illustrated by the following statement by a staff assistant to the education department of one museum:

> Education and communication must be the link between science and the public by translating the scientific research to a broad public, comprising various target groups. It must try to increase the quality of looking – looking at unique objects of the museum.
>
> (Lambrecht 1997: 90)

Museum education is a means of understanding the uniqueness of objects, not to developing the uniqueness of the spectator, which is the aim of the work in education. The historically developed difference between museums and adult education is also expressed in the terminology, museologists speak about their 'world', while adult educators speak about the 'field'.

Can change be expected? In a way. This is shown by the increasing (although still small) number of initiatives described above as examples of good practice. Most of them have been developed very recently. The situation is that the museum no longer considers, with respect to education, the aesthetic point of view as the only correct one. The same can be said about the natural historical approach. This way of looking at things could be generalised as a 'scientific approach', whereby education is reduced to compromise. Those concerned with adult education should be aware that a museum no longer implies the pursuit of an elitist policy, but that it is an open space where a variety of educational initiatives can be organised. Museums are and remain the archives of nature and culture; museums are worlds.

The Edufora project

Theoretically, the relation between adult education and museums could be stimulated by the plan that was initiated in 1997 to create educational co-operation in Flanders under the name *Edufora*. Under this plan 80 to 85 per cent of the educational offer to adults is aimed at the professions, thus leaving only 15 to 20 per cent for others. The aim is to stimulate collaboration between all sectors.

The *Edufora* has a threefold task. Within six months of its foundation, an 'educational map' of the region, showing the offer, must be drawn. Within the next six months, the organisation must link this educational map to an analysis of current and future training needs in the region. This 'needs report' will show gaps and overlaps in the offer. Finally, the *Edufora* must produce within 18 months an 'educational plan' which shows how and with what divisions of labour trainers will overcome such gaps and overlaps (De Vos 1997).

The question is whether this will result in eradicating the gaps in adult education within the museums. Indeed, adult education has its own institutions, the cultural centres and training institutions. But bridges may be built.

References

De Vos, H, 'Edufora, een nieuw geluid, een nieuwe morgen?' *Koepel*, 5(3), 1997, pp.10–12.

Elias, W *et al*, *Truth without facts: selected papers from the first three international conferences on adult education and the arts*, Brussels: VUB Press, 1995

Grosjean, E, 'Administration de la jeunesse et de l'éducation permanente: bilan 1996', *Les Cahiers DAJEP* 29, 1997

Lambrecht, G, 'Kunsteducatie en de Vlaamse musea'. Unpublished dissertation, Brussels: Vrije Universiteit Brussels, 1997

Vandendries, H *et al* (eds), *Rijkdom en diversiteit van de educatieve diensten van de musea in België: richesse et diversités des services éducatiefs des musées en Belgique*, Brussels: VMV & AFM, 1997

Van Labeke, S (ed.), *Wij horen erbij, geschiedenis van 25 jaar Toemeka Basisbeweging Vrijvilligers*, Kessel-Lo, 1995

Verlinden, J (ed.), *Museumgids van Oostende tot Maaseik*, Brussels, 1997

Watteyne, D (ed.), *Guide des musées Wallonie Bruxelles*, Brussels, 1997

Organisations

Government

Ministère de la Communauté française
    Service du Patrimoine Culturel
    44 Boulevard Léopold II
    B-1080 Brussels
    tel: +32-2-413.23.11
    fax: +32-2-413.24.15
Service de l'Education Permanente
(idem)

Ministerie van de Vlaamse Gemeenschap
    Afdeling Beeldende Kunst en Musea
    Parochiaanstraat 15
    B-1000 Brussels
    tel: +32-2-501.68.51
    fax: +32-2-501.68.43
Dienst Volksontwikkeling
    Markiesstraat 1
    B-1000 Brussels

tel: +32-2-507.42.44
fax: +32-2-507.42.39

Associated with ICOM

Vlaamse Museumvereniging (VMV)
  Commissie Educatieve Werking
  Savoyestraat 6
  B-3000 Leuven
  tel/fax: +32-16-22.69.06

Association Francophone des Musées de Belgique (AFM)
  Commission Éducation
  8 Rue Neuve
  B-7000 Mons
  tel: +32-65-40.53.08
  fax: +32-65-34.77.63

22 Luxembourg

Bettina Heldenstein and Herbert Maly

Brief overview

Luxembourg cannot claim to have a long tradition of adult education. However, the Ministry of Education has been organising evening courses for adults since 1965, and basic courses like post-primary education, languages, secretarial work have been extended to more general and cultural education, such as art history and philosophy. Some courses on art history, including guided tours or conferences, are also organised by the Ministry. Especially in more recent years, evening courses proposed by the Ministry have become increasingly popular, and there is a constant proliferation of new subjects. For example, some courses are organised to help (re)integrate women or immigrants into professional life. A spectacular growth in the number of courses can be observed from year to year.

Museums offering special educational programmes for adults is not something Luxembourgers have experienced. The National Museum for Art and History, for example, has not succeeded in installing special adult education programmes.

Only since 1995, when Luxembourg was Europe's Cultural City, has there been a general and sustained interest by the local public. The sheer abundance of events designed for a large public and the educational work (guided tours) were all efforts made to familiarise people with culture. Guided tours for tourists had, in fact, been available previously, but the people of Luxembourg did not make use of this offering and were more or less left to their own devices.

At the end of 1995 a forum for contemporary art was installed in the former nineteenth century Casino bourgeois. The Casino Luxembourg became, meanwhile, a medium for familiarising the public with contemporary art. As a forum it evolved into the long-awaited place of exchange and creativity, promotion and discussion.

Art courses, conferences, lectures and workshops are organised in the same place. It became more than just an exhibition hall, rather a place for encounters for learning and for documentation. There is no documentation centre for art in Luxembourg, and art education is still very traditional. Traditional guided tours for adults represent the normal form of adult education, although efforts are being made to encourage teachers to use the museum. Thus, at the beginning of every new exhibition, teachers are invited by the educational service to undertake a special visit. Theoretical and practical training is offered to teachers in collaboration with the Ministry for Education. Motivating teachers to transmit *their* interest to pupils seems as important as motivating children or young people.

Once a month guided tours adapted to the interests of senior citizens are arranged. Furthermore, workshops and projects lasting more than one day are organised for disabled people and immigrants.

However, all this is only the beginning of adult educational work. We often do not achieve the success we were planning to have. It is very difficult to break through because the concept of lifelong learning is not familiar or embedded in people's habits in Luxembourg.

Examples

One year (1997), the Casino Luxembourg organised, in co-production with the Centre National de l'Audiovisuel, workshops for mentally and physically disabled and socially disadvantaged people. The concept of this work was formulated by the educational service of the Casino in collaboration with the Luxembourg artist Antoine Prum.

One of the aims of the project was to produce a videotape that could be directed and edited with the participation of these people. For each exhibition, one group – coming from a Luxembourg institute or association for disabled or disadvantaged persons – was invited by the Casino Luxembourg to participate in a four-session workshop. During the first session, the group, guided by Antoine Prum, would usually 'discover' the exhibition. The subsequent sessions consisted of activities which might happen partly outside the forum but which always related to the artistic concept of the exhibition.

In most of these workshops, group members' views provided a basis for analysis and explanation of the artworks they were shown. Their choice and their perceptions guided the cameraman to focus on images and details in which they were personally interested. Afterwards, some of these themes were developed in workshops or activities in or outside the Casino Luxembourg. To our surprise, they really enjoyed the opportunity to expose themselves to the camera.

The aim of this project should not be considered as a therapy for disabled or disadvantaged persons; rather, it was to offer a positive and delightful experience to those adults who rarely had the opportunity to move out of their everyday surroundings. For once, they were the centre of interest, and they decided on their own how the project was going to be developed.

The Centre National de l'Audiovisuel offers, each year, theoretical and practical training in different audio-visual disciplines such as photography and cinema.

COOPERATIONS

The idea of COOPERATIONS is the result of projects devised to make it possible for able and disabled people to work creatively and artistically in an open forum. It was proposed by artists who used their talents to develop models for intervention in the public arena and social environment.

COOPERATIONS builds a platform upon which people with different social and intellectual backgrounds can avail themselves of offers to participate in a creative project, workshops or training; and upon which connections are made between art, social and physical environments.

The model COOPERATIONS describes, on one hand, communication and expression by people who work together in various ways, and on the other, an organisational and thematic framework which attempts to take into account the disparate interests and needs of these people. This model, which has to be flexible, is based on the criteria of resource, quality and development.

- *Resource* means the creative potential which is inherent in every person, every place and every situation, and which forms the most important starting point for the development of a project.
- *Quality* applies to innovative, authentic or intensive aspects of a person, of a communication, course or result of a project, and transmits these as ethical, social, aesthetic or financial values.
- *Development* means: at individual level – acquisition of know-how, technical and social learning, training up to formal education; at local level – participation in the cultural and socio-economic development of the city of Wiltz; at regional level: integration into the developmental initiatives of the region; at supra-regional level – participation in networks for the advancement of sharing experiences, dissemination, training and research.

The programme of COOPERATIONS consists of longer-term educational initiatives, short-term training workshops and projects of varying lengths. These initiatives are group-focused and utilise the various projects as means of training. A number of COOPERATIONS projects, such as Jardin de Wiltz or Kannersummer, were already in existence before the founding of the organisation and have influenced subsequent work methods, format and development of the programme.

Some examples of COOPERATIONS initiatives are set out below.

ArtWorkshop

This is a programme within the COOPERATIONS vocational training scheme addressing people with learning difficulties and/or mental health problems. It is supported by the Ministry of Labour and the European Commission.

Exclusion from numerous social processes, including formal learning, and marginalisation have become major aspects of the biographies of the ArtWorkshop's members. The ArtWorkshop provides an environment for individual development, artistic production and expertise for training. The personalities of the participants, their interaction and productions form an artistic framework which affects the concept and the daily working process, linking art with empowerment.

The training scheme challenges all participants, disabled and non-disabled artists

- to question, sharpen and broaden perception;
- to discover personal resources and use them for personal and artistic development;
- to learn new social competences;
- to acquire the necessary artistic skills and techniques;
- to develop authentic forms of expression; and
- to interpret their environment.

Its aims are

- the improvements of participants' individual, social and professional opportunities;
- the production of authentic and high-quality artistic products; and
- public awareness of the individual and group contributions to contemporary arts.

The project started in 1994 with a six-year pilot phase. The ArtWorkshop is located in a studio at the Project Centre Gruberbierg. Activities take place in the studio, in the Jardin de Wiltz and at events in Luxembourg and abroad.

The members of the ArtWorkshop have acted successfully as workshop leaders in Germany, Austria, Belgium, Great Britain and Luxembourg. Various exhibitions in Luxembourg and Belgium have addressed a wider public and received positive response from the media.

Creative Workshop

This is a workshop scheme, started in 1990. It has involved groups of young people and adults, mostly people with learning difficulties or mental health problems.

The scheme is developed on request. Duration, format and activities are based on and adapted to the interests and motivation of the participants and artists. The working process covers a broad spectrum of media used: theatre, video, painting, building of objects, temporary installations outdoors or cooking.

It is directed by artists who provide support

- to explore imagination;
- for experimentation with materials, colours, forms, movement, sound or rhythm;
- for broadening perception of people, subjects or the environment and relate to them;

- to enter verbal and non-verbal dialogue;
- to influence the working process, space and working products;
- to define preferences and make decisions; and
- to develop personal expression and interpretation.

The scheme is based on the idea that each participant, each working situation or space offers potential and resources. In order to discover, explore and develop them, the artists provide know-how and experience and appropriate 'tools'. The artists are both leaders and participants. They are responsible for creating a workshop structure which permits everyone involved to

- identify with it;
- enjoy themselves; and
- value their experience.

The scheme is a space for development. It does not aim to acquire techniques which are defined beforehand or specific artistic media within a teaching programme. It does involve aspects of learning, or might contain elements of therapy; but it is not defined as a teaching or therapy programme.

It needs a flexible structure, allowing

- space for individual preferences;
- group communication;
- freedom of expression;
- productive restrictions; and
- development of activities according to opportunities that may arise, available material or weather conditions.

COOPERATIONS has also initiated a non-governmental organisation (NGO) which, since 1995, connects grassroots organisations with higher education institutions. Its first project, begun in 1997, is the International Art and Environment Pilot Project which is under the auspices of the European Voluntary Service.

Since its opening in 1996, the City History Museum has offered its visitors a varied educational programme, and in 1998 the museum was awarded a special commendation at the European Museum of the Year Awards, partly because of the quality of its educational programme.

In addition to regular visits, conferences and workshops, special activities in connection with the permanent collection and temporary exhibitions have been organised. For example, the museum offered a visit-dinner-concert event during the Putty Stein exhibition, which treated the subject of the Luxembourg musician at the beginning of the twentieth century.

During the archaeological excavations at St Nicolas church in the centre of the city, the museum organised visits to the excavations and afterwards offered visitors refreshments.

In 1997, the museum featured an exhibition on the modernist architecture of the 1930s, and besides the usual visit/conference/workshop programme it arranged a bus trip for the elderly in order to see the buildings shown in the exhibition. Coffee and cake were offered after the cultural programme.

In the summer months of 1997 and 1998, the museum organised guided tours by bicycle of the remnants of Luxembourg's fortifications. Three walking tours of the old parts of the City of Luxembourg have already been planned (the Renaissance town, the medieval town, and the town of Louis XIV).

At the beginning of 1998, the museum mounted an exhibition concerning the medieval towns of Luxembourg, Metz (in France) and Trier (in Germany). Bus trips were organised, enabling the public to visit these three towns.

Training and staff development

Most of the educational staff working in museums are freelancers. In general, they are employed on the strength of their experience or qualifications.

The National Museum for Art and History, the Casino Luxembourg and the City History Museum together organised a seminar for guides employed in these three institutions. This seminar focused on methods of guiding and how to communicate culture to the public. A new seminar, with the same presenter, is being planned for the future.

As most of our guides are freelancers, they work for different institutions simultaneously. The institutions propose training and seminars for them all in *process* rather than *content* skills.

Education staff in museums are given the option of taking part in staff development programmes annually.

Potential for progress

In the last five years two new museums have opened in Luxembourg: the Nature Museum and the City History Museum. Efforts are made to attract people to these museums, and exhibitions are organised to attract not only specialists or scientists but also a much larger public.

The Casino Luxembourg has been transformed into an exhibition hall for contemporary art. Its role is to teach the public to appreciate contemporary art and, initially, to promote the new Museum for Modern Art and encourage the local public to visit and appreciate exhibitions.

The project for a Museum for Modern Art Grand-Duc Jean has been in progress for a number of years and will be completed in the year 2001. The educational work of the museum is already in preparation, and teachers, educational staff from existing museums or persons involved in the Ministry for

Culture and Education in Luxembourg are deciding how it should be organised.

Museum education in Luxembourg is relatively recent. It is open to the provision of a wide range of educational events. There is also a need for the recruitment of more staff, including adult education specialists.

Bibliography

Christophory, J, 'La Ville de Luxembourg, un carrefour des cultures', in *La Ville de Luxembourg, du château des comtes à la métropole européenne*, Anvers: Fonds Mercator Paribas, 1994, p.335

Hansen, J, 'Luxembourg', in *Manifesta 2*, Luxembourg: Agence luxembourgeoise d'action culturelle, 1998, p.246

Lunghi, E, (1994), 'L'art et la ville', in *La Ville de Luxembourg, du château des comtes à la métropole européenne*, Powers: Fonds Mercator Paribas (1998), p.351

Ouquiquoi: le repertoire culturel du Grand-Duchy de Luxembourg, Ministère de la Culture, Luxembourg

23 The Netherlands

Bastiaan van Gent

In the Netherlands, approximately 850 museums are open to the public, making it the country with the highest museum density in the world (Elshout 1990: 157). A process of differentiation and specialisation has led to a great and often confusing variety of collections in the areas of art, history, nature, ethnology, science and technology.

Generally speaking, museums can fulfil at least eight functions: a museum assembles objects (the museum as *collector*), preserves or restores them (*conservator*), does research (*investigator*), provides access to the collections and organises exhibitions (*curator*), informs people about its activities and takes care of its public relations (*communicator*), entertains its clientele (*animator*), tries to reach those who are outside (*activator*), and teaches children and adults (*educator*) (van Gent 1997: 80).

In this chapter, the term 'education of adults' is used rather loosely as an amalgam of communication, animation, activation and education. The phrase 'adult education' will refer more specifically to non-vocational liberal education with activating overtones and emancipatory intentions. It will be argued that in present-day Dutch museum education, the functions of communicator, animator and educator are often combined within the same service or even the same person, while the function of activator has practically disappeared from the stage.

Dutch museum education: an overview

After World War II, great expectations for a new beginning were disturbed by intense feelings of pessimism. 'The masses' were seen as threatened by a moral decline that was attributed to the German occupation of the Netherlands, the chaotic period of transition after the liberation and the spreading secularisation. Educational intervention and cultural diffusion appeared to be urgent tasks.

For a long period of time, subsequent Dutch governments considered art to be a 'vital condition' for individual and society. According to the text which introduced the 1949 budget, the state 'had to remove barriers and open new possibilities to allow its citizens to besome acquainted with the cultural heritage' (Oosterbaan Martinius 1990: 72). Two years later, the government appointed a Committee for the Development of Museum Visits which completed its report in 1952. Museums were said to have "a social duty". According to the committee, this implied that "through information and otherwise, these visits should be fruitful in every possible way" (Vaessen 1986: 145).

The committee advised the appointment of 'pedagogical advisers' to organise and co-ordinate specific activities for the general public. In 1952, the first Pedagogical Department within a museum in the Netherlands was founded at the Municipal Museum in The Hague, and museums in Amsterdam, Rotterdam and Leiden soon followed this example. Meanwhile, the visionary director of the Amsterdam Municipal Museum had gone a different way: whereas others tried to impose traditional norms of beauty on the working class, he preferred to show what was at that time a revolutionary kind of art. A middle course was chosen by the foundation Public Art Treasures, which was established in 1957. This organisation distributed reproductions and provided lectures, at first on the radio and later also on television, 'in order to reach the masses in all corners of the country' (Overduin 1983: 8).

Five years later, the Pedagogical Department of the Municipal Museum in The Hague changed its name to 'Educational Service' so as to sound less paternalistic. American innovations were introduced and the 'cultivation of the whole person' became the primary goal; exhibitions needed 'to touch people where soul and mind, feeling and intellect overlap' (De Gruyter 1965: 177). Guided tours were predominant, but mechanical devices like slide projectors were used from time to time. The reputation of these pioneering activities remained dubious. Although in some museums a special space was made available for educational purposes, interested visitors had to use the service entrance 'in order not to be a nuisance to the museum public' (Overduin, 1983:9). Nevertheless, these exploratory efforts would soon bear fruit.

In 1965, the arts became the responsibility of a new Ministry of Culture, Recreation and Social Work. A broad welfare policy began to take shape, now that the Dutch government was of the opinion that more provisions for cultural and social well-being should accompany the provisions for material prosperity. Two years later, a national Working Group for Educational Services was founded, in which museum educators combined their forces. The timing was fortuitous. At that moment, leading figures in the welfare state began to consider art as a way to raise the social consciousness of the underprivileged. Educational departments were set up in every major museum, and in many ways they even overshadowed the activities of other departments. Within the museums, new and provocative methods of display were being developed, while the borders between high culture and popular art, and between temporary happenings and permanent arrangements, became vague. On behalf of those who had remained outside, strategies of community organisation and adult education were often combined. Experiments took place with mobile exhibitions and expositions in windows of major shopping malls (Overduin 1983: 11).

In a memorandum published in 1976, the government announced its intention to diffuse culture as part of a strategy to spread knowledge, power and income. Museums were considered to be institutions of public interest and a branch of the welfare services (Ministerie van CRM 1976: 10). Education of the public was seen as a primary task of museums. Unfortunately, no extra money was made available for the museum world as a whole, which aggravated the feelings of unease and jealousy among the other segments. Soon, their time would come again.

During the 1980s, in the aftermath of the international oil crisis, the edifice of the Dutch welfare state began to show many fissures. The government confronted the museums with important cuts in their allocations and a drastic change of cultural policy. With regard to requests for funding, 'the criterion of artistic quality would be decisive' (Oosterbaan Martinius 1990: 72). The state exchanged its educational policy for a cultural one and gave priority to the conservation of high-quality objects. The pursuit of social emancipation was abandoned.

This provoked little protest from the traditional elite within the museum hierarchy, which had become irritated by the welfare offensive. The policy was also welcomed by those who feared that a significant increase in the number of visitors would endanger the contemplation of the aesthetic mystery or that educational directives would hinder an open-minded appreciation.

At the same time, the welfare state underwent a metamorphosis into a 'caring community'. A new memorandum, issued in 1985 by a restructured Ministry of Welfare, Health and Culture, announced that in the near future state museums would have to stand on their own feet; the government preferred to play an encouraging rather than an executive role (Ministerie van WVC 1985: 7).

In 1994, the responsibility for cultural affairs was transferred from the Ministry of Welfare, Health and Culture to a newly formed Ministry of Education, Culture and Sciences. In a way, the public care for museums returned to the house where it had been lodged from 1945 to 1965. A year later, this Ministry addressed the cultural problems of the Netherlands as a recent multi-cultural country. Culture should not be a fenced reserve but a backbone on the road towards 'unity in diversity'. As a form of permanent education, the museum was required to make the Dutch heritage accessible to ethnic minorities and to present their cultural products to the indigenous population (Ministerie van OCW 1995: 6–9, 16–17). Some interpreted this request as a promising sign of a revival of art education, others considered it as mere lip-service to the multi-cultural cause since, at the same time, museums were being asked to become market-orientated and to look for more outside support from corporate sponsors and private donors.

Educational types and activities

Different types of museums have emerged in the Netherlands since World War II. Among art museums, for example, the following types can be identified from an educational point of view:

The art museum as a temple for sacrosanct beauty: Until around 1965, museums were considered to be secular churches where a devout silence had to be observed. In a period of rapid social change and the decline of organised religion, museums could perhaps offer some compensation for increasing feelings of loss of identity. Contact with high art would have a civilising effect on the lower classes. In the struggle against 'the danger of massification', many activities of art museums were aimed at moral uplifting (Oosterbaan Martinius 1990: 51).

The art museum as a school for social emancipation: From 1965 till 1985, museums became educational institutions. To break down the image of the museum as 'an instrument of the dominant powers', methods of outreach work were applied and co-operation was sought with Neighbourhood Centres in working-class areas, and with politically motivated volunteers (Ganzeboom and Haanstra 1989: 26).

The art museum as a commercial centre of cultural excellence: From 1985 on, the government's new emphasis on privatisation compelled museums to solicit corporate sponsorship, to organise attractive and financially profitable 'mega-expositions', to sell luxurious catalogues and to run fancy restaurants. The museum director became the manager of a cultural enterprise. In many museums art promotion took the place of art education (Willink 1987: 67).

By and large, every type of museum can be characterised by a salient activity with regard to the education of adults, broadly defined. In a way, these types form a series of images with 'family resemblances'. From 1945 to 1965, the educational activities of art museums can be characterised as *edification*. *Adult education* was typical for the period between 1965 and 1985. Since then, providing *entertainment* has become the predominant activity. At present, neologisms like 'edu-tainment' and 'info-tainment' are the postmodern catchwords (Haanstra and Oostwoud Wijdenes 1996: 26).

Around 1980, museum educators held at least three conceptions of their activities. The 'disciplinary' approach stressed the elucidation of the collection through a transfer of scholarly information. In the 'thematic' approach, the collection was not seen as a goal in itself, but as a means to serve a strictly cultural purpose. The 'emancipatory' approach also emphasised the intermediary function of the collection, but strove for an explicit social goal (Haanstra and Holman 1980: 15). Nowadays, the emancipatory intentions have vanished, although natural history museums with their environmental concerns and ethnological museums with their multi-cultural interests can still represent the progressive spirit. At the same time, the barriers between the disciplinary and the thematic approaches have been removed.

The tasks which are concerned with the general public can be categorised as *active presentation* (museum education), *passive presentation* (the actual display), and *public information* (communication management) (Ministerie van CRM 1976: 48–52). A comparison between the state of the art in 1980 and the present shows little change in the methods and technology of Dutch museum education.

In the area of *active presentation*, the method most often used is still the guided tour. Since this is labour-intensive, the actual work is often done by volunteers who are trained by education officers. Lectures inside or outside museums take second place, followed by projects or trails from one art object to another, while many museums organise special events or associate themselves with nation-wide activities. As far as *passive presentation* is concerned, panels with written texts remain the most important vehicle. Videos are now more favoured than slides. The use of computers and other electronic media is much discussed, but their application is more in the field of recording the collection than of assisting the public.

With regard to *public information*, a major part of the available time is spent on the maintenance of good public relations and the development of marketing strategies. Often this work is combined with educational activities, especially since the privatisation of the state museums (Haanstra and Oostwoud Wijdenes 1996: 32,43,49). Free courses, for example, are offered to employees of a sponsoring organisation.

Museum educators as professionals

A profession can be distinguished from other occupations by several features. Its members belong to an association that sets standards for their occupational competence and ethical behaviour and tries to protect their field of expertise against invasion by other professions. The professional training takes place in institutions of higher education. These training schools strive to co-operate with universities and other specialised agencies, because fundamental to the process of professionalisation is the creation of a body of knowledge fit to serve as a basis for the development of specific methods and technology. Seen from this perspective, a modest form of professionalisation has taken place in the field of museum education.

As early as 1926, the heads of museums had founded the association Directors' Day, named after the one-day symposia which enabled them 'to share their thoughts on the difficulties facing them in their work'. World War II had interrupted these regular meetings, but in 1947 the association was re-established as Museum Day and in 1970 it became the Dutch Museum Association which was to open its doors to anyone whose work was connected with museums. A year later, the Working Group Educational Services became a separate section, but their status within the organisation was still low. In the first issue of *Museumvisie*, the professional journal of the association, its Board expressed the fear that 'the political principle of cultural diffusion will be handled in such a way that it will cause a levelling of the museum tasks' (Nederlandse Museumvereniging 1977: 4).

The Dutch Museum Association organises in-service training and refresher courses. As a forum for discussion, the symposia still constitute the centre of its activities. Recently, this association has decided to become more an organisation of museums than of individual members in order to improve the promotion of common interests in a period of increasing privatisation and commercialisation (Nederlandse Museumvereniging 1996: 5).

In 1986, the International Council of Museums (ICOM) adopted a Code of Professional Ethics. It took another four years before this subject became a matter for discussion at a general assembly of the Dutch Museum Association (Van Mensch 1989: 98). In 1991, a general 'Line of Conduct' was accepted; a separate code for museum educators does not exist.

The Reinwardt Academie, which was founded in Leiden in 1976 but transferred to Amsterdam in 1992, provides higher professional education in museum studies. It offers a four-year programme with the possibility to specialise in 'management and conservation' or in 'museum communication', under which heading fall museum education (including information), public relations and marketing. As such, it claims to be the only daytime course in practical museum work in continental Europe (Reinwardt Academie 1996: 11).

In 1973, a part-time chair in museology, seen as an interdisciplinary approach which studies the museum as a link between a specific area of interest and the general public, was established at the University of Leiden. Because of budget cuts, this chair was abolished in 1983 and has not been re-established since.

Museum education has hardly been subjected to scientific scrutiny by other disciplines. Dutch pedagogy has paid only marginal attention to the art education of children; ethics were more important than aesthetics. The same applies to andragogy (a term often used to denote the education of adults). When, in 1970, the science of andragogy was granted academic recognition in the Netherlands, the official documents referred to the 'social and cultural education of adults'. Cultural education, however, particularly in the more limited sense of art education, has enjoyed little attention from Dutch academics in this field. An exception is the SCO-Kohnstamm Institute at the University of Amsterdam which publishes regularly about its research on museum education on behalf of children and adults.

At present, two institutes outside the university world pay attention to museum education: firstly, the Boekman Foundation in Amsterdam was established in 1963 as a research institute for professional associations of artists. In 1977, it was transformed into a centre for study and documentation in the areas of art and culture (Jongbloed 1991: 58). The foundation publishes the quarterly *Boekman Cahier*.

Secondly, the LOKV, the Dutch Institute for Art Education in Utrecht, came into being in 1983. It organises workshops and gives advice to managers and teachers of institutions for art education (LOKV 1995: 47). *Kunststof* (Matters of Art) is its quarterly publication, with information on products and services.

Success and failure

Various Dutch researchers have come to the conclusion that, from an emancipatory perspective, the strategy of cultural diffusion has failed. At the same time, the number of annual visits to museums has increased in a spectacular way.

Many practical reasons have been offered for the commercial success of museums during a period in which the number of visits to theatres and cinemas has dropped dramatically. Instead of being a dreaded competitor, television seems to act as a promoter of museums because of the attention given to the potentially suspenseful auctions of masterpieces and the publicity given to blockbuster exhibitions. Moreover, museums offer a much more flexible use of free time to tourists and locals compared with the fixed programmes of theatres and cinemas. Last but not least, in recent years Dutch museums have expended a great deal of inventiveness and energy on cultivating customer relations (Ganzeboom and Haanstra 1989: 2). The Museum Year Pass can serve as a typical example.

In close co-operation with the former Ministry of Culture, Recreation and Social Work, the Dutch Museum Association has developed the concept of this pass which, for a small amount of money, allows the bearer free access to more than 400 museums. Since this was to be a commercial undertaking, a separate foundation was established in 1981 that issues the pass, publishes a list of exhibitions in the major newspapers every two weeks and organises an annual National Museum Weekend which is accompanied by intensive publicity around its special events.

Seen in the light of the philosophy of culture, the rapidly growing interest in museums is not just a fashionable trend. This process has been described by Vuyk as the 'aestheticisation of the world picture', echoing the Dutch scholar Dijksterhuis who, in 1950, referred to the genesis of modern Europe during the sixteenth and seventeenth centuries as the 'mechanisation of the world picture'. Situations, events, acts and people are seen primarily as aesthetic objects. Style and form are more important than ethical content (Vuyk 1992: 51–2). By the same token, Vaessen finds a connection between the rise of museums and the 'musealisation' of culture. A multitude and multiplicity of ideas, values and norms present themselves, free of obligation, as if they were objects in a museum. For this new version of cultural plurality 'everything goes', because preference in taste is no longer considered to be a subject for education or discussion. Contemporary society tends to treat its cultural heritage as an open treasury where everyone can find something to their liking. However, widespread cultural diffusion has not taken place, and networks between museums and socio-cultural institutions have so far not developed.

One perspective draws on Dutch research, which indicates that income and, even more, education are the main factors accounting for the highly disproportionate rate of participation. The aesthetic experience flourishes on the fertile ground of previous schooling and cultural upbringing (Ganzeboom and Haanstra 1989: 6). Likewise, a 1975 study by the American National Research Center of the Arts found that 'the more frequently people went to museums when growing up, the more likely they are to go more frequently today', and 'early exposure to the arts is a very significant factor in adult participation in the arts' (Silver 1978: 18). From another perspective, cultural competence is seen as a useful weapon in social competition. The 'process of civilisation' can be regarded as a continuous alternation of lower-class imitation of higher-class behaviour and, as a consequence, new efforts by the elite to obtain more sophisticated means of distinction (Elias 1969). The possession of 'cultural capital' is an important advantage which only has market value if it remains within the hands of the happy few (Bourdieu 1984: 10). The pursuit of cultural distinction, therefore, has impeded both the traditional goal of moral edification and the modern ideal of social emancipation.

References

Bourdieu, P, *Questions de Sociologie*, Paris: Les Editions de Minuit, 1984
De Gruyter, W J, 'Belevingstentoonstellingen', in Ten Have, T T (ed.), *Handboek Vorming,* Groningen: J B Wolters, 1965, pp.176–9
Elias, N, *Ueber den Prozess der Zivilisation*, Bern: Francke Verlag, 1969
Elshout, D, 'Verslag ICOM-congres', *Boekmancahier* 2, 1990, pp.157–9
Ganzeboom, H and Haanstra, F, *Museum en Publiek*, Rijswijk: Ministerie van Welzijn, Volksgezondheid en Cultuur, 1989
Haanstra, F and Holman, B, *Hoe musea hun publiek begeleiden*, The Hague: Staatsuitgeverij, 1980
Haanstra, F and Oostwoud Wijdenes, J, *Trendrapport Museumeducatie*, Amsterdam: SCO-Kohnstamm Instituut, 1996
Jongbloed, K, *Herengracht 415*, Amsterdam: Boekmanstichting, 1991
LOKV (1995), *Bruggen Slaan,* Utrecht: LOKVMinisterie van Cultuur, Recreatie en Maatschappelijk Werk (CRM), *Naar een Nieuw Museumbeleid,* The Hague: Staatsdrukkerij en -uitgeverij, 1976
Ministerie van Onderwijs, Cultuur en Wetenschappen (OCW), *Pantser of Ruggegraat,* The Hague: SDU, 1995
Ministerie van Welzijn, Volksgezondheid en Cultuur (WVC), *Museumbeleid,* The Hague: Staatsdrukkerij en -uitgeverij, 1985
Nederlandse Museumvereniging, 'De museumnota', *Museumvisie* 1, 1977, pp.3–5
——*Jaarverslag 1995*, Amsterdam: Nederlandse Museumvereniging, 1996
Oosterbaan Martinius, W, *Schoonheid, Welzijn, Kwaliteit,* The Hague: Schwarz/SDU, 1990
Overduin, H, *Voermannen, Gastvrouwen en Educatoren* (Reinwardt Cahier no.3), Leiden:

Reinwardt Academie, 1983

Reinwardt Academie, *Brochure*, Amsterdam: Amsterdamse Hogeschool voor de Kunsten, 1996

Silver, A Z (1978), 'Issues in art museum education', in Newsom, B Y and Silver, A Z (eds), *The Art Museum as Education*, Berkeley: University of California Press, 1978, pp. 13–20

Vaessen, J A M F, *Musea in een Museale Cultuur*, Zeist: Kerckebosch, 1986

Van Gent, B, 'Andragogy', in Tuijnman, A C (ed.), *International Encyclopedia of Adult Education and Training*, Oxford: Pergamon, 1996, pp.114–17

—— *Lessons in Beauty: Art and Adult Education*, Frankfurt am Main: Peter Lang, 1997

Van Mensch, P (ed.), *Professionalising the Muses*, Amsterdam: AHA Books, 1989

Van Mensch, P and Maurits, H, 'Museologie is de brug tussen de verschillende vakgebieden in de musea', *Museumvisie* 1, 1982, pp.4–6

Vuyk, K, 'De esthetisering van het wereldbeeld', *De Revisor* 1/2, 1988, pp.171–83

Willink, J, 'Van vorming naar werving', *Metropolis M* 5/6, 1987, pp.67–75

Organisations

Boekmanstichting
  (Boekman Foundation)
  Herengracht 415
  1017 BP Amsterdam

LOKV, Nederlands Instituut voor Kunsteducatie
  (LOKV, Dutch Institute for Art Education)
  Ganzenmarkt 6
  3512 GD Utrecht

Nederlandse Museumvereniging
  (Dutch Museum Association)
  Prins Hendriklaan 12
  1075 BB Amsterdam

Reinwardt Academie
  Dapperstraat 315
  1093 BS Amsterdam

SCO-Kohnstamm Instituut
  Wibautstraat 4
  1091 GM Amsterdam

Stichting Museumjaarkaart
  (Museum Year-Pass Foundation)
  Prins Hendriklaan 12
  1075 BB Amsterdam

24 Ireland

Ann Davoren and Ted Fleming

Background

The Irish Museum of Modern Art opened to the public in May 1991. A national institution, concerned with modern art and contemporary art, its remit from the beginning was to provide access to the best Irish and international visual art through exhibition, collection, and community and education programmes. Its aim is to foster within society an awareness, understanding and participation in the visual arts through structures and programmes that are both innovative and inclusive.

The museum presents both temporary exhibitions and displays from the collection, which cover all media from the traditional to the contemporary. The exhibitions include younger and established Irish and non-Irish artists. Regular large-scale retrospective exhibitions and those that explore specific themes are also features of the programme.

Interwoven throughout all aspects of the museum is the 'Education and community' programme, which aims to increase access to the visual arts by developing audiences which are both engaged and informed. We work through a broad range of programmes and projects and seek to develop good practice in the field of arts education through action research projects.

A variety of approaches to working with participants has been explored; some projects take cues from aspects of the exhibitions, others are developed from an individual or collective desire to express personal or social issues. All projects and programmes of work are designed to create a forum where artists and people can meet to engage in meaningful exchange so that both acquire new understandings of the issues and ideas being explored. Working with artists introduces participants to a range of materials, approaches and techniques which can open out a wide visual vocabulary and affirms the value of making work out of one's own experience (Drury 1996).

Exploring concepts through the making of work is central to the majority of artist-led workshops. Art education, located in making, in exploring materials, in working through a process, in resolving ideas, has a distinctive contribution to make to personal development in intellectual and social terms (Drury 1996).

Engaging in the art process 'makes meanings, creates ways of understanding, forms memories and binds people together through modes of understanding which are uniquely their own' (Benson 1989). Art education not only brings about personal growth but also develops potential for collective social action. Art education at the museum is informed by formal education practices and developments at community level, and so the museum's work with older adults takes place within the field of adult education and in the context of Irish society as it approaches the beginning of the new millennium.

Civil society, a sense of place and adults learning

There is a strong sense of place in Ireland. Being Irish is linked to a place (a city, a town or a landscape) and the place is peopled with friends, family and relationships. These peopled places are communities.

We live in that place sociologists call 'civil society' (Cohn and Arato 1992: 14). Civil society includes the extended family, neighbourhoods, community groups, youth clubs, local businesses, voluntary associations, women's groups, churches, farmers' organisations, trade unions and others. But society also has two other components: the state and the economy. These three parts relate to one another in a complex way, and each of the components has a different view of what is meant by adult education and a different relationship with older people. But first let us take a brief look at the three components: the state, the economy and adult learning.

The economy is interested in the free movement of capital and goods, and the maximising of profits. It creates jobs and wealth. It works closely with the state. Tax structures, incentives for business and industry and the regulation of the economy through interest rates and exchange rates all underline this close coalition of interests, policies and practices.

Whereas the state actually supports the economy, civil society is under threat from both the state and the economy. The relationships of mutuality, trust and reciprocity built in civil society develop slowly and can be easily undermined. The development of Tallaght (a new large urban development in Dublin) is a good example of how, in moving people from their original places, a vast network of connected relationships of support and trust can be demolished. The social capital of their original location and of their connected world was lost. In the subsequent restructuring of the inner city, the state and the economy rebuilt the physical fabric with grant aid and tax-free status. The residents lost cultutal capital and civil society was undermined (Fleming 1998: 3–13).

In the National Lottery the fund-raising capacity of the voluntary sector (civil society) is taken by the state, which donates back to the original organisations the money they now find difficult to raise. The economy makes huge profits by gaining the licence to run the lottery.

When the state and the economy combine, as they do frequently, they are a formidable coalition ensuring that the interests of the economy are served.

The state, economy and adult education

Learning is seen by the state as predominantly a matter of supporting the economy. Adult education has little merit, in the view of the state, unless it supports learning for jobs and work. The Irish Minister for Social, Community and Family Affairs recently restated the commitment of the government to supporting education for those on social welfare as 'further evidence of the Government's commitment to tackling unemployment' (Ahern 1998). For the state, adult education means mostly job and skills training – schooling for the Celtic tiger. But an education policy based solely on the needs of the market is deeply flawed. However, the relationship between the state and adult education is complex and frequently includes elements of resistance and contestation as well as reproduction.

There are two different kinds of adult education. One has to do with state programmes. This is adult education in the system world. The other is education for the development of civil society or community education. We are not, however, suggesting that transformative learning and education can only take place outside the system world. There ought to be a lively contest taking place in the state and economy about working in solidarities for change in the system. This raises the important question as to how one might work for a critical pedagogy within the system world of state and economy.

Civil society operates on the basis that the government is not fully representative of the people. There is a democratic deficit – a gap between actual democratic practices and the ideal. The feminist movement, for example, has always identified a democratic deficit and bias in the system world. The agenda of civil society is influenced strongly by this analysis of undemocratic or partial democratic achievements and by a certain conception of what democracy might mean. Civil society has the dual function of ensuring that those who exercise power do not abuse it and of transforming the system to regenerate more democratic practices (Amalric 1996: 8).

In this context, Youngman states that adult education is opposed to

> economic exploitation and accompanying divisions between classes and nations; imperialism and maldevelopment in the South; uncontrolled industrialisation and environmental destruction; poverty, inequality, and social domination; the exclusion of the majority from decisions which affect their lives; the processes of globalisation and homogenisation of cultures; injustice and violence; values of competitive individualism and ideologies of racism, ethnocentrism and sexism.
>
> (1996: 24)

This critique of capitalism, the state and economy informs adult education, which, at its best, proposes a change not only within existing structures but a fundamental transformation of these structures. Adult education, in this vision, will be most effective when it supports the possibilities of collective social action rather than only enabling individual development. Older adults, in particular, will, after a life of productive activity in the economy, creating families, building communities in civil society and contributing through taxes to the state, take on a different relationship with the sectors of society. They pose problems for all three. Firstly, the economy sees older people as non-productive and of no concern at all. They are, in basic terms, a drain on pension resources. The state, too, perceives older people in this way. As long as this is the case, there will be a democratic deficit.

The place of museums

Museums are part of a long tradition of engagement with art as a location for raising significant and critical questions, for reclaiming a sense of place and exploring and proposing new, more egalitarian social arrangements (Marcuse 1977; Greene 1995).

The values of care, relating, friendship and the connected world of voluntary association are the values of civil society. The kind of learning implied by civil society is learning for community, democracy and inclusion. Civil society and community stand for a different kind of learning which has an interest in living in a transformed place. The vision of a transformed place has been worked on in various exhibitions at the Irish Museum of Modern Art, such as 'Inheritance and transformation' (IMMA 1991) and 'Anthony Gormley' (Nesbitt 1993). The Education and Community Programme at the Irish Museum of Modern Art encourages the kind of learning where art acts as a 'catalyst where one's view of the world can be tested' (O'Donoghue and Davern 1996: 15). In the learning encouraged by the museum new meanings can be explored and new places discovered where justice, tolerance, equality, love, friendship and care can be developed. Taken-for-granted meanings can be made clear, obvious and transparent. Alternative meanings can be sought, tested and, if appropriate, adopted. Changing one's frames of reference and acting on more inclusive world views are facilitated in the dialogue with art and artists. Transformative learning which bridges the democratic deficit is the lifelong learning encouraged at the museum.

The programme for older people

This is the longest-running programme at the Irish Museum of Modern Art. Since its opening, the museum has worked with a group of local older people from the St Michael's Parish Active Retirement Association.

The first project created with the group revealed the shared agendas for the arts that the museum and the group held in common, and opened up a number of starting points from which to develop our access policy, education strategy and community links. The project, a document of some of the reasons why people paint, was based on a series of discussions with the group, who had come together to paint every week for a number of years.

Throughout these discussions, group members spoke enthusiastically about the excitement generated through the act of creating a painting. Many remarked on renewed energy and a sense of fulfilment. Many spoke about 'exploring new ways of seeing the world, of discovering a sense of balance and calm, of losing a sense of time, of burying oneself in paint'. Emma Doyle described how painting opened her eyes to a new world: 'You see things in a different way, it is like seeing things for the first time.' Teresa Egan discussed how she paints to express private thoughts and feelings. She sees art as a connection to life, 'If you look at television all day, you lose touch, you have nothing to compare with.' She stressed the social as well as the artistic role of the group, and this has been an important element in the developing relationship between the group and the museum.

This first project led to a structured programme of work with this group. The programme is broadly based and investigative in nature, comprising visits to the exhibitions, meetings with exhibiting artists and working with artists through a range of materials, processes and ideas.

> Our Friday workshops open up a new interest to us. A venue in which we learn many different aspects of modern art, to view it from many angles. Also it is lovely to meet and talk with the exhibiting artists. I loved the atmosphere from the start, and look forward to Fridays very much. The Museum introduced us to new interests at our time of life – the 'Golden Age' really – if we look at it properly and have a positive outlook, age is a number only and all in the mind.
>
> Phyllis McGuirk

The group's ongoing engagement with the museum acknowledges the role older people can play in contemporary visual culture. The group's contact and involvement with contemporary art and artists is felt to be essential to the exploration of new forms of expression and the nature of personal creativity for individuals within the group.

> We are all convinced that the programme is of great benefit to us. We derive immense pleasure and satisfaction from taking part and are deeply indebted to the Museum, for giving us the means to expand our knowledge of shape, texture, colour and form and the ability to design and create, even when only using scraps and waste, because in our twilight years, that is what we would be, scraps and waste, if it were not for those bodies who know and care enough to untrap the artistic qualities which everyone possesses, but few get a chance to unfurl.
>
> Teresa Egan

The programme aims to be enabling rather than directive and is informed by developments at community level to promote people's potential to contribute. The programme, jointly developed by the museum and the group, values and engages older people's perspectives and aspirations, acknowledging that they represent a cross-section of society and emphasising integration rather than segregation.

> The contact with the museum has shown that we have learnt to accept challenges, and secondly, that we are capable of a lot more than we ever dreamt. We were introduced to many famous people and their work too numerous to mention. Some we loved, some raised eyebrows. That, too, is art, it would be very dull if we all liked the same things, and we love the discussion afterwards, it's fun.
>
> May McGibney

The museum works closely with the national agency Age and Opportunity, which was set up in 1988 to change negative attitudes towards ageing. Age and Opportunity aims to encourage the full participation of older people in local communities, and to encourage older people to use their skills, to exchange ideas and to confront issues which concern them. It links closely with health boards, adult education services, arts organisations and older people's associations.

Although focused on older adults, issues arising out of this programme have implications for other sectors. Questions are highlighted about the lack of resources for a developmental and continuous art education in schools, the rights of the individual to have access to the resources that enable self-expression and creativity, and the needs of many to find a voice to raise issues in a non-verbal context. Many within the group have remarked upon 'lost opportunities due to schooling and social circumstances', and are concerned that the younger generations should have access to adequate resources to enable more people to explore and discover their own creative impulse.

Over the past seven years, artists have explored drawing, painting, print-making and claywork with the group and encouraged members to discover and utilise their own personal experiences as a rich and valid source for individual expression.

> What has surprised me is how everyone sees so differently. It has made me notice things I just did not see years ago. Especially colour, I feel I was awakened to see afresh the vividness and variety of the world, the sky, the trees, the clouds.
>
> Rose Nugent

A Sense of Place

In 1994, the group began an exploration of place through a project entitled 'A Sense of Place', which lasted almost two years and led to the making of a series of paintings which were exhibited at the museum in 1996. This was an important project, both for the group and the museum, in that it brought together the individual and collective learning that had occurred. The group was now familiar and comfortable with the museum and its staff, its collection and its programme of temporary exhibitions and visiting artists. They were familiar with a wide range of processes and materials and stimulated by contemporary art and its possibilities for expression. The museum had also learnt about working with older people, about specific needs and approaches such as the pace and rhythm of workshops. A relationship of trust and commitment had developed between the group and the museum. We were now ready to embark on a sustained investigation, to learn, to share and to make work through an organic and developmental process.

Through a lengthy series of workshops and discussions with artists and storytellers, the group explored a range of processes and materials to develop images describing the special places in people's lives and the rich layering of associated memories which evolves through experiencing a place over time.

Inchicore and Kilmainham is the neighbourhood where many in the group have lived from childhood or since marrying; it is their community where they support and care for their friends and neighbours; it is where they raised their children and looked after their grandchildren. The church, grotto, school, canal and park, the streets and avenues, the houses and homes are touchstones representing lives lived over many decades, stretching to the past and the future.

Memories of place were evoked through exchanging stories about special places and recounting how differently one negotiates a place from childhood to older age, from exploring it as a child to exploring it with children and grandchildren. Visual metaphors were developed to express specific meanings attached to those places. What emerged was a series of individual paintings which describe not only a special place but also the memories and emotions evoked by that place.

Always Little Sisters

Painting is always a new experience for me, a new adventure. I've painted the view from my house of the Little Sisters Convent and the road where I used to play when I was a child. The focus point is the convent gate where my twin sister and I used to play ball. The Little Sisters is no longer a convent, it's now an apartment block. I feel that the area I knew so well is slipping away from me, sliding out of my grasp into the hands of the new generation.

Rose Nugent

Kilmainham Gaol

I'm very interested in the history and heritage of the Inchicore/ Kilmainham area, especially Kilmainham Gaol. My painting refers to the history of Kilmainham Gaol and how this history affects how the Gaol is regarded today. I've layered different perspectives of the Gaol, one on top of the other, to show how the one building has had many and varied uses, from a place of execution of political prisoners, to a gaol for common criminals, to a place which was neglected by the new state, to a restored heritage centre.

Teresa Egan

The rose garden

The Memorial Park is the place I visit most often when I go for walks with my daughter Ann. I have been going for years since Ann was a young child. It's relaxed up there and safe, and the rose garden is beautiful. When you go there you are surrounded by roses.

Carmel Walsh

The grotto

My painting is about me being in the grotto and the feeling of being at home and being in the presence of somebody so beautiful. It's something I can never really explain in words. It's something out of this world. It's like a radiance I can feel, this radiance of our Blessed Lady. The painting tries to express that radiance, that feeling that's there inside me.

Joan Brennan

Conclusion

The programme for older people is an important part of the work of the Irish Museum of Modern Art. Through working with Age and Opportunity and the core group of older people, we have developed a programme for other older people. The St Michael's Parish group both hosts visits to the museum and visits groups around the country, therefore acting as key workers and ambassadors for the museum and for older people's involvement in the arts.

In celebrating the International Year of Older Persons in 1999, the group is currently engaged in the process of curating an exhibition from the museum's collection and in developing a programme around this show to involve other older people's groups in the museum.

The Irish Museum of Modern Art, through its programme for older adults, attempts to realise the potential of art and the museum to become a key player in the development of civil society. By engaging in art, adults make new meanings, transform their way of looking at the world and see their own place differently. This happens because the museum enables people to exercise their imagination, to imagine new ways of caring, of being a neighbour, a friend, a member of the community and so bring about a more civil society.

References and further reading

Ahern, D, *Second chance education supporting the unemployed*, Dublin: Department of Social, Community and Family Affairs, 1998, URL:http://dscfa.ie/dept/pr/pr270498.htm

Amalric, F, 'In search of a political agenda for civil society in the north', *Development 3*, 1996

Benson, C, *Art and the ordinary: the ACE report*, Dublin: Arts Community Education Committee, 1989

Cohn, J and Arato, A (1992), *Civil society and political theory*, Cambridge, MA: MIT Press

Collins, M, *Adult education as vocation: a critical role for the adult educator*, London: Routledge, 1991

Drury, M, 'Cultural analysis', in Downey, M *et al.* (eds), *Unspoken truths*, Dublin: Irish Museum of Modern Art, 1996

Fleming, T, 'Learning for a global civil society', *The Adult Learner: Journal of Adult and Community Education in Ireland*, 1998

Greene, M (1995), *Releasing the imagination*, San Francisco: Jossey-Bass

Habermas, J, *Observations on 'The spiritual situation of the age'*, Cambridge, MA: MIT Press, 1984

Irish Museum of Modern Art (1991), *Inheritance and transformation*, Dublin: IMMA

Marcuse, H, *The aesthetic dimension: towards a critique of Marxist aesthetics*, Boston: Beacon Press, 1977

Nesbitt, J, *Anthony Gormley*, London: Tate Gallery, 1993

O'Donoghue, H and Davern, A, *Intersections: testing a world view*, Dublin: IMMA, 1996

Picon, C, 'Adult education in Latin America', in Wangoola, P and Youngman, F (eds), *Towards a transformative political economy: theoretical and practical challenges*, DeKalb, IL: LEPS Press, 1996, p.79

Welton, M, 'In defence of civil society: Canadian adult education in neo-conservative times', in Walters, S (ed.), *Globalization, adult education and training: impacts and issues*, London: Zed Books, 1997

Youngman, F, 'A transformative political economy of adult education: an introduction', in Wangoola, P and Youngman, F (eds), *Towards a transformative political economy*, 1996

25 The United Kingdom

John Reeve

Museums, adults and lifelong learning

> Indeed, a museum presents probably the only effectual means of educating the adult, who cannot be expected to go to school like the youth, and the necessity for teaching the grown man is quite as great as that of training the child. By proper arrangements a museum ... becomes elevated from being a mere unintelligible lounge for idlers into an impressive school room for everyone.
>
> (from an 1853 report, quoted in Hooper-Greenhill, 1995b: 50)

'Over 70 per cent of museum visitors are adults, alone, with other adults in groups, or with children' (Anderson 1995: 14), but many museums still do not regard provision for adult education as a core function. Although adults are not usually seen as the prime concern of museum educators they are increasingly important, with the greater emphasis now on 'lifelong learning'. For example, the National Curriculum in schools is now introducing many more future adults to museums than ever before – as well as their parents and carers. *A Common Wealth*, the review of museums and education in Britain, therefore targeted lifelong learning as a priority (Anderson 1997: 43), as does its second edition (Anderson 1999). In the 1970s museum educators were often employed by local education authorities and concentrated on schools, children and teachers; adults were often an 'add-on' except in national museums, where adults often had a far better deal than children. By 1997, 33 per cent of museum educators had had previous adult education experience, 23 per cent in further and higher education, but 80 per cent in schools also (Anderson 1997: 32). The profession now has a much more varied pool of expertise to respond to more diverse audience needs. In the last decade the impact of the National Curriculum on museums has often claimed limited educational resources; but there have been many new initiatives in adult education and a growing reassessment of basic purpose.

Victorians like Henry Cole at the Victoria and Albert Museum, and enlightened curators elsewhere in Britain and North America, saw the large museum as a liberal arts college, and as a vehicle for social and cultural improvement – a message that has frequently been lost *en route* (Reeve 1988; Hooper-Greenhill 1991; Anderson 1995; Hooper-Greenhill 1995b). Local museums have normally maintained closer links with their communities and with local organisations – for example, art clubs putting on annual exhibitions, archaeological societies, and bodies such as the Workers' Educational

Association (WEA 1998). In the last 25 years differences in museum education have generally narrowed between national and local museums in provision for different ages and audiences (Hooper-Greenhill 1994a).

Twenty years ago the sociologist A H Halsey (1981) predicted a policy shift in prioritising resources from the young to the old; the Kennedy Report (DfEE 1998) has recently advocated a further shift in resources within higher and further education towards the less able and the less advantaged. The current Labour government has introduced the work-based University for Industry. Museums have begun to follow some of these trends, responding to new kinds of courses and new patterns of work or the lack of it (Hemming 1995: 79–83; Kalloniatis 1995: 75–8). The Dulwich Picture Gallery in London, for example, which was Britain's first public art gallery, has pioneered art classes for the unemployed (Wolfe 1995: 111).

Opening hours remain a problem for people in full-time employment, although many museums provide programmes at weekends, particularly for families, and now open later on a regular basis. Recently, the Royal Academy in London stayed open late for a major exhibition of works by Monet, and the National Gallery remains open every Wednesday until 10 o'clock at night. Often Friends of museums' organisations arrange evening openings: once a month 600 or more of the British Museum Society's 13,000 members come for an evening opening, with three hours of talks, music and wine, and to enjoy the galleries without tourists or school groups. As Gunther (1994: 295) emphasises, 'learning and fun are not mutually exclusive'.

Adults learning in museums

The ways in which adults participate and construct their own meaning in museums are also changing, but far more research is needed. This is another theme of David Anderson's reports (Anderson 1997, 1999). We are beginning to understand the diversity of adult audiences: different appetites, different learning styles and types of intelligences (Gardner 1983; Gunther 1994). The British Museum's adult public is predominantly from abroad, but with a large minority of regular British visitors. It is the 'tourists' (a very loose concept in museum terms) who often have the least rewarding experiences. In response to such a spectrum of users the events menu at the British Museum is increasingly differentiated, like the school curriculum, and provides 'fast food' as well as all-day feasts, with many levels for progression in between.

For the first-time visitor there are introductory tours with professional tour guides trained by the museum. Introductory 'eye-opener' tours are given in specific galleries by a team of a 100 trained volunteer guides, on Asia, Islam, the Ancient Near East and Egypt, Mexico, the Classical and Medieval Worlds; plus shorter, lunch-time 'Spotlights'. Here are non-experts informally introducing mixed-ability beginners nine times a day throughout the year, and also providing human contact in a crowded museum. The guides (half of whom are still in full-time work) are trained by curators and educators and regularly appraised to maintain quality control. These committed volunteers are providing a service that even a relatively well-funded national museum could not otherwise resource. They also take the pressure off professional staff to provide introductory talks, and so educators and curators can give their more specialised gallery talks (often two a day) and deal with special group requests.

The British Museum's 'eye-opener' tours are often reinforced by printed introductory guides dispensed in the galleries. Usually 10 objects are singled out for attention to reflect the chronological and geographical range of a gallery and the varied media, but not linked by narrative as in a children's gallery trail. Text has been reduced in length so it can be increased in 'point' size; production values have improved. The initial costs come from sponsorship and fundraising events; reprint costs are generally covered by the money collected from the leaflet dispensers. The museum is now working on more basic materials aimed at some of the 'missing audiences': working-class adults coming, for example, as parents or in groups of the elderly; and adults from ethnic communities (like the Victoria and Albert Museum, we have provided materials in Chinese and also in Turkish). The annual 'Adult Learners Week' is an opportunity to promote these materials and forge links with new organisations and individuals.

The role of museum guide books requires much greater debate. In Edinburgh, for example, the volunteer guides at the Royal Museum of Scotland have produced their own, based on their tours: very concise and object-centred rather than breathlessly attempting to be comprehensive (Royal Museum of Scotland 1996). The British Museum's guide books range from inexpensive, brief tour guides, via a *Souvenir Guide* available in many languages, to a comprehensive *A to Z Companion* (Caygill 1999) that is organised more like a website, with short essays on a very wide range of topics and exhibits. English Heritage has produced family packs for some of their historic properties, with varied activities for adults and children learning together. Requests for family learning opportunities – whether tours, workshops or specialists – rate high in visitor surveys. Sound guides offer many opportunities for flexible interpretation, including the artist's voice (Tate Gallery, London), or an actress in role (Stokesay Castle, National Trust), and with potential for a variety of layers (National Gallery, for an exhibition on 'Reflections').

Adults with time and money can move from free, introductory, informal 'drop-in' events to those that are intensive and challenging, sometimes with accreditation; they even take tours in Britain and abroad, accompanied by curators and educators, from the Royal Academy, the Natural History Museum or the British Museum, for example. Walking tours set off from the Museum of London or the National Museum of Wales; Bradford, in the North, offers printed trails around its local industrial heritage. Curators, educators and freelances run study days, lunchtime lectures, evening classes and courses at national and many other museums: one can now study hieroglyphs, botanical illustration, creative writing, gardening, Indian dance, calligraphy, sing in a choir or take a 'life class' in art, and a host of other subjects. Government funding for adult education generally has changed: these non-vocational courses do not receive funding and so have often become either quite expensive, dependent on other funding, or no longer exist. Consequently, this can become a compensatory role for museums, providing a broad context for appreciating the collections, rather than being confined to the objects on display; it is also an opportunity to build new audiences.

Museums can provide a platform for many kinds of performance. The Bowes Museum in north-east England, for example, is a remarkable collection in a town of 6,000 people, so it has to work hard to attract its wider audience. Its imaginative programme for a loan exhibition of paintings from the Royal Collection included improvisation by young musicians in response to the paintings; portrait painting workshops using life models, and several performances of a satirical theatre piece. Well-known actors and authors perform at the Imperial War Museum and the National Portrait Gallery. Artists are 'in residence' at the National Gallery in London and the Tate Gallery in Liverpool. Artists also interpret exhibitions, particularly of contemporary art, in exhibition talks at the Whitechapel and Serpentine Galleries in London. Museum film programmes range from ethnography and archaeology festivals to contemporary Japan and India, and to tailor-made videos for exhibitions. Crafts are being kept alive by adult demonstrators, often volunteers: examples are textiles and shoe-making at Golcar (an industrial museum in Yorkshire), at Ironbridge, the pioneering open air museum in the West Midlands; and at the Ulster Folk and Transport Museum. A course for women in historic crafts at the Geffrye Museum in London is accredited with the London Open College Federation (Hemming 1995: 81).

The 50,000 volunteers in museums are an increasingly significant part of adult education, as receivers and often as providers. Membership of Museum Friends' organisations is growing constantly: a local museum like that in Sunderland in north-east England may have 250 Friends, many of whom will be active volunteers. The National Trust, a national heritage organisation responsible for many country houses, landscapes and industrial heritage, has 37,000 volunteers. Volunteers may be running the information desk (as at the Victoria and Albert Museum). Warders and attendants also have an important role to play in welcoming visitors, and as adults talking to adults (Coulter 1994: 85; Hooper-Greenhill 1994b:Chapter 5). 'Everyone on the museum staff is an educator' potentially (Gunther 1994: 294).

Access

Museums, although not galleries, are much more democratic in their audience profiles than opera, ballet and the theatre [but] there are still gaps in the audience profile. ... Deep-seated cultural reasons underlie the exclusion felt by black, Asian and other ethnic groups in Britain, and indeed also by women and the white working class.

(Hooper-Greenhill 1997: 2–3).

The emphasis in British cultural policy is now on access in the broadest sense. For example, an Access Fund has been set up by the Heritage Lottery Fund which aims to encourage greater outreach from national collections, with real collaboration, audience building and increased participation in museums. There are already many models of successful practice: adults have been encouraged to curate exhibitions and share their own collections with the public, in People's Shows such as Sunderland (Anderson 1997: 45), Walsall (Hooper-Greenhill 1994a:22) and at the Open Museum, Glasgow. Ethnic community groups have been invited to present their own cultures to other museum visitors – for example, during 'The peopling of London' exhibition in 1993/94 at the Museum of London (Merriman 1997). In advance, the project team took a mobile trailer ('Museum on the move') out to supermarket car parks, street markets and public spaces to talk to local communities in areas whose residents did not usually visit the museum. The related oral history collecting generated 65 interviews, extracts from which featured in the exhibition. As Merriman described the process:

> The focus weeks formed the core of the public programme. The principle behind these was that community groups were invited to use any or all of the museum's public spaces ... to represent, in their own terms, something of the community's historical presence and cultural distinctiveness in London, to other Londoners. The community groups were to have complete editorial control, with museum staff acting as facilitators and providing publicity. No suggestion was turned down unless it was financially or logistically unrealistic.

(1997: 139)

The subsequent challenge has been how to reflect such cultural diversity in the permanent displays.

Community involvement has also featured at the former Museum of Mankind (the Ethnography Department of the British Museum), whether Arab, Maori, Mexican or African. Performance, food and dance all offer tastes of other cultures: 'multi-sensory interaction increases exhibition accessibility' (Davidson *et al*, 1994). Multi-cultural programming has, for example, involved work with the Sikh community at Gunnersbury Park, West London, in Bradford and in Walsall (Hooper-Greenhill 1997: 149–67) and at the Victoria and Albert Museum in 1999. A notable collaboration with Asian and non-Asian women – the Victoria and Albert Museum's *Shamiana* project – is discussed by its creator, the late Shireen Akbar (Akbar 1995). Museums work regularly with the community in Glasgow, Leicester, Liverpool and Birmingham, bringing in especially the older generations. Collaboration with multi-cultural arts organisations has provided a rich pattern of opportunity nation-wide: the Japan Festival of 1991 and its continuing outreach work in the Highlands and Islands of Scotland as well as big cities; and the recent Yemen Festival for which the British Museum's Arab World Programme helped to provide adult as well as schools programmes and outreach.

One consequence of the National Curriculum is that many exhibition and festival topics are no longer seen as 'relevant' by schools, and museum programming is therefore directed at adults and families (Wood 1995). Sponsors, too, are increasingly interested in young adults and families as museum consumers: the pharmaceutical company SmithKline Beecham is sponsoring the Families Programme at the British Museum, for example.

Young adults without children are another audience many museums have to try harder to attract. Bristol's new science and wildlife centre, '@Bristol', is targeting adults under 30 years of age with a child-free 'Sound Space' and 'chill-out' room (*Museums Journal* 99(3),1999: 50). Nicholas Serota, Director of the Tate Gallery, London, has argued more broadly for 'places of prolonged concentration and contemplation' in museums and galleries (Serota 1996:54). Adults can express quite forcefully on occasions their irritation with other audiences in the museum, such as school groups or foreign tourists. We do need to look at tensions between audiences as well as at audience-building.

Access for adults with physical and learning difficulties is becoming a higher priority in many museums, particularly following the 1992 Disability Discrimination Act (Hooper-Greenhill, 1994b: 107–12; Kirby 1995; Scaife 1995). Artists lead day-long access workshops at the Whitechapel Art Gallery, which integrate description, discussion and practical activity, for adults with visual impairment and/or mobility needs. For the *speed* exhibition (autumn 1998) a musician also took part. Advance information is made available on audio-tape or in large print. The British Museum also produces larger-type materials generally, as well as large-type versions of its 'Events' booklet. Tours are often sign-interpreted; a mobile sound enhancement system also helps everyone to hear the speaker through headsets in noisy galleries. Volunteers are trained to help with two 'touch-tours' of Egyptian and Roman sculpture that build on successful 'touch' exhibitions (Pearson 1991). Recent initiatives by the British Museum's Access Officer (a sponsored post) include a museum studies course in the Coins and Medals Department for adults from Barnet College recovering from mental illness. This project has resulted in a small public display, and will also be published.

The Museums and Galleries Disability Association (MAGDA) has energetically promoted good practice, as has the National Institute of Adult Continuing Education (NIACE) in many areas of access for adults. *Sharing the wisdom of age* (MAGDA 1994) records oral history and reminiscence projects in London, other parts of England, Glasgow and Dublin. The publication also describes cross-generational work with Asian audiences in Leicestershire, outreach to hospices in Manchester, and work with new pensioners in Paisley. The Tate Gallery, Liverpool, has also pioneered community outreach work, with local prisons, for examples (Jackson 1989). 'Open learning' in the work-place and distance learning via the Open University provide other models for more informal, less mediated adult education.

Gunther (1994: 295) emphasises helping adults 'to decode the museum environment'. Opportunities to see 'behind the scenes' and to understand more about the work of museums now include the Conservation Centre in Liverpool, Conservation Roadshows at the British Museum, regular open days at open-air and industrial museums, and visits to the Museum of London's Support Centre. This centre will open near the British Museum by 2003, giving access to its textile, ethnography and archaeology collections which are in store. It will also present the work of conservators, archaeologists and ethnographers. Trained volunteer guides will give 'behind the scenes' tours; special education programmes in the 'Archaeology in action' area will include 'hands-on' activities for children and adults, and the chance to see some of the processes that take objects from excavation to display case. Potters will demonstrate and lead classes for adults, families and children. The potter-in-residence project was a very successful part of the 'Pottery in the making' exhibition at the Museum of Mankind in 1997, featuring 21 potters (a different one each Saturday), relating their demonstration to a different technique or culture in the exhibition (Gaimster and Freestone 1997).

Information technologies

New developments in Information and Communication Technology (ICT) help us to address a number of persistent problems in museums: their fragmented idiosyncrasy, their incompleteness, their lack of context, the need to supply mentally and visually so much that is missing, and to relate what is in front of one to what is either lost, or a thousand miles away, or in a book not readily available. Familiarity with new media has made many visitors more critical and openly frustrated at the 'communicative incompetence' of the museum, and, particularly, of the modern art gallery (Samis 1995: 29).

ICT is increasingly making the reserve collection accessible and enabling the adult student to 'virtually' access major collections, whether in Scotland (SCRAN), the National Gallery's Micro Gallery, or the British Museum (COMPASS, on-line from 2000). COMPASS will be a selective, interactive database for 5,000 of the Museum's 8 million objects (the National Gallery has

2,000 paintings). It will make connections: between the visitor and the museum, between one part of the collection and another, between past and present, and between present question and future study. Community multimedia projects in museums include *My Brighton*, installed as part of the local history gallery in Brighton Museum, and presenting diverse personal narratives – a taxidriver, a schoolgirl and so on (Anderson 1997: 28). *Hackney voices* are reminiscences by elderly Afro-Caribbeans, recorded by Hackney Museum in east London (a museum highly responsive to its mixed audiences).

There are assumptions in the school curriculum about mixed-ability age groups and the 'spiral curriculum', where topics are revisited over a longer time-span. These are increasingly being introduced to adult education in museums. Multimedia can enhance this process: adults can be beginners, quickly sampling a website or a CD-ROM in a way they probably would not do with a book, an event or an exhibition. Hitherto 'outreach' in museum education has meant sending out travelling exhibitions, going out to community groups and (it would have been hoped) bringing some of them into the museum. Now, with the world-wide-web (www), and increasingly sophisticated multimedia, 'outreach' has even wider connotations. Reluctant museum users may use the museum by remote access via the www – it may then inspire a visit. The housebound, the disabled or infirm, the remote rural user in the Highlands of Scotland – they, too, can potentially access the formerly inaccessible. The museum user may maintain a relationship with a museum once 'visited' through regular contact on the web, both with the museum and other users; for instance, chat lines, message boards, real-time events. Students of all ages can share ideas and expertise. The museum may benefit from regular feedback in learning more precisely what its audience may want or potentially support. The static, often unhelpful language of the fixed museum display may now be mediated by a variety of voices and languages, visual and textual. The Museum of London is providing month-long small and topical displays of this kind: gay (homosexual) London, tower blocks, new archaeological discoveries. All lend themselves to web-site treatments.

One key assumption of lifelong learning is that most learning does not cease when formal education ends, and relates to the assertion by 'de-schoolers' such as John Holt and Ivan Illich that much learning is not the result of schooling – or, more radically, that much schooling does not result in learning! George Hein has recently spelt out the implications of 'constructivist learning theory' for museums (Hein 1998). Those of us who work in education have known for a long time that visitors may make their own sense of museums from a combination of what they already know, or think they know, plus what they deduce from the museum's own interpretive devices, mediated through an unpredictable chemistry of physical reactions, learning gambits and social skills. However, other museum colleagues are often still using an outmoded view of communication. Many museum educators have followed Howard Gardner, who highlighted different kinds of intelligences – the cerebral, word-based kind that traditional educators have valued most is just one of the eight he describes (Gardner 1983). Dance or calligraphy is as much a museum education activity as a gallery talk, and arguably far more memorable.

Thus a museum database or web-site can help the visitor to prepare, to 'window-shop' critically in advance: not only whether a museum can help, but which museum and in what way. It can also help to slow down the 'fast food' customer: most people still spend less than 20 seconds in front of a painting. The challenge for the museum educator is, therefore, how to bring the most 'relevant', arresting data, questions, even commands, to bear on the business of looking at a painting, a sculpture, a coin, a Zen garden. The museum physically frames that business of looking; the screen does not, although it may eliminate the distractions. 'Surfing' is no substitute for standing in or walking through the museum space. As Carol Duncan (1995) has shown, the museum building can dictate the behaviour of its users; many multimedia creators appear to aspire to similar kinds of control. In creating the 'museum without walls', through multimedia, we have to provide the frame, the structure, without imposing the inhibiting single voice or physical exhaustion of 'The Institution'. Libraries have a different relationship from museums, both to text and to users, and have already moved a long way in this direction (Carpenter *et al*, 1998; on libraries in museums see Shorley 1995: 199). Symbolically, a new kind of public library, including the COMPASS database as well as books, will occupy the famous Round Reading Room in the British Museum, no longer a 'library of last resort' for scholars and now at the centre of the Great Court, due to open in late 2000. Lifelong learning is a key component of this project which combines education centre, ICT, library, bookshop, exhibitions, restaurant and circulation space.

Prospects

One of the challenges for the museum remains how to balance its own authority with the visitor's autonomy – this can mean that 'deferential' learning styles as commonly exacted by museums are in conflict with the 'self-directed' learner's personal journey. For ICT, as for exhibitions and other resources, this means balancing structure with flexibility; and quantity of data with accessibility and sensitivity. Museums may seem comprehensive; they may claim to be 'encyclopaedic' – but they are not and cannot be. Neither can multimedia. Multimedia and museums may act together to break through the barriers of scholarly-exclusive use of languages and display, and the museum's decisions about what may be seen by the public, and how. Multimedia may help to break down barriers of age, mobility, class, education and income to provide a valued and lively museum circuit on the National Grid for Learning, now being established in Britain. But there is also the danger of widening the gulf between those with and without access to the new learning technologies (Anderson 1997: 27).

Looking ahead, there is still a great amount to do in learning from each other in museum education, and from adult education specialists. 'Museums have been deprived of the energy, commitment and sense of purpose that have been characteristic of the adult education movement, and adult education institutions have failed to utilise one of their most important educational resources' (Anderson 1997: 58). Above all, we need to learn from our adult audiences, though this is especially difficult for those of us who work in museums with large numbers of foreign visitors. There are many examples of successful collaboration, such as Goldsmiths' College and the National Maritime Museum with their Open Museum programme of courses and adult events (Coben and Lincoln 1995). The National Gallery, having already produced excellent tailor-made video for almost all their major exhibitions, and constantly innovated in programming of all kinds, has also collaborated successfully with the BBC in a popular recent series presented by its director, Neil McGregor. The British Museum has worked for two decades with the Open University, promoting day schools on Ancient Greece, the Reformation, the Age of Enlightenment and comparative religions, and also advising on film production.

The Workers' Educational Association (WEA) has initiated several collaborations with museums, including one at Brighton Museum leading to accreditation by the local Open College Network (a certificate in the History of Art and Design, covering the fifteenth to the twentieth centuries). The course also 'aimed to provide an understanding of the ways in which museums work and the problems they face'. A further collaboration with the National Trust has focused on the country house, notably Knole in Kent. A joint WEA/King's Lynn Museum course over 20 weeks is described in Chadwick and Stannett (Kalloniatis 1995: 74). As part of the European Info-Cities Project, the WEA in Manchester has been working with the Museum of Science and Industry. In Edinburgh, Preparation for Retirement courses introduce local museums, and *The Peoples of Edinburgh Project* has involved members in recording the oral history of ethnic groups. However, as they point out in the report of their Museum Working Group, there are often practical problems in attempting to collaborate: 'By no means all institutions have rooms suitable for teaching purposes, particularly during normal opening hours. Like museum staff, many WEA staff and volunteers are hard-pressed to find time to develop new projects, and there is wide variation in awareness of the potential benefits of such partnerships' (WEA 1998: 5).

In addressing our training needs we have to pay attention especially to philosophy and method when working with adults: it is all too easy to lecture. 'Andragogy' is about independent 'self-directed' learning by adults who do not have to visit museums because any curriculum tells them to do so (Knox 1993;

Knowles 1993; Dufresne-Tasse 1995). We need to respect their own styles and pace of learning and provide them with flexible and varied modes of delivery (Matthew 1996): handling sessions, sound-guides, trails, different voices offering varied opinions, whether artists, collectors, writers, members of ethnic communities. Debate and questioning work well: the National Gallery pairs two speakers who like and dislike a picture to debate in front of it, with a vote at the end by the adult audience, as part of an evening opening. Paolozzi's provocative exhibition 'Lost Magic Kingdoms' at the Museum of Mankind prompted debates between unhappy anthropologists and approving art educators. We need to relate to adults' changing roles through life and build on their experience, knowledge and misapprehensions (Jensen 1994: 274). Nelson Graburn (1992: 201) has also reminded us of that 'reverence' (a special concern of art historian E H Gombrich), and 'association' are also important factors in the adult experience of the gallery or museum (Falk and Dierking 1992:201). Many American museums cater extremely well for the social side: some organise successful evenings for single visitors with jazz, a pay bar and a background of art; many open late at weekends.

American museums are generally much more 'upbeat' about all this. Willard Boyd, President of the Field Museum of Natural History, Chicago, talks, rather extraordinarily, about 'lifelong learning, a subject second only to the weather in concern' (Falk and Dierking 1992: ix). Adults are a significant source of income generation for their education departments, and increasingly here in the United Kingdom, also; but with that comes an even greater concern for quality control. In advocating the importance of adult audiences to our own museums we should remember, as Eric Midwinter (1994: 7) points out, that persons retiring at the age of 60 in Europe have on average 8,000 days of leisure ahead of them. Already 18 per cent of the British population is retired; soon it will be 20 per cent across the European Community. Many Europeans will spend as long in the Third Age as in the Second (MAGDA 1994: 7), The museum is perhaps unique as a cultural institution in straddling all the ages. Other media and institutions, even libraries, provide less continuity. Museums, while remaining reassuringly stable, can still be responsive to changing audiences and their needs.

References

Akbar, S, 'Multicultural education: the Mughal tent project at the Victoria and Albert Museum', in Chadwick, A and Stannett, A (eds), *Museums and the education of adults*, 1995, pp. 84–91

Anderson, D (1995), 'Gradgrind driving Queen Mab's chariot', in Chadwick, A and Stannett, A (eds), *op.cit.*, pp. 11–33

Anderson, D (1997), *A common wealth*, London: Department of National Heritage

Carpenter, L *et al* (eds), *Towards the digital library*, London: British Library, 1998

Caygill, M (1999), A to Z Companion to the British Museum, London: British

Museum Press

Chadwick, A and Stannett, A (eds), *Museums and the education of adults*, Leicester: NIACE, 1995

Coben, D and Lincoln, M, 'The open museum: a case study in cooperation', in Chadwick, A and Stannett, A (eds), *op.cit.*, 1995, pp. 115–18

Coulter, S, 'Quiet revolution', *Museums Journal* 93(6): 1993, pp. 30–2

Davidson, B, 'Increased exhibit accessibility', in Hooper-Greenhill (ed.), *op.cit.* (1994b), pp. 179–94

Department for Education and Employment, *Further education for the new millennium*, London: DfEE [Kennedy Report], 1998

Duncan, C (1995), Civilising rituals: inside public art Museums, London: Routledge

Dufresne-Tasse, C (1995), 'Andragogy in the museum', in Hooper-Greenhill, E (ed.) *op.cit.* (1994a), pp. 245–59

Fahy, A and Sudbury, W (eds), *Information: the hidden resource; museums and the internet.* Paper at 7th Museums Documentation Association conference, Cambridge: MDA, 1995

Falk, J and Dierking, L, *The museum experience*, Washington, DC: Whalesback, 1992

Gaimster, D and Freestone, I, *Pottery in the making*, London: British Museum Press, 1997

Gardner, H, *Frames of mind*, London: Paladin, 1983

Graburn, N, 'The museum and the visitor experience', in Falk, J and Dierking, L, *op.cit., 1992*, p. 201

Gunther, C, 'Museumgoers: life-styles and learning characteristics', in Hooper-Greenhill, E (ed.), *op.cit.*(1994b), pp. 286–97

Halsey, A H, *Change in British society*, 2nd edn, Oxford: Oxford University Press, 1981

Hein, G, *Learning in the museum*, London: Routledge, 1998

Hemming, S (1995), 'Community-based adult education programmes at the Geffrye Museum', in Chadwick, A and Stannett, A (eds), *op.cit.,* pp. 79–83

Hooper-Greenhill, E, *Museum and gallery education*, Leicester: Leicester University Press, 1991

—— *Museums and their visitors*, London: Routledge, 1994a

—— (ed.), *The educational role of the museum*, London: Routledge, 1994b

—— (ed.), *Museum, media, message*, London: Routledge, 1995a

—— 'A museum educator's perspective', in Chadwick, A and Stannett, A (eds), *op.cit.,* 1995b, pp. 49–64

—— (ed.), *Cultural diversity: developing museum audiences in Britain*, Leicester: Leicester University Press, 1997

Jackson, T, 'Reaching the community: modern art and the new audience', in Hooper-Greenhill, E (ed.), *Initiatives in museum education*, Leicester: University of Leicester, 1989, pp. 16–17

Jensen, N (1994), 'Children, teenagers and adults in museums', in Hooper-Greenhill, E (ed), *op.cit.*(1994b), pp. 268–74

Kalloniatis, F (1995), 'Collaborative ventures at the King's Lynn Museums', in Chadwick A and Stannett, A (eds), *op.cit.*, pp. 73–8

Kelly, T, *A history of adult education in Great Britain*, 3rd edn., Liverpool: Liverpool University Press, 1992

Kirby, W (1995), 'Access to learning for adults with disabilities', in Chadwick, A and Stannett, A (eds), *op.cit.*, 1995, pp. 103–6

Knowles, M, 'Androgogy', in American Association of Museums, *Museums, adults and the humanities*, Washington, DC: AAM, 1993, pp. 26–37

Knox, A, 'Motivation to learn and proficiency', in American Association of Museums,

Museums, adults and the humanities, Washington, DC: AAM, 1993, pp. 56–8

Matthew, M, 'Adults learning', in Durbin, G (ed.), *Developing museum exhibitions for lifelong learning,* London: Stationery Office, 1996, pp. 70–2

Merriman, N, 'The Peopling of London project', in Hooper-Greenhill, E, *op.cit.,* 1997, pp. 119–48

Midwinter, E, 'Europe in retirement: ageing and leisure in the 1990s', in Museums and Galleries Disability Association, *op.cit.*, 1994, pp. 5–11

Museums and Galleries Disability Association (MAGDA), *Sharing the wisdom of age*, London: MAGDA, 1994

OAL, *Volunteers in museums and heritage organisations*, London: HMSO, 1991

Pearson, A, 'Touch exhibitions in the UK', in *Museums without barriers*, Fondation de France/ICOM, London: Routledge, 1991, pp. 122–26

Reeve, J, 'The British Museum', in Stephens, M (ed.), *Culture, education and the state*, London: Routledge, 1988, pp 65–93

Royal Museum of Scotland, *Under one roof,* Edinburgh: RMS, 1996

Samis, P, 'De-connecting meaning', in Fahy, A and Sudbury, W (eds), *op.cit.,* 1995, pp. 25–38

Scaife, S, 'Welcoming adults with learning disabilities at Wakefield Museums and Galleries', in Chadwick, A and Stannett, A (eds), *op.cit.*, 1995, pp. 107–10

Serota, N, *Experience or interpretation: the dilemma of museums of modern art*, London: Thames & Hudson, 1996

Shorley, D, 'Noble kin and a mission shared', in Fahy, A and Sudbury, W (eds), *op.cit.*, 1995, pp. 197–202

Wolfe, G, 'Programmes for disadvantaged people at Dulwich Picture Gallery', in Chadwick, A and Stannett, A (eds), *op.cit.*, 1995, pp. 111–14

Wood, R, 'Museums, means and motivation: adult learning in a family context', in Chadwick, A and Stannett, A (eds), *op.cit.*, 1995, pp. 97–102

Workers' Educational Association (WEA), *Working in partnership: the Workers' Educational Association and museums*, London: WEA, 1998

26 European initiatives

Alan Chadwick and Annette Stannett

Adult Education and the Museum

As mentioned in the Introduction, this project, supported by SOCRATES, arose out of a presentation made at the General Assembly of the European Association for the Education of Adults in 1995. The project represents one of the first European initiatives on the theme of collaboration between adults and museums, continued over two years (1996–98), and has just published its final report (in German: English version to follow). Its main aim was to involve all (then) 15 members of the European Union in a wide-ranging overview of the *status quo* of educational provision for adults in a variety of museum settings and with a variety of adult groups. It set out to encourage an 'exchange of case studies of existing collaborative activities and discussion of inter-cultural work for mutual enrichment and stimulation, taking into account the diversity of the regions involved' (publicity brochure, August 1996).

There were four principal concerns:

1. that the growing educational potential of museums appears not to be realised to the extent necessary, given the wide range of challenges faced in contemporary Europe that the adult education/museum partnership is particularly well placed to address;
2. that isolated examples of good practice are not being publicised;
3. that, in order to exploit and develop good practice, it is necessary to persuade policy makers of the benefits of partnerships;
4. that there is a fundamental need to assess policy and resource requirements, e.g. in respect of training, if the potential is to be realised.

The report contains a large number of short case studies from European Union countries, as well as Switzerland. The projects described cover a wide range of initiatives with different community groups. One of the innovative features is an emphasis on collaborative work with 'opposites' – for example, laymen with artists; unemployed adults with employees; women re-entering the work-place with female students just completing their studies; able-bodied people with the disabled; foreigners with indigenous inhabitants. The overarching aim was to foster mutual learning, become aware of different perspectives and develop more tolerant attitudes.

The project has already been influential in leading to several national collaborative ventures in Austria, Germany, Greece, Italy, Scotland and Switzerland. Similar efforts on a transnational scale have to date been minimal, and consist mainly of seminars and conferences: the seeming lack of European political will in this area calls for further initiatives, efforts and, particularly, dissemination.

Further details of this AEM Project can be found on the web-site
(http://www.mhie.ac.uk/aem/Home.html).

Museums, Keyworkers and Lifelong Learning

Another research project, also partially funded by SOCRATES and titled as above, is currently in progress and just reaching the end of Phase 1 (1998–99). This initiative is based on the hypothesis that keyworkers, such as youth and community workers, volunteers, public employees who work on city streets, arts workers and adult educators, may be able to provide a bridge between museums and those adults with whom they currently have little or no contact. There are six project partners, each from a different European country: The Irish Museum of Modern Art (IMMA) in Dublin, the City of Stockholm in Sweden, the Casino in Luxembourg, the Bureau for Cultural Mediation in Vienna, the Municipal Museum in Sobralhino in Portugal, and the Victoria and Albert Museum (V&A) in London. Each partner is developing initiatives relevant to their own cultural contexts, with different adult audiences. IMMA, the V&A and Stockholm have completed the first phase of their projects and the Final Report has been submitted to Brussels. It is hoped that the other three partners' projects can be progressed during 1999–2000.

IMMA is targeting older people living on estates adjacent to the museum who, in turn, draw in other older people living nearby; in contrast, the V&A is addressing its project to arts and community workers who work with young people living locally in London. The Stockholm programme is aimed at public employees such as taxidrivers, police officers, traffic wardens and others who come into daily contact with local citizens and tourists (see Chapter 3). In each case the target group consisted of adults who had rarely visited museums, if at all.

The project is co-ordinated and led by the University of Surrey in Guildford, UK. Although it has not yet been formally evaluated, there is already strong evidence that the employment of keyworkers to engage excluded groups of adults as museum users can be a very effective one. As the project develops, the University of Surrey plans to establish prototype training programmes for keyworkers in association with partner museums. Increasingly, the initiative for development of the project is passing from museum staff to keyworkers and their contact groups. In London, for example, the programme's young people have interviewed several hundred of their contemporaries about their perceptions and expectations of the V&A, and have started web-based newsletters for distribution to other groups of young people. Interviews conducted at IMMA reveal that the artwork viewed and undertaken at the museum has given the older participants new perspectives on their own lives and increased their feeling of well-being. And in Stockholm, the public workers who have taken part in the educational tours of the city state that the new knowledge they have gained thereby has been instrumental in making their jobs more enjoyable and satisfying.

It is hoped that such effects can be conveyed to museum policy makers in order that similar projects may be mounted in the future, leading to possible changes in museum policy on currently excluded groups of adults.

Further details of this Project can be found on the web-site
    (http://www.surrey.ac.uk/Education/MKLL/)

27   Israel

Nina Rodin

In this chapter I shall present a model of adult learning and learning from adults, both taking place in an Israeli modern history museum, of the type known in Israel as a 'settlement museum'. Today, we have 187 museums in Israel, one-third (67) of which relate to the centenary of the re-settlement of *Eretz Israel* (the Land of Israel). As such, they represent a new museum category.

The chapter will open with a definition of the settlement museum category and its different types of museums. I shall then present the 'Khan' History Museum of Hadera as a case study, firstly as a project carried out by an association of adult volunteers, for whom the establishment of the museum 17 years ago was a fascinating, multi-faceted learning process; secondly, I shall focus on the 'Khan' Museum as a learning arena for the elderly. This section will highlight 'inverted' learning which has been employed at the 'Khan' Site Museum since its inception and was recently given expression through the activities of reminiscence groups on the one hand, and through the high level of involvement of elderly volunteers on the other. In conclusion, the 'Khan' Museum will be viewed as a community in which young people, adults and the elderly fulfil roles in a simulation of inter-generational community life.

Settlement museums

Museums referring to the story of the settlement have existed in Israel since the 1940s, but their significant proliferation took place in the 1970s and 1980s. During this period, many of the museums dedicated to local history, or to the history of organisations and ideological groups, were established. The uniqueness of these museums, which deal with the re-settlement of *Eretz Israel* since 1870, is their connection to the sites where historical events took place. This uniqueness is expressed in their definition:

> A settlement museum represents material and/or archival aspects of the renewed Yishuv (the Jewish population) in Eretz Israel, in most cases in relation to the museum's location.
>
> (Ministry of Education and Culture 1991)

Museums which have an integral contact with the places whose history they reflect are called 'site museums'. This term was coined by ICOM (International Council of Museums) in its 1982 report, quoted by Kenneth Hudson with reference to ICOM's third category of history museums. It defines a 'site museum' as 'a museum at a place where, at some time in the past, an event occurred which was important in the history of a community' (Hudson 1987: 144).

Interactive relationships between the museum and its community pinpoint the establishment of the Israeli settlement museums, many of which were founded by citizens interested in their history or cherishing the newly formulated Israeli heritage. Each one of these initiators was highly motivated by ideological and educational goals.

According to their subject matter, settlement museums can be divided into six categories: local, regional, of events, of organisations, relating to individuals, and relating to lifestyle/folk life. It should be noted that settlement museums are primarily museums of narrative. Many of them convey a sequence of stories or a central narrative divided into sub-episodes, the material of which the museum presents, collects, documents, narrates and uses to build its overall story.

The foundation phase of these museums is clearly societal. The people who have initiated them have some personal (familial or ideological) connection to their themes. In small communities such as the *Kibbutz* (rural communal settlement), the museum's narrative reflects the collective memory of the members, and serves as the community's identity card. In settlements with an urban orientation, in semi-urban towns or cities, there may often appear a similar momentum within the framework of sub-communities such as groups of immigrants from one specific country. In these instances, the interaction among the museum founders may reflect a certain unifying factor: a mutual past, a mutual ideology or a mutual one-time experience.

The 'Khan' Museum of the History of Hadera

General background

Today, Hadera is a coastal city with a population of 80,000, spread over 7,000 acres. On its foundation in 1891, this large tract of land was purchased by four Associations of Russian Zionists from a Lebanese Christian Arab *effendi*, for the defined purpose of agricultural settlement. At that time, *Eretz Israel* was under the oppressive regime of the Ottoman Empire. Land policy and corruption amongst Turkish officials created extremely difficult conditions for Arab farmers and Jewish settlers alike. Hadera's land was purchased by 150 members of the *Hovevei Zion* (Lovers of Zion) Movement, who joined together to emigrate from Russia to Zion out of fear of anti-Semitic pogroms. At the centre of their newly bought estate stood an impressive, mid-nineteenth century sandstone farmhouse. In its mouldy, dark rooms, the first 30 families were compelled to live for six years of suffering and impoverishment, while waiting for Turkish building permits for their private homes. Their lethal enemy was malaria, which was rampant due to the vast swamps in the area. In time, the story of the founders of Hadera, their struggle and endurance, became a symbol of the history of resettlement in *Eretz Israel*.

One hundred years later, the 'Khan' (Turkish for *caravansarai*) building in which the pioneers had lived was declared a Registered National Site. A local association of Hadera residents restored its remaining 11 rooms and established a museum containing archives and museum exhibitions of the history of Hadera.

Museum founding as a learning process

The volunteers who established the 'Khan' Museum can be defined as a group undergoing a transformation from amateurism to professionalism; in other words, they are perpetual learners. The ten devoted activists who were involved in the founding of the museum in the late 1970s lacked information, let alone research experience. At the time of collecting materials, formulating the programme and mounting the first exhibition, very little historical and environmental research on Hadera was available. Hence, these citizens had to conduct their own research, based on oral histories of veteran local residents. Every aspect of founding the museum involved learning, such as constructing exhibits, organising a museum office, building an archive (including classification, cataloguing and restoration of documentary materials and objects of material culture), renovating an historic building, and much more.

Written sources of information were difficult to find. The academic establishment was not interested in local-historical subjects of the early settlement, but the use of local secondary sources was of some compensation. Oral history became the most important source for verifying the documentary evidence collected.

The learning process of adult and elderly museum volunteers continues to the present in the dynamic activity of adults aiding the professional staff by creating workshops for students, writing historical dissertations, collecting material for exhibitions, restoring objects from the museum collection, or cataloguing documentary material.

This mode of learning is distinguished by two characteristic features. Firstly, it is a goal-orientated activity (Knowles 1981). Learning in this instance can be described as a functional activity practised in order to achieve a specific goal. Secondly, it is definitely a group-learning process, conducted through interactions among team members, in order to solve problems mutually. Our experience has shown that individualists drop out of this kind of group activity fairly early on. We came to the conclusion that when involved in a demanding project, the learning activity of museum staff and of volunteers is an interactive and co-operative one.

Conventional and unconventional modes of adult learning at the 'Khan' Museum

The 'Khan' Museum operates under the regulations of a voluntary association, established long before the foundation of the museum itself. These regulations have put the service of the community as its base structure. At the heart of the service there is a commitment to the city's heritage and culture. In this spirit, the association has proposed activities for the adult community such as the 'enrichment' programme of lectures and seminars on subject matters related to the history of *Eretz Israel*. This activity was initiated by a sincere desire to enhance contacts between the local community and their museum. Local residents had to be taught that the 'Khan' is there for them; in other words, that their own identity could be found in their history museum.

These lecture meetings also included representatives of sub-communities and neighbourhoods eager to listen to the memories of their founders. Reminiscence evenings created unpredictable dynamics; the atmosphere was not always tranquil; there were arguments and disagreements. The 'Khan' Museum staff use the audio-cassettes and photographs of these meetings as a valuable source of oral and documented history, and allow access to the material to any members of the public who may be interested. The material is already used routinely. Recently there were several cases in which relatives of interviewees, searching for their family and ethnic identities, consulted our archival services. It is often a very emotional experience for them.

'Inverted' learning: reminiscence activity for the elderly

In the course of its activity since 1982, the 'Khan' Museum has developed two means of collecting information from the adult population, which can be considered two variants of the same activity. One method is the recorded interview. Museum staff conduct interviews documented by either videotape or audio-cassette. The aim is to collect oral historic information through individual sessions with interviewees.

Another way of collecting information from the elderly is through reminiscence groups, a well-known museum practice, further developed by the 'Khan' Museum to take into account the conditions and personal dynamics of the elderly community in Israel.

This population is accessed through nursing homes and clubs for the elderly. The museum initiates the contact (the contact person is a volunteer retiree). The meeting is conducted as a tea party at the participants' place of residence, their clubs or at the museum. After watching a museum video film and meeting an actor portraying one of the pioneers of Hadera, each group of 4–5 participants receives a suitcase filled with objects for them to identify. The museum educators encourage them to handle the objects and discuss them with other members of the group. Finally, they are encouraged to share reminiscences with the entire group and the attentive museum staff.

These activities, for groups of around 20 participants, take into consideration factors such as shortage of time and the requirement to speak in public, which is very difficult for many elderly people. The result may often be that people who are very articulate are not necessarily those who have valuable stories for the museum. On the other hand, we have witnessed the awakening of memories as a result of experiences and/or knowledge shared by other members of the group. For example, in a meeting with a group of elderly participants, a coal iron elicited at least four different stories, from different cultural backgrounds. As a result of one of these stories, the museum uncovered valuable information about an Arab attack on Hadera in 1929.

On initiation of the activity, our original goal was to acquire information on specific items from the museum collection, in order to increase our knowledge. In time, we have developed a form of interaction in which objects act as triggers that 'open up' personal episodes, life stories and memories that people share with us.

In both types of encounters, the individual and the group sessions, there is a dynamic of 'all-knowing' adults sharing knowledge with 'naïve' young museum staff members, a dynamic which creates a learning atmosphere of 'give-and-take'. A spirit of co-operation is created, and above all, one of respect for the valuable knowledge of the elderly. Very often, participants in these happenings discover meanings beyond the pleasure of sharing personal nostalgic moments, and express satisfaction in the fact that things long forgotten are of historical value to the museum. The quality of documentary material acquired during reminiscence meetings depends on the interviewees' intellectual level, education and clarity of expression.

For the most part, these meetings create a mosaic of life comprising 'bits and pieces', which a creative, intelligent member of the museum staff can fit into the museum's historical narrative.

Terms for acquisition of information

Reminiscence meetings of any kind create intimate connections between the museum staff – 'the student' and the adult – 'the teacher'. In this scenario, the interviewer is seen as a substitute for the institution (the museum), and therefore any amount of information, however small, that the elderly are prepared to share becomes an act of presentation to a representative figure.

On the other hand, in order to be worthy of receiving such oral information, which is often accompanied by photographs, certificates, personal objects, or documents, the interviewer must 'prove' that they have a degree of prior knowledge. The 'giving' party (the elderly narrator) wants to confide in someone with whom they have something in common. Therefore the second test which interviewers must pass after displaying interest and attentiveness, is their historical knowledge, such as dates and places, which will be discussed. The interviewer intends to learn, but their ability to carry on a discussion is a valuable catalyst for the interviewee. An example is a 91-year-old woman, granddaughter of a founder of Hadera, who has a habit of calling me at all hours of the day (and night) whenever she remembers a story of the early days in Hadera, customs of her family, or the agricultural lifestyle of those days. Each time she shares her knowledge with me she says, 'I can talk to you about these things; you come from a founders' family'.

The Museum's path of perpetual learning for adults

Since its inauguration 17 years ago, the 'Khan' Museum of the History of Hadera has worked with a group of active volunteers. Today, the professional paid staff is augmented by some 20 permanent volunteers involved in the daily activities of the museum. They participate in building pupils' workshops, recording and cataloguing archival materials, translating documents, organising the collection, maintaining the library, restoring and conserving historical objects, helping out with bookkeeping and retaining contacts with the municipal bureaucracy. The ability to cope with multiple assignments is, without question, an outcome of a combination of devotion to commitments, together with a will to learn from younger 'tutors'.

The acceptance procedure for museum volunteers is a learning process as well. As people are unfamiliar with the 'inner' or 'behind-the-scenes' workings of a museum, an important condition for successful, long-term integration in the museum is learning its *modus operandi*. The learning process at the entry stage of work is individualised (details of the procedure developed to deal with this issue are discussed later).

Museum volunteers come from middle to upper socio-economic classes; they are generally well educated and extremely self-confident, and selective as to their fields of contribution to the community. Their giving depends on their receiving: they are willing to contribute if the conditions which they have set for themselves prior to their involvement in the museum are met. What they are looking for are intellectual interests and interrelations with agreeable people.

Acknowledging the importance of their sense of well-being, the 'Khan' Museum held a three-months-long academic course from December 1996 to February 1997 for veteran volunteers and new 'recruits'. Twenty-six volunteers participated. The subjects covered in the course included museum studies, the history of Hadera and its environs, and gerontology. Participants signed a service contract to volunteer at the 'Khan' Museum or in similar cultural institutions for the period of one year. Several lessons were taught by museum staff members who shared 'professional secrets' with the new volunteers. This paid off later in their volunteer activities at the museum. The course students were extremely conscientious in the learning experience they were undertaking. They took notes, were very co-operative in sharing their life experience, and became enthused by the sheer fact of having a 'second chance' to study. Some confided in me, saying that having been able to cope with academic studies made them proud of their intellectual potential. At least half of the participants would gladly have continued their studies for the rest of the year.

Having completed the course, the participants received honorary certificates in a ceremony attended by the city mayor and other officials. The course, in which two members of the museum's Board of Directors participated, enhanced the museum staff with intelligent, efficient volunteers.

The next stage in adult volunteer learning is the 'exploratory' stage, in which the prospective volunteer learns about the practicalities of working in the museum. This is a stage of individualised learning which takes place partly in the museum where each volunteer accompanies a staff member, and partly at home where the volunteer reviews material provided by the museum. Once volunteers are accepted to work at the museum, they are invited to participate with staff members in meetings, enrichment courses and social functions.

Adult volunteers: an irreplaceable asset of the museum

Recently, with the application of the Tamuz Museum Computer Program for museum collections, initiated by the Ministry of Education and Culture, it became clear that there was an urgent need to sort, organise and catalogue the 'Khan' collections. As part of the museum's policy to integrate volunteers into all phases of its professional work, volunteers were invited to take part in all phases of discussion, training and contact with computer consultants from the Ministry. Because this interaction required programmatic and practical answers, a 'study group' of volunteers was formed to manage the discussions and propose solutions for current queries.

In the process of registering and sorting the museum's objects, we discovered that, due to the lack of professional literature in the settlement museums' specific field, the personal experience and knowledge of each of these adults provided the only source of information in many cases. This led to consultation sessions with the restoration workshop volunteers and members of staff. As a rule, the museum director took part in these discussions, during which an object would be introduced in order to identify its date, origin and function.

In an unprecedented act, the Head Restorer of the Israel Museum attended a five-hour session with three volunteer 'restorers' of the 'Khan', in the course of which professional questions were raised by the volunteers, and an in-depth discussion ensued. Subsequently we received the consultant's appreciation of the knowledge and goodwill demonstrated by these people.

Conclusion

Having been created by a community for a community, a local history museum should maintain an atmosphere of closeness and friendly personal relationships. Where such relationships exist, a new concept emerges – the 'museum as a community'.

Every individual in this community should see their part as a contribution to a mutual enterprise. When the overall perception of the museum is an ever-developing co-operative venture, learning activities become acts of giving rather than acts of receiving.

References

Hudson, K, *Museums of influence,* Cambridge: Cambridge University Press, 1987

Knowles, M S, 'Andragogy', in Collins, Z W (ed.), *Museums, adults and the humanities,* Washington, DC: American Association of Museums, 1981, pp.49–60.

Ministry of Education and Culture, Center for Cultural Information and Research, *Annual Survey of Israeli Cultural Institutions,* Tel-Aviv, 1991

28 Conclusions

Nicole Gesché

It has been a difficult yet pleasant task to attempt to draw together the main trends of this publication. The editors have met the challenge of gathering a wide range of contributions from more than 20 countries across Europe, and have included an unsolicited but welcome addition from Israel. This 'patchwork' of provision showing what is going on in Europe and a brief view beyond it is surely one of the strengths of the book.

An 'increase in leisure time and an increase in the demand for training' have led many museums to revise their attitudes towards the museum visitor and to propose lifelong learning processes to young and old in an evolutionary way; this has tended to transform the 'education/edification' museum into an entertainment if not 'edu-tainment' place. But as one may read in John Reeve's chapter (pp.197–209), 'learning and fun are not mutually exclusive'. One is, nevertheless, increasingly inclined to abandon the notion of education when speaking of museums, and place the emphasis on learning.

This study, focusing on museum education in Europe, is rich in the variety of experiences described. The fact that a museum can, as in Israel, learn from its visitors had already been acted upon in Liverpool, as presented at the CECA meeting in Jerusalem (Horwich 1993); even if those undertaking the experiment in Israel (also described at that CECA meeting) were unaware of the Liverpool experience, it is always comforting to discover that one's idea has been developed fruitfully elsewhere. That museums may emanate from a community as an 'ever-developing co-operative venture where learning activities become acts of giving rather than acts of receiving' has not only been developed at the Khan Museum in Israel: the same purpose led to the Canarian project of the *Museo vivo la Ganania* and to the Basque experience of the *Museo comarcal de les Encartaciones* (Suarez Espino and Sanchez 1996–97; Antonanzas 1996–97). The Portuguese paper summarises the whole process very well: 'The museum has to be created from "inside" the community' in order to 'become an institutional point of reference in the community'.

A journey of discovery

The creation of Europe is only possible through the taking of different journeys. Ideas have been the most important phenomena to have travelled along the Roman roads. For example, the Royal Art and History Museum in Brussels organises museum visits, *'invitations au voyage'*, preparatory to a trip abroad in the same spirit as the Gallery Bus in Hungary takes individuals on 'different journeys'.

The preparation of this Conclusion follows my immediate past participation in two particularly relevant events: firstly, in a seminar on the creation in Austria of a new training centre for cultural mediators as part of a SOCRATES project; and secondly, a two-day international symposium in Brussels on 'The borders of Europe', organised by the Museum of Europe and planned for Brussels. The Director of the Brussels Opera, Bernard Foccroulle, mentioned that a museum 'lives through the eye not of its works of art but through the eyes of its visitors and the potential of complicity between the public and the exhibit'. Nevertheless, it is our duty as museum people to offer visitors the clues necessary to understand the exhibit and thus appreciate it.

International collaboration

This can only help to create new synergies between cultural and adult educational bodies. It is a stimulating possibility and suggests a tool for progress. At the Museum of Europe symposium, Julia Motoc of the University of Bucharest proposed a similar idea in order that former Eastern European countries might enter more rapidly into a wider European arena. This sentiment is also seen in the creation of a new Academy in Linz. With an eye towards wider European co-operation, discussions with consultants from the Ecole du Louvre, the Université Libre de Bruxelles, and the Remscheid and Wolfenbuttel Academies in Germany consider it essential from the beginning to meet local needs.

One of the aims of the CECA project, *All roads lead to Rome,* has been to explore the different roads which have led and are leading to our common roots in Europe. Let me add to the detailed description of the Croatian activities, that Croatia participated in this programme with more than one project. *Hit the Road* was of great importance due to the number of museums involved. The projects *To grow on the way to Rome* and *Arhimir* in Zagreb, as well as the *Natural landscape* workshop in Rijeka, also contributed hugely to the success of the final encounter in Rome. All the participants from 10 European countries were deeply impressed by the quality of the work achieved and the motivation, both of students and museum staff. This came as no surprise to me: at the Zagreb Museum's Day in May 1997, I had been very moved by the final gathering of the *Flower ('Civjet')* project whose purpose was to bring some happiness to Croatian hearts and art after the years of war they had just undergone. As there were, alas, no more works of art, in the strict sense, to display, the women of Vukovar brought their 'art' in the shape of flower biscuits.

Liberty and funding

What museums can offer to adult visitors varies from one country to another, and the problems they face differ widely when one speaks of, for example,

France, Germany and the United Kingdom in comparison with Luxembourg, Slovenia or Malta. Some general trends may, nevertheless, be discerned, and it is fascinating and exciting to realise that even after many years of museum education there are still new ideas to gather and exploit. I would complete the quotation at a lecture by H Wissmann of the University of Heidelberg that 'liberty is the only movement able to open the path to knowledge', by adding 'and to pleasure'. Yet this requires appropriate financing, and many European countries still face important funding problems, as reflected in this publication and the fact that grants are sometimes sought well beyond European borders.

Museums as human enterprises

As human beings we are a mixture of emotion and reason, and it is the role of the museum to discover how best to meet both. We should never forget that behind every museum object there is a human being with their own existence and story. Generally speaking, these individuals belong to the past. Only objects of their past lives remain today, and we – museum mediators and adult educators – have to analyse these objects carefully in order to grasp the quantity and quality of messages they contain. Nevertheless, each of our interpretations is partly subjective. We, too, are human beings living at a certain period of time with our own particular ways of thinking and philosophy, and our public is composed of a multitude of individuals with many different social and cultural backgrounds.

We should always remember to address the public at its own level (the 'threshold level'), not at the level we consider it should have when exposed to museum experiences.

This is the reason why I found the Stockholm education programme so convincing: that museums have the potential to create an 'open society where one feels secure, is met with knowledge and respect, and where intellect is activated' (see chapter 4) is most challenging when it comes to evaluation and to the fact that this programme has 'changed more than one's working life'. Similar programmes are to be found in Portugal and in Brazil (*Neighbourhood gardeners' project*, 1996–97), or in Belgium with nursing students trained to understand their patients better by first visiting museums and artworks surrounding them and learning to 'look' at them. The same idea underpins the *Photographic details* described by colleagues in the contribution from Cyprus (see chapter 13).

The recognition of the importance of families is quite positive. Society evolves and it is interesting to see that in some countries the traditional Sunday gathering in churches has evolved into family outings to museums, as in the Portuguese example, (see chapter 16).

Personal involvement and cultural identity

Inviting people to change attitudes and move from being 'passive receptors' to 'active protagonists' is another important idea contained in this book, be it in Italy, Ireland (where active involvement 'has transformed the visitor's way of looking at the world' (chapter 24)), or Slovenia, where the aim is to have museums engaging more closely with an expanding public (chapter 12).

One of the museum's new roles is the promotion of the 'return of trust between people, reconciliation in the broad sense of the word as well as in the creation of a new identity'. This reflection on the current thinking of museums is dealt with by a number of countries, mainly in projects dealing with the revival of traditional crafts, a search for a cultural identity, and the 'development of a nation's spirituality', such as in Russia or Poland.

A brief description of a fascinating project in Slovakia three years ago may be relevant here: the Slovak National Museum has found a solution to the threat of the disappearance of many traditional musical instruments by encouraging new instrument makers, which in turn has led to stabilising of production and to the organisation of annual competitions and challenging concerts. In this way traditions and skills are being preserved.

Cultural, social and other minorities

Many chapters in this book deal with museums and minorities and art as being 'a way to raise the social consciousness of the so-called underprivileged': examples include the Shamiana project and the 'Peopling of London' exhibition in the United Kingdom, and the different exhibitions organised by the Children's Museum and the Historical Museum in Amsterdam; also the activities in Malta at the Zabbar Museum or the National Folklore Museum at Vittoriosa.

The handicapped, or, as currently perceived in some quarters, 'people with other capabilities', may be considered as additional 'minorities' targeted in museums. Generally speaking, the majority of special programmes are planned for the blind. Belgium has played a pioneering role here, together with the Youth Section of the Dalhem Museum in Berlin.

A wider opportunity of encompassing several handicaps is the purpose of Don Rankin's Access Sculpture Trail in the Yorkshire Sculpture Park in the United Kingdom. Rankin considers that in certain circumstances (for instance, a mother pushing a pram, an elderly person) we are all 'handicapped', and that one of the best ways to cope is never to forget to preserve one's sense of humour (Bowman 1993).

Following the example of the Louvre in training deaf guides for a deaf public, the Royal Museum for Fine Arts in Brussels has recently undertaken a similar scheme that involved establishing a special vocabulary in sign language, which had not previously existed.

Museums' dialogue with their public

The museum has to go out to the public; multi-disciplinary should effect better communication and understanding of museum objects. To reveal its contents is a social mission which aims at a real dialogue between museum and society that can only be achieved through collaborating with the public. Such collaboration is clearly stated, for example, in the contribution from Norway (see chapter 3). I would add that the Forestry Museum in Elverum has also achieved this aim.

To optimise museum collections both physically and intellectually, they should be opened to society at large, using many approaches, such as special publications, interactive programmes, collaboration and/or partnerships between adult education and other organisations and institutions and local authorities. The consideration, as in the Hungarian example (the Press Coffee House) (chapter 8), of journalists as social links between the museum, the press and the media, provides an idea which has also been developed more recently in Belgium and in Holland with radio lectures 'to reach the masses in all corners of the country'.

With regard to cultural awareness being brought into people's homes, museums must rely more on the use of new technology to disseminate information and use new channels to sensitise the public to the fragility of our common heritage. Different European projects have been set up to address this theme. The popular Raphael programme *Let's protect our heritage together* aims at preventive conservation in the widest sense by involving the public more consciously.

In the end, museum and adult education personnel have the same goal: to bring the public to 'see better, to understand better in order to feel more intensely'.

Whatever roads they follow, whatever their evolution – museum education and adult education can be summarised by three fundamental concepts: 'to understand, to love and to serve' the public (Gesche-Koning 1994), in order to 'form for the future a museum visitor able to converse and communicate with the works and beyond with society' (Destree 1976).

References

Antonanzas, V, 'El museo comercal de las Encartacione', *ICOM Education* 16, 1996–97, pp. 28–30

Bowman, A, 'A voyage of discovery: Access Sculpture Trail', *ICOM Education* 14, 1993, p. 36

Destrée-Heymans, T (1976), 'Le rôle éducatif des musées – Dynamusée: l'atelier créatif des Musées roylaux d'Art et d'Histoire à Bruxelles', *Vie des Musées, pp. 24–6*

Gesché-Koning, N, 'La mission d'éducation du musée', in *Musées, civilisation et développement*, Proceedings of the Encounter held in Amman, 1994, Jordan, 26–38 April, p. 386. Paris: ICOM

Horwich, D, 'First and second chance to learn: oral history workshops for all', *ICOM Education* 14, 1993, pp. 38–40

Neighbourhood Gardeners (1996–97)[co-ordinated by the Casa de Rui Barbos Foundation, Rio de Janeiro, Brazil], *ICOM Education* 16, 1996–97, pp. 15–16

Suarez Espino, J P and Sanchez, L, 'Museo Vivo Lal Granaria, Gran Canaria', *ICOM Education* 16, 1996–97, pp. 15–16

Abbreviations

ICOM   International Council of Museums

ICOM/CECA International Committee for Education and Cultural Action

IIZ/DVV   Institute for International Cooperation of the German Adult Education Association

SOCRATES the funding arm of the European Commission for projects on adult education

UNESCO   United Nations Economic, Scientific and Cultural Organisation

Notes on contributors

David Anderson is Head of Education at the Victoria and Albert Museum, London.

Daniel Artymowski works in the Royal Castle in Warsaw, Poland, as an education officer, conducting art workshops for all age groups.

Carmel Paul Borg is a lecturer in Curriculum Studies in the Department of Primary Education, Faculty of Education, at the University of Malta.

Lida Branchesi is an art historian and co-ordinator of projects on arts and museum education at the European Centre for Education (CEDE) in Rome.

Alan Chadwick is Senior Lecturer in the School of Educational Studies at the University of Surrey, Great Britain. Among his publications are *The Role of the Museum and Art Gallery in Community Education* (1980), and (co-edited with Annette Stannett), *Museums and the Education of Adults* (1995).

Tončika Cukrov is Educational Curator at the Museum Documentation Centre, Zagreb, Croatia, and an associate on research projects at the Institute of History of Arts.

Ann Davoren is Curator for Education and Community Programmes at the Irish Museum of Modern Art in Dublin, Ireland. She has been working on the Programme for Older People since 1991.

Dorothee Dennert is Museum Educator in the Museum of Contemporary History of the Federal Republic of Germany (Haus der Geschichte) in Bonn.

Ana Duarte is Professor of Aesthetic and Art History, and of Sociology of Art, at the Superior School of Education in Setubal, Portugal.

Willem Elias is Professor and Head of the Adult Education Department at the Free University of Brussels (VUB), Belgium.

Tatjana Dolzan-Eržen is Curator Ethnologist at Gorenjski Museum, Kranj, Slovenia. She has been running study circles since 1994.

Elizabeth Esteve-Coll worked as Chief Librarian of the National Art Library before being appointed Director of the Victoria and Albert Museum, London (1988–95). Subsequently, she was Vice-Chancellor of the University of East Anglia, Norwich, and now works as freelance consultant.

Edi Fanti is a trainer in adult education and an associate in the Department of Educational Sciences at the University of Florence, Italy. She has worked on several SOCRATES projects.

Gianna Maria Filippi works as researcher for the Regional Institute of Research, Experimentation and Current Education (IRRSAE) in Florence, and is responsible for European projects on adult education at the University of Padova.

Aija Fleija is Director of the Latvian War Museum in Riga. Formerly she worked at the History Museum of Latvia.

Ted Fleming is Lecturer in Adult and Community Education at the National University of Ireland at Maynooth, Ireland.

Helena Friman was Head of Education at Stockholm City Museum and Head of the Cultural Department of Skansen Stockholm. She initiated and carried out the *Stockholm Education* project during the city's position as Cultural Capital, 1998.

Jean Galard is Head of Education (*service culturel*) at the Louvre Museum, Paris. Formerly he worked as Cultural Attaché at French Embassies in Morocco, Turkey, Mexico and the Netherlands.

Nicole Gesche-Koning has been editor of *ICOM Education* since 1978. She is immediate past chairperson of CECA and co-ordinator of the CECA programme *All roads lead to Rome*.

Loukia Loizou Hadjigavriel is Director of the Leventis Municipal Museum of Nicosia, Cyprus, where she was responsible for the creation and organisation of the collections before the museum's opening in 1989.

László Harangi is a researcher in the field of adult education for the Hungarian Institute for Culture, and chairman of the Adult Education section of the Hungarian Pedagogical Society, Budapest.

Pavel Hartl is a psychologist and Associate Professor at Charles University in Prague, Czech Republic. He is the author of the *Dictionary of Psychology* and of textbooks on the psychology of lifelong learning.

Bettina Heldenstein is in charge of the Education Department of the Casino Luxembourg.

Irina Mikhailovna Kossova is Head of the Department of Museum Studies at the Institute of Retraining Workers (in the fields of) Art, Culture and Tourism of the Russian Federation, Moscow. She is Professor and Director of the Workshop 'Museum Education'.

Eva Maehre Lauritzen is Head of the Education Department and Associate Professor of the Natural History Museums and Botanical Garden of the University of Oslo, Norway.

Flavia Krogh Loser is an adult educator and founder-member of KUBIKO, the organisation formed to promote cultural mediation in eastern Switzerland. Her work focuses on educational theory for museums and interactive tours for adults and families.

Herbert Maly is Director of the non-profit-making company COOPERATIONS in Wiltz, Luxembourg, developing art and social integration programmes at local, regional and supra-regional levels.

Ivo Maroević is a Professor in the Faculty of Philosophy at the University of Zagreb, Croatia. He has worked as curator and conservationist, and is founder and Head of Museology. His *Introduction to Museology: the European approach* was published in 1998.

Peter Mayo is Lecturer in the Faculty of Education at the University of Malta. His main focus is on the sociology of education, with special emphasis on adults.

Virgil Stefan Nitulescu is editor-in-chief of *Revista muzeelor*, the Romanian Journal for Museums, and works as an expert with the Committee on Culture, Arts and Mass Media of the House of Deputies.

Paolo Orefice is Professor of Adult Education in the Department of Educational Science, and Dean of the Faculty of Science of Education and Training at the University of Florence, Italy. He is a founder-member of the Italian Associations for Adult Education (AIDEA) and Community Education (AIEC).

Gabriele Rath works as freelance curator and museum educator in Austria. She is co-founder of KOM.M.A., the Office for Communication in Museums and Exhibitions, Innsbruck, lectures at the Institute for Culture in Vienna, and has recently published a national survey of Austrian museum visitors.

John Reeve is Head of Education at the British Museum, London, and Visiting Fellow at the Institute of Education, University of London, where he teaches on the Museums and Galleries in Education course.

Nina Rodin is Curator and Director of the 'Khan' Local History Museum of the city of Hadera, Israel. She lectures on the University of Haifa's Museum Studies Certificate Course, and is a member of the Israeli National Museum Council.

Radka Schusterová studied philosophy and the theory of culture, and is currently Head of the Public Relations Department of the National Museum, Prague.

Annette Stannett works as consultant in the fields of adult and museum education. Among her publications are *Perspectives on adult education in Europe* (with P Jarvis, 2nd edn. forthcoming); *Museums and the education of adults* (with

Alan Chadwick, 1995); and *Museum education bibliography 1988–1996* (1997).

Bastiaan van Gent was, until 1998, Professor of Androgogy and Head of the Department of Adult Education at the University of Leiden, The Netherlands. He has published widely on andragogy, adult education, philosophy and art.

Helena von Wersebe works as Co-ordinator of Visitor Services at the Haus der Geschichte, Bonn.

Index

Note: Individual museums and other institutions are listed under the country or city in which they are located.

action research 93, 188
active protagonists, museum visitors as 102, 112, 224
admission charges 50, 124
adult education
  definition of 179
  diversification of 143
  for economic purposes 189–90
  integrated concept of 148
  policies for 10, 86–7, 96, 150, 159
  popularity of 147
  potential for development of 134
  programmes of ix–xi, 1–2, 4–5, 8, 31–2, 35, 42–3, 49–50, 59–60, 63–4, 65–9, 70, 83–5, 86, 89–90, 103–6, 116–17, 126, 130–37 *passim*, 168–9, 172, 197, 206
Adult Education and the Museum (AEM) project 1, 210
Adult Learners Week (UK) 199
advisory services of museums 57
African communities 8, 119, 204
Agren, Per Uno 117
Ahern, D. 190
Akbar, Shireen 202
Allen, Ricky Lee 108
Amarant organisation 160, 166
amateur organisations 16–17, 167
Amsterdam
  Children's Museum 224
  Historical Museum 224
  Reinwardt Academie 184
  SCO-Kohnstamm Institute 184
Anderson, David 103–4, 131, 197–8, 206
andragogy 184, 206
Antwerp
  Museum of Modern Art 160, 165
  Royal Museum of Fine Arts 160
Apple, Michael W. 106
archaeological excavations 51, 176, 203
archaeological museums 32, 34, 60–61, 91
Arts Electronica festival 10
audiophones 110

audiovisual presentations 126, 140–41, 150, 161–2, 173
Austria 123–9
  Bureau of Cultural Mediation, Vienna 211
awards 56, 176
Azores, the: Rural and Ethnographic Museum, S Miguel 120–22
Azzopardi, John 110

Bakar 34
Bartolo, E. 107
Basle 149, 155
Belgium 158–70, 223
  Amarant Study and Exhibition Centre 166
  Centre for Amateur Arts 167
  Gaasbeek Castle 16
  Gallo Roman Museum, Tongres 165–6
  government departments for culture 160, 163, 167
  Musée du Petit Format 167
  Muséum Préhistosite de Ramioul 168
  Ostend Provincial Museum of Modern Art 165
  political structure 158–9
  Royal Institute for Natural Sciences 164–5
  Royal Museum for Fine Arts 164–5
  Royal Museum of Mariemont 163
  see also Antwerp; Brussels; Charleroi; Flanders; Ghent; Walloon provinces
Benson, C. 188
Berlin 224
Bern
  Adult Education Centre 152
  Kunstmuseum 150–52
Biofitum club 71
Biskupin 60–61
blind visitors to museums 16, 36, 134, 164, 168, 224
Borg, Isabelle 107–8, 112
Bourdieu, Pierre 107–8, 186

Boyd, Willard   207
Bradford   199, 201
Brazil   223
Brennan, Joan   195
Brighton   204, 206
Bristol   202
Brussels   158–9, 162
    Archive and Museum of Flemish Life   163
    Royal Museum for Art and
        History   163–4, 221
    Royal Museum for Fine Arts   224
Budapest
    Agricultural Museum   57
    Kiscelli Museum   54
    Museum of Hungarian Literature   54
    Transport Museum   57
Bydgoszcz   62

canning industry   119
Ceausescu, Nicolae   65
Cesnola, Luigi Palma di   81
Charleroi
    Industrial Museum   168
    Musée des Beaux Arts   168
Choay, Françoise   135
Church museums   105, 112; see also parish
    museums
citizenship   117
civil society   189–91, 195
club activities   71
club-schools   148, 152
Cole, Henry   131, 197
collective memory   120, 214
collective social action   190
colonial legacies   104, 107–8
'colour-blindness'   4
commercial pressures on museums   66, 90,
    182–5
'common sense'   6–7, 10, 108, 116
Communist Party   65
community education   190–91, 195
community institutions and initiatives   55–6,
    62, 103, 117, 121–2, 180, 197, 201, 211,
    214–16, 219–20, 221
COMPASS database   203, 205
computers in museums, use of   9–10, 33, 63,
    96, 110, 126, 161–2, 183
concerts   45, 54–5, 74, 176, 200
constructivist learning theory   204

contemporary art   34, 61, 84, 91, 172, 175,
    177, 188, 192, 194, 200
'conversations'   151
COOPERATIONS programme   173–6
Council of Europe   89, 91
Couto, Joao   115
Cracow   63
craft skills   14, 20, 38, 61–2, 67, 72, 121, 200,
    224
creativity   7, 10
critical pedagogy   106–10
Croatia   31–9, 222
    Academy of Science and Art   38
    Archaeological Museum of Istria   32, 34
    Bakar Naval School   34
    Ilok Museum in Exile   36
    Kumrovec 'Old Village' Museum   38
    Museum Documentation Centre
        (MDC)   32–4, 37
    Nuštar Art Colony   37
    Pula Teaching College   34
    Technical Museum   33
    Vinkovci Municipal Museum   37
    Vukovar Municipal Museum in Exile   36
    see also Rijeka; Zagreb
Cukrov, Tonèika   33
cultural activities, participation in   6–7, 23
cultural communication   136
cultural education   184, 188, 193; see also
    heritage education
'cultural engineering'   135
cultural events   37; see also concerts; festivals;
    plays; readings
cultural heritage, protection and promotion
    of   2, 43, 50, 65, 79–80, 86, 88, 93, 97,
    104, 115, 123–4, 179, 185–6, 214, 216
cultural history, courses in   22, 26
'cultural mediation'   91, 97, 135, 149, 155–6,
    222
cultural policy   10, 108, 132, 180, 201
Cyprus   81–5, 223
    Byzantine Museum   82
    Cyprus Museum   81
    Folk Art Museum   82
    'Struggle Museum'   82
    see also Nicosia
Czech Republic   41–7
    Association of Bohemian, Moravian and
        Silesian Museums and Galleries   41
    Beskydy Museum, Frýdek Místek   46

Masaryk Institute for People's
Education 43
Náprstek Museum of Asian, African and
American Cultures 44
National Museum Journal 44
Numismatics Papers 44–5
see also Poděbrady; Prague

Danish-Romanian Institute of Adult
Education 68–9
databases 18, 203, 205
Davern, A. 191
Davidson, B. 201
Davie, George 6
De Gruyter, W.J. 180
deaf visitors to museums 134, 224
Delphi study 41
democratic deficit 190–91
democratic society 6, 8, 190
democratisation 69, 110, 163
Destrée-Heymans, T. 225
digital technology 10
disabled visitors to museums 16, 36, 67, 91,
126–7, 134, 173, 202–3, 224
discussion meetings 55, 191–2
distance learning 71, 134, 148, 203
Docents 138–45
DOMUS surveys 4–5
Doyle, Emma 192
drama *see* plays
Dufresne-Tasse, C. 95
Dulwich 198
Duncan, Carol 205
Dynamusée initiative 163

ecological programmes 24, 34, 109
Edinburgh 199, 206
Edufora project 169–70
Egan, Teresa 192, 194–5
Elderly, the, University for (Norway)
15; *see also* Third Age
elitism 110, 169
Elverum 225
emigrants returning to their country,
programmes for 60
Emiliani, Marisa Dalai 88
empowerment 110, 175
Encarta *World Atlas* 41–2
English Heritage 199
English language, use of 111

entertainment at museums 182, 221
environmental stimuli 96–8
ethnic minorities, programmes for 67, 90,
126, 180, 199, 201; *see also* African
communities
ethnographic and ethnological museums 37,
61, 67, 75, 109, 120–22, 123, 182
European Association for the Education of
Adults 1, 210
European City of Culture 25, 172
European Commission 1, 10, 174
European Info-Cities Project 206
European Museum of the Year 176
European Union 210
Ministers of Culture 25
see also European Commission
European Voluntary Service 176
evening opening 90, 150, 198, 207
exile, museums in 36
expert services provided by museums 14, 37
'explanation', cognitive 97–9

families, provision for 60–61, 68, 70, 72–3,
125, 151, 164, 199, 202, 223
family history 80
family museums 72
Fentress, J. 120
festivals 15–16, 61
film clubs 53
Flanders 159–62, 165
Centre for Adult Education 159
Federation of Registered Cultural
Centres 166
Museum Decree 160
Museums Advisory Council 160
Museums Association 161
Florence 90
Foccroulle, Bernard 222
folk museums, folk art and folklore 16, 57,
61, 73, 123, 200, 224
food, traditional 121–2
France 130–37
Association of Popular Education 132–3
Ministry of Culture 133
Musée du Louvre 108, 130–32, 134, 224
Réunion des Musées Nationaux 134
free admission 50, 124
freelance staff in museum education 128–9,
177
Freire, P. 109–10

friends of museums, organisations of 38,
50–51, 53, 66, 77, 82–4, 143, 198, 200
Frýdek Místek 46
funding of museums 50, 63, 69, 77, 153–4,
156, 180, 223; *see also* private sponsorship
Fuur 4

game of concepts 95
Gardner, Howard 204–5
Geneva 154
Genoa 90–91
Germany 127, 138–45
Dalhem Museum, Berlin 224
Haus der Geschichte der
Bundesrepublik 138–45
Humanistische Union 144
Institut für Museumskunde 143
Institute for International Cooperation of
Adult Education Association
(IIZ/DVV) 1
Gesche-Koning, N. 225
Gharb 109
Ghent
Doctor Ghuislain Museum 166
Museum for Industrial Archaeology and
Textiles, Ghent 166
Glasgow 201
Going Graphic project 9–10
Golcar 200
Gombrich, E.H. 207
Gozo
Folklore Museum 109
Heritage Museum 104
Graburn, Nelson 207
Gramsci, Antonio 108, 111
'Great Museum' metaphor 22
guidebooks to museums 73, 199
guided tours of museums 126–7, 132,
139–40, 143, 150–52, 161–3, 166–7,
172–3, 180, 183, 198–9
Gunnersbury Park 201
Gunther, C. 198, 203

Hackney 204
Hadera 213–19
Halsey, A.H. 198
Hatvan 55–6
hedonism 135–6
Hein, George 204

heritage education 87–8; *see also* cultural
education
Heritage Week (Italy) 91
'high art' 182
Holt, John 204
Hooper-Greenhill, E. 105, 197, 201
Horváth Matiszlovics, Eva 55
Hudson, Kenneth 22, 82, 213–14
Hungary 48–57
Grassalkovich Community Art Gallery,
Hatvan 55–6
Jósa András Museum, Nyiregyháza 50–51
Museum and Institute of Military
History 53
Museum of Applied Arts 48, 57
Museum of Fine Arts 48
National Association of Museums'
Friendship Societies 51
National Gallery Education
Department 57
National Museum 48
Press Coffee House 52, 225
socialist brigade movement 49
see also Budapest

identification of objects 14
ideological pressure on museums 28, 65–6,
70
Illich, Ivan 204
illiteracy 86, 110, 133
Ilok 36
immigrants, programmes for 15, 67, 133,
173, 214; *see also* refugees
Inchicore and Kilmainham 194–5
individual visitors to museums 145, 162, 207
information technology *see* computers
integrated concept of adult education 148
intelligence, different kinds of 205
interactive technology 101, 126, 136–7, 140,
161
International Art and Environment Pilot
Project 176
International Committee for Education and
Cultural Action (ICOM/CECA) 34,
91, 115, 221–2
International Council of Museums
(ICOM) 34, 37, 66, 95, 123, 161, 168,
184, 213
Newsletter 2
International Museum Day 37

International Year of Older Persons   195
Internet, the   9–10, 17, 136, 161, 165
interpretation
    of the environment   96–8
    of history   73
    of museum exhibits   100–102
Ireland   188–95, 224
    Age and Opportunity (agency)   193
    Kilmainham Gaol   194–5
    Museum of Modern Art   8, 188, 191, 195,
        211–12
    National Lottery   189
    St Michael's Parish Active Retirement
        Association   191, 195
Ironbridge   200
Israel   2, 213–20, 221
Istria   32, 34
Italy   86–102
    Cagliari Archaeological Museum   91
    Centre for Museum and Territory
        Education   89
    Egyptian Museum, Turin   90
    Ministry of Heritage and Culture   89
    National Commission for Museum and
        Territory Education   88–91
    National Museum of Folk Arts and
        Traditions   90
    Pecci Museum, Prato   91
    Pigorini Anthropological Museum,
        Rome   90
    Sant' Agostino Ligurian Architecture and
        Sculpture Museum   91
    Uffizi Gallery, Florence   90
    see also Veneto region

journalists   52, 225
József, Attila   54

Kalisz   61
Kaluga   72
Kašpar of Sternberg, Earl   44
Kazan   73
keyworkers   211
King's Lynn   206
Knole   106
Kranj   77–9
Krasnoyarsk   75
Krúdy, Gyula   54
KuMen project   167–8

Kumrovec   38
Kunstkader project   167

laboratory work   91
labour market trends   42
Lagrange, Léo   133
Lambrecht, G.   169
language issues   111, 158–9
Lapira, Rosa   107
Laszlo, Želimir   33
Lather, Patti   108
Lattanzi, V.   90
Latvia   28–30
    Museum of Revolution   28–9
    War Museum   28, 30
law on museums and collections   68
Lawton, Dennis   106
Layer, Leopold   78–9
Leal, Eusebio   23
learning
    alternative expressions of   100
    ideology of   131
    museums as centres for   9–10, 24, 105–6,
        120, 215, 218–20
    perceptions of   4
learning environment   ix, 217
learning process   101–2, 137
lectures   4–6, 13–14, 18, 23, 36, 45, 49, 51,
    56, 62, 70, 105, 126, 134, 162, 183, 216
legitimacy of particular kinds of
        knowledge   106
Leicestershire   203
Leiden University chair of museology   184
Leiner, Vesna   34
leisure time   x, 134, 145, 185, 221
library facilities   162, 205
Libštejnský, František   44
lifelong learning   1, 19, 25, 90, 96, 106, 141,
    145, 163, 173, 191, 197, 204–5, 207, 211,
    221
Linz   222
literacy see illiteracy
Liverpool   221
    Conservation Centre   203
    Tate Gallery   200, 203
living history   118
local museums   12, 17, 37, 55–6, 61–2, 110,
    115, 117, 197, 200
Locus project   93–102
London

British Museum 108, 198–9, 201–3, 205–6
Dulwich Picture Gallery 198
Geffrye Museum 200
Goldsmiths' College 206
Hackney Museum 204
Imperial War Museum 200
Museum of London 199, 201, 203–4
Museum of Mankind 201, 203, 207
National Gallery 198–200, 203–4, 206–7
National Maritime Museum 206
National Portrait Gallery 200
Natural History Museum 109, 199
Royal Academy 198–9
Serpentine Gallery 200
Tate Gallery 199, 202
Victoria and Albert Museum 9–10, 197, 199–202, 211
Whitechapel Gallery 200, 202
'lost' history 110
Louvain, Catholic University of 168
Lublin 60
Lucerne 154
Luxembourg 172–8
Casino 172–3, 177, 211
Centre National de l'Audiovisuel 173
City History Museum 176–7
Grand-Duc Jean Museum of Modern Art 177
Gruberbierg Centre 175
Ministry of Education 172
National Museum for Art and History 172, 177
Nature Museum 177
Lyons 131

McGibney, May 193
McGregor, Neil 206
McGuirk, Phyllis 192
McLaren, P. 106, 108
Madách, Imre 54
Malraux, André 132
Malta x, 103–12, 224
Cathedral Museum 111
Corradino Prisons 111–12
Folklore Museum, Gharb 109
Fondazzjoni Patrimonju 111
Grand Harbour area 112
the Hypogeum 104
Karmni Grima Museum 109

Ministry of Education 105
National Archaeological Museum 111
National Folklore Museum, Vittoriosa 109, 224
National Maritime Museum 110, 112
National Museum of Fine Arts 107, 111
St John's Co-Cathedral, Valletta 107
University Faculty of Education 103
Vittoriosa Historical and Cultural Society 105
Xaghra Windmill Museum 109
Zabbar Sanctuary Museum 104, 108–9, 224
see also Gozo; Mdina; Rabat
Mamo, Gwamm 107
management of museums 66, 109
Manchester 203, 206
marginal role of museum education 128–9
marginalisation of cultures 107–8
Mariemont 163
master classes 72
Mdina
Cathedral Museum 104, 110
Dungeons 104
Natural History Museum 109
media, the 9–10, 225
mediation see 'cultural mediation'
mentoring 77–9
Merriman, N. 201
Metz 177
Midwinter, Eric 207
Miercurea Ciuc 67
military history museums 28, 53
military personnel, programmes for 29–30
Moldvay, Gyözö 55
Molnár, Ferenc 54
Moscow
Kremlin Museum 70, 73
Polytechnical Museum 72
State Biological Museum 71, 73
University Department of History 73
Motoc, Julia 222
Mravik, László 52
multiculturalism 116, 180, 182, 201–2
multi-disciplinary work 225
multimedia technology 101–2, 136, 161, 165, 204–5
municipal museums 8, 37, 43, 180
'musealisation' 185

Museum Day and Museum Weekend
  (Netherlands)   183, 185
Museum Sunday (Belgium)   165
Museums, Keyworkers and Lifelong Learning
  project   1, 211
museums, numbers and distribution of   24,
  41, 104, 115, 123–4, 160, 179

National Curricula   17, 103, 133, 197, 202
national identity   39
natural history museums   14–19 *passim*, 182
needs, educational, analysis of   93, 99
Netherlands, the   160, 179–86
  Dutch Institute for Art Education,
    Utrecht   184–5
  Dutch Museum Association   183–5
  The Hague Municipal Museum   180
  Public Art Treasures (foundation)   180
  types of museums in   181–2
  see also Amsterdam
networking   95, 186
Nicosia
  Leventis Municipal Museum   82, 84–5
  Municipal Arts Centre   84–5
Norway   12–21, 225
  Association for Adult Education   18–19
  Association of Museum Educators   13, 16
  Council for Cultural Affairs   15
  Museums Association   20
  Official Report on Museums (1986)   20
  State Council for Museums   20
  Tromsö Museum   20
  Tröndelag Folk Museum, Trondheim   16
  university museums   12–13
  see also Oslo
Nugent, Rose   193–4

O'Donoghue, H.   191
'official knowledge'   106
older people
  economic and social role of   190–91
  programmes for   8, 14–15, 46–7, 60, 74–5,
    105, 126–7, 151, 173, 191–5, 207,
    211–12
  as volunteers   213
  see also reminiscence projects
Olsztyn   60–61
open-air museums   14, 38, 67, 200–201, 203
opening times   90, 124, 150, 198
Oporto   115

Ópusztaszer   51
oral history   8, 110, 201, 203, 206, 215–17
Oslo
  Botanical Gardens   14, 16
  International Cultural Centre and
    Museum   15–16
  Kon-Tiki Museum   15
  Mineralogical Museum   17
  Museum of Applied Art   13–14
  Palaeontological Museum   17
  University course in museum
    studies   19–20
  University Museum   12
Ostend   165
outcomes from arts experiences   8
outreach   111–12, 182, 201, 203–4

Paisley   203
Palacký, František   44
parenthood, education in   148, 154
Paris   108, 130–32, 134, 224
parish museums   108–9, 120
participation
  in cultural activities generally   6–7
  in museum activities   9, 71, 94, 100,
    174–5, 201
partnership   ix, xi, 143–4
pedagogy   68, 89, 103
  of answers   109–10
  see also critical pedagogy
pensioners *see* older visitors
Petofi, Sándor   48, 54
Pharos   34–5
Pierides, Demetris   81
pilot projects   144
Pingelap   4
place, sense of   189, 191, 193–5; *see also*
  territory
plays, performance of   54, 74, 200
Poděbrady
  Polabské Museum   45–6
  School of Economics   45–6
Poland   59–64
  Biskupin Archaeological Museum   60–61
  Bydgoszcz District Museum   62
  Kalisz District Museum   61
  Lublin Castle Museum   60
  Masovian Village Museum, Sierpc   60, 62
  National Museum, Poznan   59–60
  Olsztyn Museum   60–61

Royal Castle, Cracow   63
Warmia and Mazury Museum   59
see also Warsaw
political control of museums   28, 86–7, 147
politics of knowledge   106
popular culture   108–9
popular education   132
Portugal   115–22, 223
   Associacao Portuguesa de
      Museologia   115
   Instituto Portugues de Museus   115
   Instituto Portugues do Patrimonio
      Arquitectonico   115
   Museo comarcal de les Encartaciones   221
   Museo vivo la Ganania   221
   National Museum of Ancient Art,
      Lisbon   115
   Sobralinho Municipal Museum   8, 211
   see also Azores; Setubal
Poznan   59–60
Prague
   College of Information Services   45
   Czech National Museum   43–4
Prato   91
Preti, Mattia   108
private sponsorship   148, 182
privatisation   182–4
professionalisation   149, 155, 183
public relations   127, 183, 185
Pujoulx, Jean-Baptiste   130–31

quizzes and competitions   51, 66, 151

Rabat
   Natural History Museum   109
   St Paul's Collegiate Museum   110
radio and television programmes   27, 132,
   180, 206, 225
Rankin, Don   224
readings of literature   71
reflective practitioners   106
refugees, programmes for   35–6, 67; *see also*
   immigrants
regeneration, social and economic   8
regional museums   43–6, 61–2, 74
religious exhibitions   111
reminiscence projects   62, 119–21, 203, 213,
   216–17
research facilities   111–12
reserve collections   203

retired people *see* older visitors
Ribeira de Cha   116, 120
Rijeka
   Gallery of Modern Art   38
   Natural History Museum   34
Rodriguez, Espinosa   107
roles of museums   7–9, 24, 28, 31, 49, 116,
   124, 130, 136, 179, 191, 223–5
Romania   65–9
   Centre for Training and Education for
      Personnel from Cultural Institutions   68
   Ministry of Culture   68
romanticisation   107
Rome   90
Russia   x, 70–75
   Academy of Sciences   70
   Institute for Retraining Workers in Art,
      Culture and Tourism   70
   Kaluga family museum   72
   Kazan University   73
   Krasnoyarsk Cultural and Historic
      Centre   75
   Museum of Theatre and Music, St
      Petersburg   74
   Novozybkovsk Regional Museum   74
   Russian State Museum   74
   Shushenskoe Museum of History and
      Ethnography   75
   Tatarstan State Museum   73
   Tol'yatti Museum   72
   Vologda Museum   71–2
   see also Moscow

Sacks, Oliver   4
St Gallen   153–4
St John, Sovereign Order of   107–8
St Petersburg   74
Samsung Electronics   55
science and technology museums   123–4
Scotland
   Highlands and Islands   202
   Parliament   6
Second World War   52, 132, 179
self-directed learning   205–6
Seniorgymnasium project   46–7
Sergiev Posad   75
Serota, Nicholas   202
settlement museums   213–14
Setubal

Michel Giacometti Museum of
    Work   116–20
  Professional Theatre Group   117
  S Bernardo's Hospital   117
  Trade Association   117
Shushenskoe   75
Sierpc   60, 62
Silver, A.Z.   186
site museums   213–14
Slovakia   224
Slovenia   77–80, 224
  Centre for Adult Learning   77
  Gorenjski Museum, Kranj   77, 79
Smith, Chris   10
SmithKline Beecham   202
Sobralinho   8
social class of museum visitors   24, 160, 186
social emancipation through
    museums   180–82, 186
SOCRATES funding   1, 27, 210–11, 222
Sogn og Fjordane   18
soirées   66
spiritual dimension of museums   8
staff of museums
  multi-functional skills of   106
  numbers of   12, 50, 87
  selection of   140–41
Stari Grad   34–5
Stockholm
  City Museum   22, 26
  as Cultural Capital of Europe   25
Stockholm Education   23, 25–7, 211–12,
    223
Strazisce   79–80
student visitors and placements   73–4
study circles   77–80
study tours   56, 105, 160, 199
Suncokret organisation   35
Sunderland   200–201
Surrey University   211
Sweden   22–7
  Educational Broadcasting Company   27
  National Report on Museums   24
  see also Stockholm
Switzerland   127, 147–56, 210
  Academy for Adult Education,
    Lucerne   154
  Association for Adult Education   148, 154
  Association of Professionals for Education
    and Mediation in Museums   154–5

Basle University courses in
    museology   149, 155
  Educational Institute of the
    Christian-National Trade Union   148
  Geneva University course in adult
    education   154
  Henry Dunant Museum   155
  KUBIKO Centre for cultural education
    and communication, St Gallen   153–4
  KUVERUM course   155
  structure of museum education   149
  see also Bern
Széchenyi, Ferenc   48
Szendrey, Julia   54

Targu Mures   67
teachers
  courses for   13, 60, 74, 106, 144, 148, 151
  museums' links with   74, 86, 91, 132–3,
    164, 172
television programmes *see* radio and television
Tentori, Tullio   90
territory, relationship of museum to   88–9
theatrical performances *see* plays
Third Age, the, University of
  in Malta   103, 105
  in Poland   60
  in Slovenia   77, 79–80
'threshold level' of cultural knowledge   97–
    100, 102, 223
Toemeka Base Movement   167
Tongres   165–6
tourists, provision for   29, 75, 90, 105, 143,
    172, 185, 198
trade unions   148
tradition *see* cultural heritage
training
  of museum staff   x, 19–20, 68, 104, 128,
    138–44, 149, 160–61, 168, 177, 184,
    218–19
  of participants in museum
    programmes   175
  see also craft skills
travelling exhibitions   111, 180
Trier   177
Tromsö   20
Trondheim   16

Ulster   200
unemployed people, provision for   14, 42–3,
      60, 67–8, 190, 198
uniqueness of objects and of spectators   169
United Kingdom   103–4, 106, 127, 131, 160,
      197–207
United Kingdom
   Arts Council   7
   @Bristol (science and wildlife
         centre)   202
   Bowes Museum   200, 206
   Brighton Museum   204
   Department of Cuture, Media and
         Sport   4, 10
   Glasgow Open Museum   201
   Golcar industrial museum   200
   Heritage Lottery Fund   201
   Ironbridge open-air museum   200
   Kennedy Report (1998)   198
   King's Lynn Museum   206
   Museums and Galleries Commission   4–5
   Museums and Galleries Disability
         Association   202–3
   National Grid for Learning   205
   National Institute of Adult Continuing
         Education (NIACE)   203
   National Museum Directors'
         Conference   9
   National Museum of Wales   199
   National Trust   200, 206
   Open University   203, 206
   Royal Collection   200
   Royal Museum of Scotland,
         Edinburgh   199
   Stokesay Castle   199
   Ulster Folk and Transport Museum   200
   University for Industry   198
   Yorkshire Sculpture Park   224
   see also Liverpool; London
United Nations Economic, Scientific and
      Cultural Organisation (UNESCO)   1,
      34, 93
United States   125, 186, 207
universities see under individual names or
      locations
Utrecht   184–5

Vaessen, J.A.M.F.   185
Valletta   107
valuation of objects   37

values, transmission of   124
van Gent, B.   179
Vance, Cyrus   48
Veneto region   93–102
   Institute for Educational Research and
         Training   94
Vienna   211
Vinkovci   37
'virtual' visits to museums   136, 204
visitors to museums
   diversity of   138–40, 143–4
   frequency of visits   140
   motivations of   139, 145
   numbers and characteristics of   4, 12, 24,
         39, 46, 50, 65, 70, 133, 138–9, 150, 185–6
   surveys of   139, 145, 162
   see also disabled visitors;   individual
         visitors; older people; student visitors
voluntary associations   191
volunteers, museums' use of   5, 123, 128,
      167–8, 183, 198–200, 213–15, 218–19
Vukovar   36
Vuyk, N.   185

Wales   199
   Assembly   6
walking tours of cities   26–7, 84, 166, 172,
      177, 199
Walloon provinces   167–8
Walsall   201
Walsh, Carmel   195
war damage   32
Warsaw
   Asia and Pacific Museum   60
   Centre of Contemporary Art   61–2
   Ethnographic Museum   61
   Laboratory of Creative Education   62
   Museum of the Earth   60
   Royal Castle   59, 62
web-sites   9–10, 136, 161, 204–5
Wickham, C.   120
Wignacourt, Alof de   108
Wiltz   174–5
Wissmann, H.   223
wood painting   71–2
Workers' Educational Association
   in Switzerland   148
   in the UK   197–8, 206
workshops
   for museum staff   62–3, 184–5

for museum visitors   35, 37–8, 59, 61–2, 90–91, 134, 143, 151, 175–6, 188, 192, 194

Xaghra   109

year passes   185
Yemen Festival (UK)   202
young people
    museum programmes for   33–4, 53, 59, 62–3, 67, 82–3, 85, 86, 105, 115, 125, 143
    participation in the arts   7
    syllabus-oriented programmes   125

see also families
Youngman, F.   190

Zabbar   104, 108–9, 224
Zagreb   222
    Archaeological Museum   34, 36
    Kloviæevi dvori   35–6
    Mimara Museum   38
    Museum of Arts and Crafts   38
    Museum of Contemporary Art   34
    Technical Museum   36
    Typhlological Museum   36
Zelenograd   74

Also available from NIACE

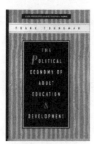

The political economy of adult education and development
Frank Youngman
ISBN 1 86201 080 3, 2000, £15.95

This book provides a theory of applied political economy to explain the interface between society and adult education in developing countries. Youngman analyses specific issues which affect adult education: the impact of foreign aid; gender and ethnic inequalities; and the relationship between state and civil society in peripheral capitalist societies.

The book draws on a wealth of empirical information and case studies from various parts of the world and whilst the approach is broadly influenced by the Marxist tradition, *The political economy of adult education and development* seeks to transcend many of the limitations and rigidities often prevalent in the past.

Teaching culture: the long revolution in cultural studies
Nannette Aldred and Martin Ryle (eds).
ISBN 1 86201 045 5, 1999, £14.95

This book reviews the politics and practice of cultural studies as an academic discipline, from the perspective of teaching and learning. By looking at questions of pedagogy and knowledge, contributors examine the changing curriculum of the field and assess how it can be sustained in light of policies, discourses and constraints which dominate higher education.

Learning in social action: a contribution to understanding informal education
Griff Foley
ISBN 1 86201 067 6, 1999, £12.95

This book helps to increase our understanding of the informal circumstances in which people learn. Using case studies, Foley argues that adult educators should not neglect the importance of the incidental learning which can take place when people become involved in voluntary organisations, social struggles and political activity.

The author shows how involvement in social action can help people to unlearn dominant, oppressive discourses and learn oppositional and liberatory ones. In this book Griff Foley points the way to a more radical agenda.

Books can be ordered from
Publications Sales
NIACE
21 De Montfort Street
Leicester LE1 7GE
England
Phone 44 (0) 116 204 4216; fax 44 (0) 116 285 4514; email orders@niace.org.uk

Forthcoming titles from NIACE

Stretching the academy: the politics and practice of widening participation in higher education
Edited by Jane Thompson
ISBN 1 86201 091 9, 2000, £15.95

A major new intervention in the Widening Participation debate by academics active in radical politics. This collection of essays brings together critical analyses and inspirational prose, rooted in the authority of experience and practice. Essential reading for all those concerned with the part played by Higher Education in widening participation.

Perspectives on adult education and training in Europe – 2nd edition
Peter Jarvis and Annette Stannett (eds)
ISBN 1 86201 022 6, 2001, price to be confirmed

A completely updated and revised edition of Peters Jarvis' best-selling book. This is the only book to cover adult education and training right across Europe. Written by practitioners in the field, this book gives historical comparisons and shows the growing influence of adult education in Europe. Lessons from Central and Eastern Europe are distilled for practice in the West.

Rural learning: a practical guide
John Payne
ISBN 1 86201 089 7, 2000, £19.95

This useful new guide sets the context for rural learning and provides excellent advice about contacting learners, sustaining projects and developing networks for effective learning support. It is aimed at adult education workers, community development workers, health and social workers, and members of voluntary organisations with an education brief in rural areas. This is an essential 'how to' book that cuts a dash through rural learning.

Further details about these and other publications by NIACE can be found on the internet at www.niace.org.uk